Contents

Part III: The Jet-Set Millionaire

Part IV: The Crypto Millionaire

Epilogue

★ NEW FRONTIERS ★

HOW AND WHERE TO FIND, GROW, AND PROTECT YOUR FORTUNE

By LIEF SIMON and VICTORIA HARMER

Published by Lahardan Books

Published by Lahardan Books

ISBN 978-1-958583-13-5

Book and Cover Design by Cristian Landero

This book is intended for general informational purposes only. It does not constitute legal, tax, financial, immigration, investment, or professional advice, nor should it be relied upon as a substitute for consultation with qualified professionals. Readers are strongly encouraged to seek independent advice from appropriately licensed legal, tax, financial, immigration, or other professional advisers before making any decisions or taking action based on the information provided herein.

About The Author

Lief Simon has lived and worked on five continents and traveled to more than 75 countries.

His real estate investment career began with a $5,000 down payment on a three-flat building in Chicago. Less than three years later, Lief sold that building for a leveraged return of 3,000%. That translated to $150,000 in profit after closing costs and commissions.

From there, Lief turned his attention overseas. He has since bought property in 24 countries including France, Croatia, Portugal, Ireland, Spain, Panama, Belize, Argentina, Mexico, Cyprus, Romania, and beyond. Thanks to his decades-long career as a global property investor, Lief has built a multi-million-dollar portfolio that includes rental properties, significant land holdings, and seven personal residences.

In 2008 Lief and wife Kathleen Peddicord made the most important investment of their lives—a 225-acre oceanside finca known as Los Islotes. There, on Panama's largely undiscovered Veraguas coast, they've installed underground electricity, water, and internet and built a forever family home that sits at the heart of their ultimate vision: a gold standard private residential community for those in search of a true safe-haven escape.

Over the decades he's spent living and doing business around the world, Lief has learned many lessons about how to succeed in business and in life offshore. He shares those lessons and his ongoing journey with readers of his *Offshore Living Letter* e-letter and *Simon Letter* monthly newsletter.

Lief has built a network of reliable and expert contacts—attorneys, bankers, tax consultants, and other advisors—both stateside and in the jurisdictions where he spends time and money. With their help, he stays on top of the ever-changing world of offshore business and opportunities in real time.

As Lief says, "You don't have to be a millionaire to take up the ideas of banking, doing business, and investing offshore. There are different levels to this game. Only you will know what makes sense for your circumstances and what's within your comfort zone.

"Your strategy might be as simple as opening a bank account in another country... or perhaps establishing a backup residency. You don't have to leave the United States to do either of these things.

"Or you can get more complex and diversify into real estate or precious metals, form an offshore corporation, move overseas, and even acquire second citizenship, as I have.

"Either way, *Offshore Living Letter* and *Simon Letter* will help get you started on your path to relying on yourself for your future prosperity... not some government."

Stay in touch and get regular updates from Lief by signing up FREE for *Offshore Living Letter* at offshorelivingletter.com or by scanning the QR code below.

Acknowledgements

Publishing this book is another milestone on the journey my wife Kathleen Peddicord and I began when we started our life together in Waterford, Ireland, in 1998.

The past thirty years of traveling the globe in search of opportunity, establishing residencies and businesses, buying and selling real estate, banking, acquiring second passports, and more have taught me a lot of lessons. That's one reason for this book—to share my hard-won, sometimes expensive wisdom. Please, learn from my mistakes.

Things have changed a lot since I set out on my path to diversification. Today's world is more unstable in parts than ever before.

At the same time, in other locations, greater opportunity exists that at any time in history. That's the other reason I wrote this book. To help you pinpoint the places that make sense for you now. Places where you can find, grow, and protect your wealth and build a legacy that will stand strong for generations.

This book would not exist if not for the efforts of my longtime editor Victoria Harmer who keeps me on track, on deadline, and connected in real time with many dozens of invaluable contacts and colleagues on the ground across the globe.

Work by numerous other writers and editors at *Simon Letter* and Live And Invest Overseas has likewise gone into bringing this project to life, including Kathleen Peddicord, Lee Harrison, Harry Kalashian, Kat Kalashian, Mónica Linares, Sophia Titley, and Jeremy Savory. Thank you, all.

INTRODUCTION

★ ★ ★

New Frontiers How And Where To Find, Grow, And Protect Your Fortune

In the 15th century, European explorers set sail in search of new trading routes, riches, knowledge, and adventure...

The Age of Discovery.

Over the two centuries to follow, these journeys resulted in fortunes made, lands mapped, and doors to a new world of opportunity thrown wide open.

Today, for those of us exploring options overseas, the driving motivation remains the same.

You can find your frontier—the place where you can create, grow, and protect your wealth while enjoying the adventure of a lifetime—recognizing that not everywhere is for everyone. Your challenge is to identify the best match for your circumstances, tastes, finances, desires, and preferred lifestyle.

If you like the idea of going off-grid and getting back to basics and would rather be riding horseback than reclining in a jet, you likely won't feel comfortable in a ritzy marina lined with designer boutiques and glitzy yachts.

For others all the conveniences of home where their dollars translate into double or triple the ROI is the dream...

And for others finding a country where you can keep more of your wealth is a priority far above climate, language, or access to a Starbucks.

Whichever category you fall into there's likely more than one place that meets your desires. This book is designed to pinpoint the best of those places and to detail how to get yourself to your chosen spot quickly and efficiently.

Whether you're a millionaire or just want to live like one... want to join the jet-set or go off the grid... are looking to grow your wealth or simply keep your nest egg safe and secure... there's a place in these pages for you.

To identify the locales I spotlight, I've used a time-tested approach...

The 5 Flags

Perhaps the most important thing for anyone looking to move themselves or their assets offshore to understand is that this world is forever changing.

Tax laws and treaties, residency visa requirements, opportunities for obtaining second citizenship, documentation required to open a bank account, as well as the political situations, the values of local currencies, and the ease of coming and going... all these things change all the time.

The key to surviving and prospering in the current global climate is to internationalize your life. The best strategy for that is known as the Five Flags.

I didn't invent it, but I knew the guy who did. He went by "Grandpa," and he was last seen in Panama City.

Grandpa's "Five Flags" are to do with residency, citizenship, banking, assets, and business.

Not everyone needs all five flags planted, but the goal should be to plant whichever ones you do need in different jurisdictions. Moving to another country and taking all your cash, investments, and business activities with you to that new country doesn't achieve the goal of going offshore.

For the goal is diversification.

Fortunately, different countries shine for different reasons.

Some are better for banking, others for investing, some for residency, and yet others as places to incorporate your business. No country gets "A" ratings on all fronts, but some get closer than others.

The Five Flags are simply reference points, and they overlap. Residency and citizenship are related, banking and assets are related, business and banking are related, business and cyberspace can be related. But that's not the point.

The point is that understanding the Flag Theory and taking this Five Flags approach allows you to create a road map you can use to simplify the very big-picture concept of internationalizing your life.

Planting your flags is about identifying which country (or countries) work best for your agendas and priorities. Break it down. Consider the options flag by flag.

Flag #1: Banking

The easiest first step can be a bank account in another country. It doesn't require a move or any big commitment. But it does diversify the risks associated with holding cash.

You've got options in dozens of jurisdictions. Don't get caught up trying to choose the "best" offshore banking jurisdiction. Shop for what's best for you based on your goals.

The problem in the current climate is that banks and even whole jurisdictions worldwide are closing accounts owned by Americans. In many cases, the banks are providing either no explanation or ridiculous ones for the abrupt closures.

It has happened to me. I've been three times presented with a check from a bank where I'd been holding money, in each case for years. Accounts closed without warning or apology and me left to figure out what to do with the funds.

Fortunately, I had backup accounts in each case where I was able to deposit the bank checks, but I've known others over the years who didn't have redundancy accounts in place and so were unable to deposit their cashed-out checks anywhere.

This is the current reality of banking around the world, especially for the American. And it's a great example of why you need to protect yourself by internationalizing your life.

Open a foreign bank account when you can. Don't hesitate or put it off. The window for opening an account at any bank can close, sometimes overnight.

And don't approach this as one and done. You need at least two accounts offshore in case one bank decides it's no longer okay with the color of your passport.

Two accounts are particularly essential if you're operating a company offshore. You don't want to be left scrambling to open a new company account so you can deposit a bank check before it expires. As I said, I've known people in that position. It's not pretty.

Flag #2: Residency

Maybe you're not ready to move to another country just yet, but you recognize the benefits of planting a residency flag somewhere offshore.

Residency rules can and do change as quickly and as often as banking rules, so, as with banking, my strong recommendation is that you take steps toward establishing a backup residency in another country as soon as you are able to.

Don't wait until you think you need it. Getting the documentation together to apply for residency in another country can take weeks or months. In that time, the rules can change.

One important thing to consider before establishing residency in another country is the tax consequences.

Example: Colombia taxes residents on their worldwide income once they are considered a fiscal resident and imposes a wealth tax (that you may or may not qualify for, as the tax kicks in at about $1.3 million at current exchange rates). Establishing a backup residency in Colombia may not make sense unless you plan to spend a lot of time in Colombia.

Flag #3: Second Citizenship

An offshore plan could and I'd say should include plans for a second passport. Many people think that a second passport wouldn't be beneficial to them. I say *au contraire*. A second passport is an important part of diversifying your life internationally, no matter your circumstances.

At the most practical level, a second citizenship is useful for travel. The EU isn't the only economic community in the world. You also have MERCOSUR in South America, for example, whose member nations include Argentina, Brazil, Uruguay, Venezuela, and Paraguay.

While MERCOSUR is fundamentally an economic treaty, holding a passport for a MERCOSUR member country simplifies travel to, from, and among other MERCOSUR countries.

CARICOM is a group of Caribbean nations where you can travel around more easily if you come from (that is, hold a passport from) a member country.

ASEAN is a similar group in Asia, and others exist in other regions of the world.

These groups are smaller and less organized than the EU, but so was the EU at one time. The primary objective for all these groups is to facilitate trade, but, again, holding a passport in one means much easier travel among the others.

It can also mean residency and work options. This is the case and the serious benefit of holding an EU passport. Being a passport-carrying member of any EU nation means you can live or work not only in that nation but in any other EU nation, as well, with no application or permit process required. That's a big deal.

Again, having the right to live or work in another country is an enormous benefit. Maybe it's not one you imagine yourself taking advantage of right now... but who knows where life leads you five or seven or 10 years down the road?

Unless you're eligible for a second passport through ancestry, it takes either a lot of time (a minimum of three years and up to 10 or even 20, depending on the country) or a lot of money (typically hundreds of thousands of dollars) to obtain a second passport. You want to start the process when you can so that you've got that backup plan in your back pocket when you need it.

Another benefit of holding a second passport is visa-free travel. This is an increasingly big deal for Americans. As the United States continues to make it more difficult for citizens of many other nations to visit that country, those other nations are reciprocating.

The final reason to get a second passport is if you want to give up your current citizenship. You can't be stateless. If you're considering formal expatriation, the first step is to acquire a second passport. Without this, you will face a series of hardships.

We recommend connecting your backup residency to this agenda if possible—that is, consider establishing residency in a country where it can lead to naturalization.

In that context, pay attention to how long it takes to qualify for citizenship in any country where you're considering residency, as well as the likelihood of being approved for citizenship.

While the tail shouldn't wag the dog (that is to say, don't choose a country for residency solely based on its timeline to naturalization), you don't want to end up in a country where you can't get naturalized according to an acceptable timeline if that is your goal.

Flag #4: Protect Your Assets

Simply put, asset protection means protecting what is yours. Many people tell you how to increase your wealth. Asset protection is the other side of the coin. It is a defense—safe-guarding what you already have.

Focusing on making more and more money without planning for protecting what you already have creates a sieve. You have income coming in the top but running just as fast out the bottom. That gets you nowhere.

An asset protection plan could mean putting your money into property. It could mean forming a corporation. It could be an international trust or a generational insurance product...

Maybe it's as simple as taking your teenaged daughter's credit card away from her.

Asset protection can be many things, but I'll tell you what it isn't. Asset protection is not a scheme to evade taxes. Many imagine that operating in the offshore arena means you can take liberties when it comes to reporting income and paying taxes.

Don't go down the path of diversifying your life and your investments and assets offshore because you want to "get away with something." In today's world, you can't, and nobody looks good in an orange jumpsuit.

An offshore asset protection trust is considered by many experts to be the strongest asset protection vehicle available when done right. When done wrong (that is, for purposes of evading taxes), it's fraught with risk.

That said, you do have legal opportunities for deferring and minimizing the amount of tax you pay... and you should pursue every one relevant to your situation.

Flag #5: Overseas Business Incorporation

The key to maximizing the tax benefits of incorporating offshore is to retain profits over and above the Foreign Earned Income Exclusion (FEIE) in an offshore corporation.

Since the 2017 tax changes, profits retained in a U.S.-controlled foreign entity pay corporate taxes in the United States. That change was a bummer for those of us who'd already been doing business offshore and who had become accustomed to being able to defer 100% of profits for the purposes of U.S. taxes.

Still, under the current law, structured correctly, the rate of tax can be at least 50% less than the regular U.S. corporate rate.

Let's walk you through it...

If you intend to operate a business outside the United States, you should use an offshore corporation.

Operating a small business through an offshore corporation

allows you to draw a salary of up to the FEIE amount. In addition, the offshore corporation eliminates payroll and self-employment taxes, saving you 15% in most cases.

For a simple offshore corporation to be able to defter U.S. tax on business profits, the offshore business must be active and profitable and must retain profits in the corporate bank account.

If you are an American who might generate significant profits in your international business, it's important to use the proper structure from the start... and that structure should be created by a tax advisor with experience both in the United States and overseas.

The basics are these: You must use a corporation (not an LLC, foundation, partnership, or other pass-through entity) that is incorporated in a country that will not tax your profits. It does not matter where you live except that you must be legally resident outside the United States to take advantage of the FEIE.

Where you operate your business matters for local taxes on the business operations. Two top options are Panama and Belize, both jurisdictions where you can base a business without becoming liable for much or any local income tax.

I've used this approach to identify locations that make sense overseas but as I've said, there's no one size fits all answer. You will likely find more than one jurisdiction that suits you. That's no bad thing. It serves your diversification objectives well... though it will cost you a bit more in airfare. So it goes.

Finding *Your* New Frontier—What Kind Of Millionaire Are You?

In the predecessor to this book, *Cowboy Millionaire—The New American Pioneer*, I detailed my three decades investing outside America, obtaining residencies and second passports, opening bank accounts and offshore corporations, cutting tax bills, and much more.

This book is designed to show you how and where you can do the same in today's world.

Start by profiling yourself. You need to identify which of the following categories best describes you and your objectives.

Bear in mind, "millionaire" here doesn't have to mean you have a million dollars in your bank account right now. Maybe you do. Maybe you have more. Maybe you're working toward it... or maybe you're just hoping to find a place where the money you do have stretches to afford you the millionaire lifestyle of your dreams.

All of those are great starting points for the conversation to follow in these pages.

You may also find you fit into more than one category, as I do. Not a problem. It means you have more solid options to choose from.

The Cowboy Millionaire

When the pioneers set out to settle the American West, they had nothing—no jobs, no homes, no land. They traveled thousands of miles in search of one thing: Opportunity.

They wanted a chance to find their fortunes and change their lives for the better, cultivating new territories and building bright futures where nothing existed before.

The West has long been settled, but there are parts of this world where you can still pioneer in that same way.

I'm doing it at Los Islotes, the 225-acre former finca where I'm building my own "intentional community." Here on Panama's untamed Veraguas coast amidst lush jungle and fronted by the most beautiful coastline imaginable, colonial-style homes constructed to the highest standards dot the hillsides.

Kathleen and I spend much of the year here in this place where our neighbors are others who likewise want the freedom to live in paradise and be left alone.

We're four to six hours from Panama City, depending on who's driving—far enough off the beaten track that I don't see the government ever paying much attention to us or the troubles of our increasingly troubled world encroaching.

Bigger picture, we're in Panama... and Panama is the world's number-one choice for today's Cowboy Millionaire. More on this later in these pages.

Los Islotes is about privacy. It's also about legacy.

The world Kathleen and I have created for ourselves over the past three decades, including at Los Islotes, is predicated on the 5 Flags strategies I laid out above. We've used this program to create wealth, to protect that wealth, and to foster a lifestyle that we've worked hard to help our children appreciate as much as we do. We want them to be ready and able to carry forward with everything that we've built for them... while adding to it for their children and on and on.

Kathleen and I consider ourselves stewards of the land and protectors of the legacy we're creating at Los Islotes. We intend this community to grow and thrive for hundreds of years.

That's the big idea of the Cowboy Millionaire agenda—to set you and your family up for the very long-term.

This is also about adventure. The opportunity to cultivate new lands and blaze new trails. To build things where nothing existed before. To embrace the freedom of open spaces and uncharted territory.

If you, too, are looking for a corner of the world where you can escape prying eyes, get back to basics, reconnect with the land, and enjoy a way of life lost back home, then consider yourself a Cowboy Millionaire, like me.

The Millionaire Next-Door

You may be a small business owner or an entrepreneur or maybe you've worked diligently in your career for decades. You've built wealth through discipline, frugality, and smart financial habits. You're not looking to flash the cash.

Instead, you're looking for a place where you can continue

to protect and grow what you've got while also enjoying a better standard of living on the money you've worked hard to accumulate.

Community, like-minded souls, and easy living are high on your list of priorities. You're the Millionaire Next-Door.

The Jet-Set Millionaire

You like to enjoy the finer things in life but haven't got the budget to embrace that lifestyle Stateside, so you want to find a location where what you do have will afford you a luxury lifestyle... one that includes things like regular massages, boat trips, a country club membership, a maid, a gardener, a cook...

A location that provides access to activities like golf, skiing, boating, and watersports, as well as opportunities for high-end shopping, fine dining, and travel are key priorities for the Jet-Set Millionaire.

The Crypto Millionaire

Crypto is an increasingly important component of the wealth-creation story globally. Over 560 million people worldwide own cryptocurrency and of those some 200,000 have $1 million or more in crypto holdings.

Cryptocurrency tax treatment is a key consideration. As are a country's legislation regarding digital assets, banking and financial infrastructure, security and privacy, and access to international markets.

And, of course, as anywhere for anyone, residency, lifestyle, and environmental factors also come into play for the Crypto Millionaire.

Now that you know what kind of millionaire you are (or want to be), let's consider the world map.

The pages that follow are divided into four sections, each detailing five countries that make great sense for each millionaire profile.

Of course, as I mentioned, you may well fit into more than one category.

Perhaps you've made your fortune in crypto but your dream is to live on a remote ranch in the wilds or Argentina...

Maybe you've got champagne dreams but a beer budget...

Or perhaps you have a singular priority—like obtaining a second passport or reducing your tax bill...

Worthy objectives, all.

Within the pages of this book, you'll find a place where you can meet them.

Happy hunting,

Lief Simon

PART I

THE COWBOY MILLIONAIRE

CHAPTER I

PANAMA

The Ultimate Offshore Haven

Today's Cowboy Millionaire should have Panama squarely in his crosshairs. It is the world's best place to be a pioneer... especially if you've also got an appetite for making money.

Panama uses the U.S. dollar. That means zero currency risk if your home base currency is likewise the dollar, making financial planning and projecting much easier.

Panama is a business hub at the center of the world. Location, location, location.

The country offers tax advantages you won't find back home. Its approach to taxation is as good as it gets.

Its banking sector has never had a crisis.

More than all that, however, Panama is the world's safest haven at a time of unprecedented global uncertainty.

Foreign investors, businesspeople, retirees, expats, and tourists are seeking out these shores in ever greater numbers. Everyone paying attention wants to be in Panama and for sure wants to put their money to work for them in the safe, stable Hub of the Americas.

Kathleen was the first to identify Panama as the world's top retirement haven. That was in 1997. She and I moved to Panama full-time in 2008 not as retirees and not for the lifestyle but with entrepreneurial agendas. Kathleen that year founded the Live And Invest Overseas publishing business... and I purchased the finca called Los Islotes with the intention of creating a private community of like-minded folk.

By the time we arrived in Panama, we'd already bought a pre-construction ocean-view condo in the heart of Panama City, bought and renovated an historic building in Casco Viejo, and invested in a teak plantation in the Darien. Boots firmly planted on the ground we looked around and were nearly overwhelmed by the opportunities to invest further... so we did, including in commercial space and land for banking.

Kathleen and I came to Panama to start businesses and make money. We've stayed for two decades because it turned out Panama is also a great place to build a new life. In the years since we've called Panama home, we've watched this country grow up. Panama City has always been the only real city in the region, but today it's taking its place at the table alongside global brand-name cities like Singapore and Dubai.

I've been all-in on Panama for a long time, and I'm happier all the time with that position. The good news for you is that it's not too late. Panama makes more sense right now than ever.

Panama's origins as a global hub can be traced back to the completion of the Panama Canal in 1914.

As the First World War broke out across Europe and that continent fell into darkness, this engineering achievement in this tiny Central American country was a beacon of progress. A sign that—though the Great Powers were at war with each other half a world away—there were better days ahead for globalization and peaceful progress through trade.

Today, 6% of all world trade passes through the Canal, some $270 billion annually, serving 80 countries.

The Panama Canal set Panama up for success... but it was not inevitable that Panama would become the global triumph it is today.

That's down to some sound decision making. Panama has no central bank, so there is no monetary intervention. The maximum rate of income tax is 25%, with income up to $50,000 taxed at just

15% (and the first $11,000 exempt entirely).

Panama City's infrastructure is First World. It even has a metro system.

Plus, Panama has the second-largest duty-free zone in the world, and the people are pragmatic and business minded.

Panama was ready for prime time by the time the eyes of the world turned toward it in the 2000s when three seasons of the hit reality show "Survivor" were filmed here, bringing the natural beauty of this isthmus into American living rooms and leading to further tourism and business growth.

Then the blockbuster beauty contest "Miss Universe" was held at the Panama Canal, again drawing the eyes of the world to this small country of 4 million people.

In 2008 Panama was given a seat on the Security Council of the UN, alongside China and the United States. The country has gone from strength to strength since.

Panama has two big advantages that give it a competitive edge for both investors and expat living.

First, as I've mentioned, is its location.

Thanks to the Panama Canal and the country's continually expanding international airport, Panama is a gateway for the 700 million people of Latin America.

Second, as I've also mentioned already but want to repeat because it bears repeating, this country is an icon of stability in an unstable world. The market here cycles up and down like any other, but the dips aren't dramatic and the time to recovery is quick.

Planting Flags In Panama

When sizing up Panama in the context of our Cowboy Millionaire agenda, here are key considerations...

Banking In Panama

Panama's banking industry is big in context. The country is home to 54 operating banks (40 general licenses and 14 international licenses) and 10 representative offices. It's where not only businesses and the wealthy of the region bank; banks in Panama attract clients from around the world.

The big appeals, again, are the stability and location of the country... and the seriousness of the Panama Banking Superintendent. The cherry on top is that Panama doesn't tax bank interest.

Historically, banks in this country haven't wanted to deal with small client accounts unless the client was living or doing business in Panama. Owning property and establishing residency helps.

Today, even if you're placing a large amount of money on deposit, banks in Panama want you to have a connection to Panama... a reason you're using a Panama bank. I've known people who have been able to open accounts without being a resident of Panama and without buying property in the country, but they are few and far between.

Heck, I've lived in Panama for nearly 20 years, hold permanent residency, have businesses in the country, own two residences and many other pieces of property, and have held accounts with 12 different banks, including five currently. Still, opening a new account is more painful than going to the dentist.

Once you have an account open, as long as your account activities stay within the parameters you outlined in your application documents, you should be fine. Vary from those parameters, say, by wiring a large amount of money to purchase a property, and expect the bank to want a lot of back-up documentation. It's the world we live in.

If, rather than a business or operating account, your interest is in an offshore account for holding money as part of your Plan B, Panama probably isn't the best choice. You must visit in person to complete the Know Your Client due diligence, and most banks aren't interested in foreign customers unless you make an outsized deposit.

Finally, frankly, customer service at the retail banking level is abysmal even if you speak Spanish.

Panama banks can make sense if you're looking to open an investment account. That's the private banking side of any bank, for which most banks require a deposit of $250,000 to let you in the door. That's a lower account requirement than most European banks... and several European banks have branches in Panama with lower requirements than those of their offices on the other side of the pond. It can be a back door into a Euro bank.

I've had maybe three-dozen accounts across those 12 banks I mentioned above. Based on that breadth of personal experience, I prefer not to make any specific recommendations. All banks in Panama are maddening. For retail accounts, much depends on the branch you walk into and the personnel working there.

Again, if you're resident in the country, it'll be easier to open an account. If you're not resident, a referral from an attorney in Panama or an account holder at the bank can help.

A good way to get your foot in the door can be to open a CD with say $10,000 or more. This can give you a leg up when trying to open an account. Remember, the interest you earn isn't taxable in Panama.

Residency In Panama

Most countries offer more than one path to becoming a legal resident. Panama offers more than a dozen. The three to consider first are the Pensionado, the Friendly Nations, and the Qualified Investor visas. One of these likely will work for you. If not, speak with a Panama attorney about other options.

When formalizing our residency in Panama two decades ago, Kathleen and my first choice was the Forestry Investor Visa. This program allows foreigners to qualify for residency by investing in approved reforestation projects, such as teak and other hardwood plantations, certified by Panama's Ministry of Environment.

At the time, our teak investment qualified us only for temporary residency. We would have needed to renew that status before becoming eligible for permanent residency. We wanted something more straightforward, so we pivoted to the Friendly Nations Visa.

Regardless which residency path you choose to pursue, you begin your Panama residency process by registering with immigration in the country. In some countries, in Europe, for example, you must begin your residency process in your home country. In Panama, you start in Panama. Your attorney will take your passport to the immigration office for you, but, obviously, it means you must be physically present in the country.

To apply for any Panama residency permit, you'll need to meet these requirements:

Your original passport must be valid for at least another six months or more from the date of application. If your passport expires before this time, you must have it renewed before submitting your residency application. To be safe, the passport should be good for a year from the date of application, in case of any delays.

If you are married, you need an original copy of your marriage license and an original copy of the birth certificates for any dependent children.

You need to get a background check from the national law enforcement agency in your home country. This document must be notarized.

In addition, these documents must be "authenticated" at a Panamanian Consulate or apostilled.

It is not necessary to translate your documents into Spanish. This will be done by your attorney in Panama.

Along with these basic requirements, each residency permit option comes with its own requirements, as follows...

Pensioner Visa (*Pensionado*)

The *Pensionado* Visa is by far the most popular residency option in Panama. It has become the Gold Standard worldwide thanks to its generous packages of retiree benefits. To reap these benefits, you don't need to invest a cent up front. You need only receive a pension or an annuity that meets the requirements.

The government of Panama is relaxed with regards to the minimum age to apply for this program. Typically if you are over the age of 18 and if you receive a guaranteed pension from any government entity, Social Security, Armed Forces, or private company, you can apply.

Your pension must be at least $1,000 per month, plus $250 per month for each dependent, including children under 18.

Once you've qualified, you enjoy all *pensionado* discounts. These are also available to all legal residents in Panama of the requisite age, but the age restriction doesn't apply to holders of a *pensionado* permit. The discounts include 50% off entertainment anywhere in the country (movies, theaters, concerts, etc.); 30% off bus, boat, train fares; 25% off airline tickets; 50% off hotels stays Monday through Thursday; 25% off hotels stays Friday through Sunday; 25% off at sit-down restaurants; 15% off at fast food restaurants; 15% off hospital bills (if no insurance applies); 25% off utility bills; 10% off prescription medications; 20% off medical consultations; 15% off dental and eye exams; 20% off professional and technical services; and 50% off closing costs for home loans.

Used to be you'd hear stories of *pensionados* being challenged or declined when requesting their discounts. That's no longer the case. One of the biggest ongoing benefits can be savings on your electricity bill. And, again, you can take advantage of these *pensionado* discounts even if you aren't resident in the country under the *Pensionado* Visa program. You simply need then to meet the age requirements.

You need to use an attorney for your residency process in Panama, regardless which residency program you choose.

Here's a pro tip: Don't pay the attorney fees in full up front. They should charge you as the process progresses, including for the government fees, which aren't payable until a certain point in the process.

If you are retiring with a government pension, you must present a letter or form from your government pension plan (and/or pension administrator, if you are retiring before you receive a government pension) showing that you will be receiving at least $1,000 a month for you and an additional $250 for each dependent. These forms/letters must be authenticated.

If you are receiving your pension from a non-governmental agency or business, you will also need to provide a check stub or statement of account showing the pension being deposited, along with a good-standing certificate from the company issuing the pension. This also must be authenticated.

The Friendly Nations Program

This is the second-most-common residency path in Panama. If you're from one of the countries on the Friendly Nations list—Andorra, Argentina, Australia, Austria, Brazil, Belgium, Canada, Chile, Costa Rica, Croatia, Cyprus, Czech Republic, Denmark, Estonia, France, Finland, Germany, Greece, Hong Kong, Hungary, Ireland, Israel, Japan, Latvia, Liechtenstein, Lithuania, Luxembourg, Malta, Mexico, Monaco, Montenegro, Netherlands, New Zealand, Norway, Paraguay, Peru, Poland, Portugal, San Marino, Serbia, Singapore, Slovakia, South Africa, South Korea, Spain, Switzerland, Sweden, United Kingdom, United States, and Uruguay—then this residency option is likely your best option if you don't qualify for the *Pensionado* Visa program and don't want to invest (or don't have) the $300,000 required for the Qualified Investor program.

In addition to the principal applicant, the following dependents are also eligible for residency: spouse and parents of the main applicant; children under 18 years old; children with disabilities; and children 18 to 25 who are single and registered at universities.

For the Friendly Nations option, you can either obtain a work offer from a Panamanian company or invest $200,000 in real estate. If you're planning to start a business in Panama anyway, then setting up a corporation and giving yourself a work offer letter is the easiest, most efficient residency path. You also have to deposit $5,000 into a bank account in Panama as part of the process, but you can access the funds immediately after getting a letter from the bank indicating the funds are there.

You'll be granted first a two-year temporary residency. At the end of those two years, you can apply for permanent residency if you still meet the requirements of the program. Five years after qualifying for permanent residency, you're eligible to apply for Panamanian citizenship.

Qualified Investor (QI) Residency

The Qualified Investor program is the most recent addition to Panama's long list of residency options. It was designed to attract larger investors to the country by offering fast turnaround times (30 days) for processing and permanent residency out of the gate as opposed to the temporary residency most other options in Panama start with, thereby fast-tracking, in essence, the total time before being eligible for naturalization.

Qualifying investments for this program include $300,000 in real estate, $500,000 in the Panama stock market, or $750,000 in a five-year bank CD.

Besides the higher investment requirements, the QI program comes with much higher government fees than the other options—$10,000 for the main applicant and $2,000 for each dependent.

This program makes sense for someone wanting the fastest route to citizenship and for someone from a country that isn't eligible for the Friendly Nations program.

Citizenship In Panama

Panama allows you to apply for naturalization after five years of permanent residency. This means you can apply five years after you're approved for the Qualified Investor permit. If you qualify for residency under one of the residency options that require renewals before converting to permanent residency, your timeline doesn't start until you convert from temporary residency to permanent residency.

Panama does allow for dual citizenship if you're born with Panamanian citizenship. If you're naturalized, you're meant to renounce all previous citizenships. For someone looking to give up their current citizenship, that's not a problem. However, most people are looking to hold multiple passports.

Panama doesn't specifically require proof of renunciation, so most people who get naturalized don't bother giving up their previous citizenships... and the reality is that it probably doesn't matter. Just be aware that if you do maintain your previous citizenships, it's possible your Panama naturalization could be revoked at some point down the line... though I've never heard of a single incident of that happening.

It can take a year or more to be approved for naturalization. One friend waited more than two years from applying to receive his passport.

Once you have a Panama passport, you'll be able to travel to 138 countries without getting a tourist visa in advance. That's a good number, but 68 other passports currently have more countries they can visit without a visa. The countries that most people would want to visit—most of the Americas and Caribbean as well as Europe—are included in the 138 countries as well as some Asian and African countries.

Additionally, Panama became an associate member of the MERCOSUR trade bloc in 2024. Should Panama eventually become a full member, as is intended, holding a Panama passport would allow you to live or work in any of the MERCOSUR countries. It'll be like holding a passport to an EU-member country... but for the Americas.

Doing Business In Panama

In 2008, Kathleen took her leave from the publishing company where she'd been working for 23 years. At the time, we were living in Paris. Kathleen spent the next three months enjoying very early retirement, exploring that city on foot, early to late each day, and getting to know Paris well.

She learned that three months is her limit for doing nothing, even in Paris. She returned home from a long walk one afternoon to announce that she wanted to start a business of her own.

"We'll need to leave Paris," I replied.

She and I both knew from experience that France is no place to build a business. It's not a country that values entrepreneurs, and running a business there is expensive and hassled. Labor law and the French perspective make every employer the enemy, and French taxes can take half of every dollar your business earns.

We were in the fortunate position of being able to move anywhere, so, as much as we loved living in Paris, the question became:

If France is among the worst places in the world to invest in a business, where would be among the best?

By this time, Kathleen and I had managed businesses in eight countries. Based on that experience, we made a list of things important to the expat entrepreneur, as follows:

- Quality and cost of infrastructure, especially Internet and banking
- Quality, availability, and cost of English-speaking labor
- The country's approach to taxation
- The current administration's perspective on foreign business and foreign investment
- Residency and work permit options
- Cost of doing business, especially office rent
- Ease of setting up a company
- Stability of the local currency (if other than the U.S. dollar)
- Time zone relative to the business' intended marketplace

- Local labor law
- Local standard of living

We considered the countries we knew from experience and others, too, in the context of these 11 questions, and one stood out—Panama.

The infrastructure in Panama City is the best in the region, in part thanks to the decades-long U.S. military presence here while the Americans ran the Panama Canal. Panama as a whole is a safe, stable, affordable country that uses the U.S. dollar as its currency, meaning no exchange-rate risk. The standard of living is comfortable, even international standard if your budget stretches to allow for it.

Those things, though, are true for many other places that could also make sense for the would-be entrepreneur, including in Latin America but also in Europe and Asia.

Panama's trump card is the approach it takes to taxation, both personal and corporate. It's possible to live and run a business you own in Panama, paying little in taxes, even if you're an American. The list of places around the world where that is true is short. I'm speaking of legal and compliant strategies. It's not difficult to organize, but you need competent advice from a tax expert who understands both Panama's approach to taxing corporate income and the obligations to Uncle Sam of an American living and earning money in another country. Really, you need two tax experts, as finding one who understands both sides of this tax picture will be near impossible.

Because I understood Panama's tax advantages, this country rose quickly to the top of the where-should-we-locate-the-new-business list.

The second reason we focused early on Panama and, in the end, chose it as the place to base Kathleen's new Internet publishing business is Panama City's labor pool.

Over the past 20 years, Panama City has evolved into a global melting pot. In addition to Panamanians and Americans, who've been a part of this landscape for more than a century, today's

Panama City is home to Venezuelans, Colombians, El Salvadorans, Hondurans, Costa Ricans, Guatemalans, and Nicaraguans who've migrated to Central America's most developed city in search of safe haven. Included in this population of regional migrants are investors, who've bought real estate and started businesses; unskilled labor in Panama mostly illegal and working as maids and restaurant staff; and, relevant for us, the cream of the regional labor crop, people who recognize they can get better jobs and make more money in Panama City than anywhere else in Central America.

That labor pool was enough to get our attention back in 2008. Then something important happened four years after we moved to Panama that made Panama City an even more interesting place to be an employer...

In 2012, Panama's then President Ricardo Martinelli issued an Executive Order creating this country's Friendly Nations visa program. Overnight, Panama was targeted by eager, educated, and English-speaking 20- and 30-somethings from North America and Europe in search of employment opportunities. Thanks to the Friendly Nations program, these enthusiastic youngsters, then and today, can obtain both easy residency and work permits. It's a uniquely turnkey program that makes it possible for anyone holding a passport from one of the 50 countries on the "friendly nations" list to be able to live and work legally in Panama almost immediately. Martinelli issued his decree in a creative attempt to provide more qualified labor for the dozens of foreign businesses setting up shop in his country. In the near two decades since, the program has done precisely that.

Over the years, thanks to this open-minded, open-borders visa option, we've been able to hire staff from the United States, Canada, Ireland, the U.K., France, Germany, Spain, Belgium, Australia, and New Zealand, none of whom we would have been able to employ (legally) otherwise.

Nearly two decades later, we've built a successful, continually growing business. What have these years of focused effort in Panama taught us?

Panama Entrepreneur Tip #1:

Panama City is home to a bigger and better-educated pool of English-speaking labor than anywhere else in Central America and perhaps than anywhere else in all Latin America. However, a sizable percentage of it is what I've come to think of as "accidental labor."

As Panama continues to be an easy place to establish legal residency and get a job, kids from across North America and Europe are doing that. Not all of them are interested in working, though. Some are on walkabouts, the post-graduation equivalent of a gap year, wandering around to see what they might see and experience what they might experience. Panama makes it possible for them to get jobs and earn a little money to refill their coffers before setting out for their next stops. We've hired 20-somethings from North America and across Europe who've worked for us for six months or so, long enough to save up enough to buy plane tickets onward. Just as we've trained them to the point of becoming worth something to the business, they bug out.

On the other hand, we've also hired 20-somethings from North America, across Europe, and beyond who've been with us for more than a decade and who are now fully fledged, world-class professionals helping us to push the Live And Invest Overseas business ever to next levels.

Panama Entrepreneur Tip #2:

Panama celebrates three independence days, all in November, plus 11 other national holidays each year. Almost everyone extends every holiday to include at least one other day off, officially or unofficially making the bridge between the holiday and the nearest weekend.

In addition, Panama labor law calls for four weeks of paid vacation every year, starting from year one of employment, and stipulates that employees earn into a "sick leave fund" that allows for up to 18 sick days per year with signed doctor letters. I've been told by many, including my attorney, that signed doctor letters can be bought on many street corners for $5.

Ours is a deadline-intensive business. We've finally built a team that understands that and works hard to work ahead to cover all the out-of-the-office time.

Panama Entrepreneur Tip #3:

A third piece of advice for the Cowboy Millionaire considering starting a business in Panama would be to be prepared for the culture shock.

Panama's is a booming economy, and all the foreign investment in the country can give you the impression that this is a real-world business culture. It is that much more so today than it was 20 years ago when we began doing business here... but, still, this is not the United States when it comes to getting things done. This is still a country of *fiestas* and *mañanas*. For most, business is not the priority, and work is not a vocation but a way to pay the rent. You'll encounter exceptions but you should be prepared for the typical Panamanian perspective on the employer-employee relationship.

Panama Entrepreneur Tip #4:

Panama labor law, like that everywhere in the world that is not the United States, favors the employee. You need a good reason and a lot of documentation to fire someone. No matter how good the reason, you'll be required to pay what I consider an overly generous "liquidation," or severance, depending on how long the about-to-become-former employee has worked for you.

In addition, Panama labor law equates to some particular land mines that we wish someone had told us about from the jump. For example, if you have any doubt about someone's long-term value to the business, make the decision to remove them from the business before their two-year anniversary. Again, it's always tough and costly to fire someone. After the two-year mark, it gets tougher and more costly.

I recommend hiring someone well versed in Panama labor law to manage HR for you while you learn the ropes and maybe forever.

All that said, I'm more convinced today, after doing business in this country full-time for two decades, that Panama is the best place in the world to be an entrepreneur. Kathleen and I don't spend many days swinging in hammocks or lazing on the beach. Those pastimes are ever-available, but, for us, that lifestyle has never been the point. We chose Panama because we believed it would support the business-building dream Kathleen conceived in 2008, and I doubt we would have been able to accomplish what we've accomplished these years since anywhere else.

As I mentioned, we chose the Forestry Investor Visa when we moved to Panama then switched to the Friendly Nations program when it was launched as it allowed for a quicker path to permanent residency. Another option that could have worked for us and that could be right for you if you, too, are looking to Panama with the eye of the entrepreneur is the country's Investor Visa.

To apply for an Investor Visa, you must invest a minimum of $160,000 in a new or established business in Panama. If you are applying with dependents, you must increase your minimum investment by $2,000 for each dependent.

The company you invest in must be registered in Panama's Social Security program, and the investment funds must come from abroad.

A minimum of five permanent Panamanian employees must be hired by your company. The employees must be given Social Security benefits, and they must be paid no less than minimum wage, which differs throughout the country.

Only one Investor Visa request can be made by any company.

Once approved, you are provided with a two-year provisional residency permit. After the two-year period, a permanent visa is issued. After five years with permanent resident status, you can apply for citizenship and a passport.

To apply for the Investor Visa, you must provide a sworn declaration letter from the company's secretary or treasurer attesting to your investment in the company. The investment must be at least $160,000.

You will also require a Certification of the Public Registry that credits the following:

- Purpose of the corporation
- Capital
- Your appointment as director of the corporation
- Copy of the Social Security payroll certifying that the company is operating
- Declaration before a notary certifying the investment
- Employer's Social Security payroll (minimum five Panamanian employees)
- Social Security good standing certificate
- First tax return
- Lease agreement or property title deeds and public utility bill

Kathleen's plan that brought us to Panama was for an Internet publishing business. Panama is an ideal place for any kind of Internet business you can imagine. In addition, this business and trade hub has now long been attracting many big-deal international brands that are locating their Latin American regional offices in Panama City. The country has the second-largest free-trade zone in the world along with several smaller incentive zones for businesses to operate out of.

The Cowboy Millionaire entrepreneur should begin by considering what type of business you want to start—one for local markets or one for international clientele. If local, then is your target market Panamanians, foreigners, or both.

I've known many local businesspeople in Panama. The ones who have done well know their market. One couple of French expat entrepreneurs I know started two businesses—a restaurant targeting the middle-class Panamanian market with "Ejecutivo

Lunch Specials" that they say are a cash cow and a French bakery and café targeting the expat market that does great happy hours.

Forming A Company

The most popular options for forming an offshore company in Panama are corporations and limited liability companies.

In the case of a corporation, an attorney drafts the documents, including a list of subscribers and bylaws, then records it in the registry. After that you'll need a RUC/Tax ID and a social security employer's number if you intend to hire staff.

Wages

Minimum wage in Panama varies depending on economic activity, business size, and region. The median monthly wage is around $1,288 with significant regional variations. The minimum wage for household help is $350 per month.

A 13th bonus month is paid to workers, split over three payments annually. Social security is paid at a rate of 12.25% by employer and 9.75% by the worker. Worker's comp is 0.98% to 5.6% depending on the risk of the job. Day shifts work up to a 48-hour week and are paid an additional 25% for overtime thereafter.

Tax Incentives

Industrial promotion certificates are available for industrial, agroindustry, marine, raw material, and forestry investments qualify for tax credits through industrial promotion certificates. Tax credits are also available for qualifying tourism investments.

In addition, a company operating in one of Panama's free zones can be exempt from import duties, income tax, sales tax, export tax, and certain consumption taxes.

Real Estate Opportunities In Panama

In 1996, Kathleen got a life-changing call from a property scout she had sent on a mission to Panama City.

"You need to see this place yourself," her scout Bob Fordi reported. "I believe Panama is shaping up to become the greatest investment opportunity of our lifetimes."

Kathleen followed Bob down to this little isthmus and confirmed everything he'd said was true.

The first big investment opportunity she identified was the sale of former U.S. military housing. Officers' former homes hit the market for $20,000. Today they sell for a million dollars and more.

From there she and I targeted Avenida Balboa in Panama City, where we bought a pre-construction condo that we still own. Over the years it's been a rental—earning us as much as 20% per year—and today it's our home when we're in the city. It's also worth twice what we paid for it.

On and on the deals rolled... from the City Beaches to booming Boquete and beyond.

And now, three decades on, for our money, Panama remains the surest property investment market in the world. We are more invested in Panama than anywhere else... and we're actively expanding our holdings.

In the face of a dramatically shifting global landscape, Panama continues to stand out as the world's safest haven. Here's why:

- **Strategic location:** As the isthmus connecting North and South America, Panama enjoys a unique geopolitical position. It's home to the Panama Canal, the expanded Tocumen International Airport (the "Hub of the Americas"), and a booming financial sector.

- **Strong economic fundamentals:** According to the IMF, Panama is "converging to U.S. living standards faster than any other country in the region."

- **Safe-haven resilience:** In our world of political instability and market volatility, Panama has proven itself a steady performer with low inflation. The local currency is the U.S. dollar, meaning no currency risk for U.S. investors.

- **Solid infrastructure:** From the Canal expansion to the new Panama Metro system and cruise ports, Panama's mega-projects continue to support long-term growth.

- **Headquarters of business.** More than 188 of the world's largest multi-national corporations, including Caterpillar, Pfizer, L'Oreal, and more, have made Panama City their regional base.

- **Growing middle class:** From 2008 to 2023, Panama's middle class grew from 45.7% to 59.9%. This means more internal demand for quality housing, both to buy and rent.

- **Favorable expat climate:** Panama offers investor-friendly residency options, excellent health care, and a tax regime that is territorial and welcoming to foreign capital.

- **Tourism and rental growth:** With close to 3 million visitors a year, Panama's rental market is thriving—especially in key urban and lifestyle hubs.

Successful investors in Panama are targeting high-demand, yield-generating rentals. They're also capitalizing on resale opportunities where units are trading below replacement cost.

There's strong interest in turn-key short-term rental units located in licensed buildings in popular Panama City neighborhoods such as Costa del Este. These investments offer high yields with legal certainty, professional management, and built-in diversified demand from both tourists and business travelers.

Bank foreclosures remain one of the best-kept secrets in this market. Privately circulated and often deeply discounted, these properties can deliver 20% to 30% savings on market value—if you know where to look.

Lifestyle investors are drawn to emerging beach destinations and cool mountain towns like Boquete, where tourism and remote work trends are generating strong rental demand.

In all cases, clear goals, well-researched plans, and on-the-ground expertise are crucial.

Panama continues to be a land of opportunity... but the market is not for uninformed buyers or speculative flippers. For a long while, you could have bought anything in this country and counted on making money. That's no longer true, especially in Panama City. You need to know where to look. However, for those who understand how to assess local regulations, builder reputations, and neighborhood dynamics, the opportunities remain significant, even once in a lifetime. Focus on cash flow and value-based buying.

Bottom line, whether you're looking for a second home, a lifestyle asset, or a pure investment property play, Panama deserves a place in your portfolio.

Taxes In Panama

Panama takes a jurisdictional approach to taxation. In addition, it offers several tax exclusions for certain kinds of income.

All that to say that the tax scene in Panama is as good as it gets anywhere.

A jurisdictional approach means that only money earned in the country is taxed in the country. This benefits entities set up in Panama that aren't doing business in Panama, but it also benefits residents of Panama who earn their money outside the country.

You will still be likely to be taxed in the country where the income is earned, but you don't have to worry about reporting non-Panamanian income in Panama for your company or for yourself if you're living there.

Panama also doesn't tax interest income earned from banks, so your CDs in Panama incur no tax in Panama.

If you're an American, it's moot as you'll still pay taxes in the States on that interest income, but if you're a non-American, depending on where you live and your overall tax situation, it could mean no taxes at all on the interest income. Specifically, if a non-American is a tax resident in Panama, that would be the case.

Revenue from agriculture is also exempt in Panama up to $350,000. Invest in a farm operation in Panama and you can pay no taxes in Panama. However, the same caveats apply for Americans who will have to report the income in the States and pay taxes to Uncle Sam on the income. Again, a non-American living in a jurisdictional taxation country whether it's Panama, Costa Rica, Malaysia, or elsewhere could owe no tax anywhere on their Panamanian farm income.

If you're operating a business in Panama that is earning its money from Panama, the company will pay taxes in Panama. The tax rate is 25% of net taxable income or 1.7% of gross taxable income, whichever is higher. Only companies with taxable revenue of more than $1.5 million are subject to the 1.7% alternative tax calculation.

For individuals earning an income from work done in Panama, the first $11,000 is exempt, the next $39,000 is taxed at 15%, and income over $50,000 is taxed at 25%. Few deductions are allowed but include medical expenses and insurance as well as mortgage interest.

Entities In Panama

A Panamanian corporation not doing business in the country is highly efficient from a Panama tax perspective. That does not mean, though, that you need or should have a Panama corporation.

I've heard too many stories over the years from Americans

who have bought property in Panama and been told by Panamanian attorneys that they "needed" to use a Panama corporation to hold that property. That can be costly advice for an American when it comes to U.S. taxes.

A foreign LLC and corporations in certain countries can be disregarded for U.S. tax purposes. That means the income from the entity flows through to your personal tax return for U.S. tax purposes. However, a Panama corporation is specifically excluded by IRS code. It cannot be disregarded.

This means an American who sets up a Panama corporation to hold a rental property in Panama, for example, is subject to the Passive Foreign Investment Company tax rules.

Under the Tax Cuts and Jobs Act, U.S.-controlled foreign corporations are taxed at the U.S. corporate rate of 21%, any associated rental income is taxed at 21%, and, when the profits are distributed to the owners of the corporation, they are taxed again.

A Panama corporation only makes sense if you intend to use it for an active business.

Panama does have an entity that can be disregarded for U.S. tax purposes. It's called a *Sociedad de Responsabilidad Limitada* (SRL). However, like a Panama corporation, which requires three directors, an SRL in Panama requires three members.

Unlike directors—who aren't owners of the company—members are owners of an SRL. Therefore, an SRL in Panama doesn't make sense for most people, as most people using an offshore entity to hold real estate or other passive investments are individuals or couples.

The other Panama entity that can make sense for an American who wants to hold real estate (and for Canadians who can't use an LLC due to Canada's tax rules) is a Panama foundation. A foundation is the civil law equivalent of a trust. It's a juridical entity like a corporation, but its set-up and structure are governed by different rules and its purpose is to hold assets while also accommodating automatic succession of beneficiaries—like a trust.

A Panama foundation is a reasonable alternative to a Panama corporation for people wanting to hold assets in an entity. However, for Americans, a foundation is treated like a trust, which means you'll have to file tax forms required for offshore trusts—both when the foundation is set up as well as annually.

Annual tax forms are required for Americans owning offshore corporations and LLCs, but they are less complicated than the offshore trust tax forms.

If you do set up a corporation in Panama, even if the corporation doesn't do business or have income from Panama, you're required to maintain financial statements and file them with your registered agent each year.

The bottom line is that a Panama corporation is less attractive than a corporation from another jurisdiction that doesn't require the regular filing of financial statements with the registered agent. Plus, Panama doesn't have a usable pass-through entity.

A Panama foundation is really the only entity to consider—unless you plan on doing business in Panama, in which case a Panama corporation is a must.

PANAMA

For The Cowboy Millionaire

For a small isthmus, Panama offers the Cowboy Millionaire a rich array of lifestyle options from cosmopolitan Panama City to the highlands of Boquete, from Playa Bonita just outside Panama City to Bocas del Toro in the Caribbean, and from established hotspots like Venao on the eastern coast of the Azuero Peninsula to the Veraguas frontier along Azuero's western coast. That's where you'll find Kathleen and me, at Los Islotes.

I discovered Panama more than 25 years ago but wasn't turned on to the west coast of its Azuero Peninsula until a decade later. When I began spending time on this country's Veraguas coast, no one else had ever heard of it... not foreign investors and not Panamanians either. On this coast, Kathleen and I were pioneers.

Look at Panama on a map, and you see a clear path of development along its Pacific coast, starting from just outside the capital city and moving westward. The Azuero Peninsula sits directly in this path.

Back in 2006, Kathleen and I explored the far side of the Azuero Peninsula, where the expat haven of Pedasí is located. My take? The terrain wasn't compelling. Neither were the prices.

A year later, we came down the other side of the peninsula and looked at pretty much every property that was available to be purchased at the time, as well as some that weren't. That's when we found Los Islotes.

Finding Los Islotes took a lot of research and legwork.

Getting here was no joke either.

There wasn't a direct road to the property. To gain access you had to hike in from the neighbor's property or come in from the beach. Los Islotes was originally a cattle farm. The ranchers got their livestock in and out via the beach. They didn't spend money even to put in an access road.

The pioneer life isn't without challenges. Azuero's western coast is remote and undeveloped; services can be unreliable, roads rutted.

The flip side of remote is private. For us, that was a priority agenda when we targeted this stretch of the Pacific.

I won't sugar coat it. It's been work. We've installed underground electricity, water, and fiber optic internet. We've built our dream home, which we're now planning to expand into a private family compound with room for the kids and all grandkids to come. This is a legacy undertaking.

Spanish colonial-style homes dot the hillsides. Just back from one of the two beaches you'll find Panama Jack's Bar where owners and guests meet for cocktails, cookouts, and great company. Our Equestrian Centre stands strong with mighty beams hand-hewn on-site by local craftsmen and features a grand central social area with a bar.

Our teams continue infrastructure and construction projects. Our long-term vision incorporates a Town Square with a church and a Student Center with a library.

Everybody who visits is awestruck by how beautiful this place is, but this is still a frontier. It's not for everyone. That's okay. We don't want everyone.

We want the people who appreciate the vision and the sense of community and privacy that we're building here.

Los Islotes is a refuge from a crazy world and an incubator for an independent way of life that went out of fashion in the United States a long time ago.

For me, Los Islotes... and Panama overall... are the ultimate Plan B.

CHAPTER II

★ ★ ★

BELIZE

A Freedom Seeker's Paradise

The small country of Belize nestled on the Caribbean coast of Mesoamerica doesn't really fit in...

Belizeans speak English, so they aren't part of the Central American region culturally, and, as the country itself is tucked below Mexico on the Yucatan peninsula, Belize is not really part of Central America geographically either.

European settlement in Yucatan was initiated by the Spanish, but the area around Belize became a buccaneer's haven as English pirates realized that Belize's coastline served as a good base for their attacks. Eventually, they also started logging logwoods for textile dyes.

While Spain and England disputed control of the area for more than a century, the English settlers were left to their own devices.

Finally, at the end of the 18th century, the Spanish lost a naval battle off the coast, and Spain stopped trying to expel the English from the region. The settlers were mostly left alone, and the large landowners established their own local government.

This buccaneer background and the long-ignored status of the settlers set the stage for the Belizean culture that persists these centuries later.

Belize today continues to follow its own independent path. Belizeans keep to themselves, and the government interferes little with day-to-day life. That mentality helps to explain why Belize has developed into the unique offshore jurisdiction it has.

When it gained independence from Great Britain in 1981, Belize had no real economy. The financial services industry that the British had initiated (including writing banking privacy into the constitution for the new country) took hold and became an important part of how the country has developed since.

Offshore services may be only a small percentage of Belize's GDP, but the country continues to foster this industry and remains one of my favorite offshore jurisdictions, all things considered.

Belize offers essentially the same banking and structures products as all the better-known players in the offshore world but with a much lower profile. In today's world, a low profile can be a big advantage.

The country is home to around 430,000 people with a Gross Domestic Product (GDP) of about $3.5 billion. Tourism is the most important source of foreign exchange in Belize today, followed by agricultural exports and services.

With hundreds of islands and the barrier reef just off its shores, Belize is a popular diving and snorkeling destination. And, as infrastructure in the interior of the country improves with more hotels and resorts, more tourists are also coming to explore the mountains, rivers, and Mayan ruins of the mainland.

Why else (other than its ability to date to stay off the offshore world's radar) am I a fan of Belize as an offshore haven? To answer that, let's look at the country in the context of how well it serves the sovereign individual in key areas...

Banking In Belize

Opening an offshore bank account is the easiest and usually the best first step for anyone looking to diversify their life internationally. In this regard, Belize stands out as a very user-friendly option. In most countries where you might want to plant your offshore banking flag, you're going to have to travel there to open an account in person. Not so in Belize.

You can open an account with an international bank in Belize remotely. In addition, it's possible to open an account in Belize with a modest initial deposit—even, in some cases, with no initial deposit.

This is very unlike the requirements in Switzerland, Austria, and Andorra, for example, jurisdictions where minimum account requirements can start at $1 million or more.

In fact, banks in Belize don't typically have formal minimum balance requirements for opening an account, though they may require minimum amounts for activating an account (as low as $1,000).

These low account balance requirements help to make Belize a good "starter" jurisdiction for anyone looking for where best to open a first offshore bank account.

However, while there may be no official minimum requirement, I'd suggest that you'd want to build up a balance to the point where the interest earned on the funds on deposit offset the monthly bank fees, which can be relatively high.

I'd also suggest that once you approach the $1 million mark, you diversify your offshore banking flag further by opening an account in another jurisdiction.

Belize banks are stable but small. Belize banking regulations require all banks in this country to maintain liquidity ratios of at least 24%. That means that 24% of all deposits in a Belize bank must be in liquid assets—cash or very short-term instruments.

One potential pitfall to the banks here being small is, once you have a biggish chunk of money, say $1 million plus, in any one of them, you risk becoming an overly big percentage of the bank's balance sheet. That's not a situation I'd want to be in.

Belize grants two kinds of banking licenses—international and domestic. A bank with an international license in this country can have only non-Belizean clients. Belizean citizens and permanent residents (excluding Qualified Retired Person, or QRP, residents) are not permitted to open accounts at an international bank in

Belize. They can hold accounts at local banks only.

Belize is home to three international banks: Belize Bank International Limited, Caye International Bank Ltd., and Heritage International Bank & Trust Limited. They exist outside of the hard currency controls that the Central Bank of Belize has, meaning they can trade in dollars, euro, pounds, yen, Swiss Francs, etc.

Belize Bank International and Heritage Bank have domestic banks as well but they are separate—so opening an account at Heritage International Bank & Trust Limited, for example, won't get you an account on the domestic side at Heritage Bank Limited.

On the domestic side, there are four banks, Heritage Bank Limited, Atlantic Bank Limited, The Belize Bank Limited, and the National Bank of Belize Limited. There are also 10 Credit Unions.

If you're planning to obtain permanent residency in Belize, you'll want to open an account with one of the domestic banks. It's not a requirement, but you're going to need to be able to write local checks to pay local bills.

Requirements For Opening A Local Belize Bank Account

- A valid passport and second form of photo ID—e.g. your driver's license.
- Proof of address—e.g. a utility bill.
- Two bank references—these must be original and signed by a bank official. They should be addressed to the manager at the Belize bank where you're applying for an account and state that you hold (and have held for a least two years) an account, confirm your address, state that your banking relationship has been satisfactory, and cover the facilities held with the bank in question. Plus, a letter of intent self-stating your reason for opening the account.
- A work permit (if applicable) or proof of economic interest in Belize—e.g. investments, property, etc.

The next step, upon receipt of the above documents, is Central Bank approval which is requested from the Central Bank for a fee of BZD$50 ($25).

Currency Controls

There's an important caveat to do with domestic banks in Belize that you should understand before opening an account with one. A domestic bank in Belize can open an account in U.S. dollars for certain types of businesses. However, you, as an individual, will only be able to get a Belize dollar account at a domestic bank.

Belize imposes currency controls to help manage its hard currency balances.

The practical consequence of this is that you may not be able to repatriate your funds back into U.S. dollars and send them out of the country easily or quickly. You'll first have to apply for the transfer with the Central Bank.

As an individual looking to move your cash out of Belize, you'll be at the bottom of the totem pole for any hard currency transfer. Import businesses and others that require U.S. dollars to keep operating will always have priority over you.

One secret to navigating this restriction can be to request your transfer during tourist season, when the Central Bank is flusher with hard currency. Of course, having to manage your personal financial affairs around the tourist season seems a little absurd. Welcome to Belize.

Belize's currency controls do not apply to the country's internationally licensed banks. Your U.S. dollar account at one of Belize's international banks will be liquid... as liquid as the bank... and any request to transfer funds out of it is not required to go through the country's Central Bank.

Note that, while some may tell you differently, as a resident in Belize, a domestic bank account is the only kind of bank account you're legally able to have in this country. Technically, if you open an account at an international bank before obtaining residency, you could get away with keeping that international account after you've become a resident, as long as nobody put the pieces together.

Also note that QRP residents aren't considered actual residents. They are considered "tourist residents" (which is why the tourist board manages the program). Therefore, QRP residents can legally have an international account in Belize (as well as a domestic one).

Residency And Citizenship In Belize

Residency status in Belize affects not only which types of bank accounts you can open. It also affects your ability to bring personal goods into the country and your eligibility for citizenship, if that is an objective.

You have two primary options for obtaining residency in Belize. The first is the QRP program, created by Belize to attract foreign currency.

To qualify to become a QRP, the applicant must age 40 or over and have a retirement income of at least $2,000 a month. You can either transfer that $2,000 to your Belize bank account each month or you can send $24,000 annually. The point is to be able to show that you're bringing at least that much hard currency into the country each year.

Accepted retirement income sources include pensions and annuities, Social Security benefits, investment accounts, inheritance, reverse mortgage, personal savings, and retirement contribution plans.

Applicants must also pass a security clearance check and spend a minimum of 30 consecutive days annually in Belize.

The QRP program is managed by the Belize Tourism Board (BTB), not the Ministry of Immigration. Therefore, QRP residency is technically a long-term stay visa... which, as I've mentioned, is not the same as permanent residency. Further, QRP status comes with none of the benefits of permanent residency, including and especially the potential for a Belizean passport and the right to work.

However, QRPs can conduct business in Belize with the approval of the BTB. For this, you need to provide a detailed business plan that includes the employment of a minimum of five Belizean citizens, proof of investment capital of at least BZ$1 million (US$500,000), and proof of having resided in Belize for a minimum of 90 non-consecutive days.

A QRP granted approval to carry on business in Belize is eligible for permanent residency after five years.

Plus, QRP residents get to bring all their personal and household belongings into the country duty- and tax-free, including a vehicle (could be a car, boat, plane, or, if you're going to live on Ambergris Caye, a golf cart).

You also can import another vehicle into the country every four years if you sell your previous one and the duties and taxes are paid at the time of disposal. For this purpose, duties are calculated on the current rather than the initial value of the vehicle. Additionally, any car must be newer than five-years-old to qualify for importation under QRP.

You can also purchase your "QRP" vehicle from a local dealer and be exempt from duty and taxes and avoid the hassle of shipping.

QRPs are also exempted from all taxes and duties on income received from sources outside Belize, capital gains tax, and inheritance tax.

QRP Application Requirements

Your QRP application must include:

- Completed, signed, and dated application forms for applicant and each dependent.
- Notarized or certified copies of birth certificates of each applicant and each dependent.

- Notarized or certified copy of your marriage certificate (if applicable).
- Original police record or certificate no older than six months from the last place of residency for the main applicant and each dependent.
- Notarized or certified copy of a complete valid passport (including all blank pages) for the main applicant and each dependent.
- Proof of income amounting to a minimum of $2k monthly or $24k annually in an approved foreign currency.
- Bank statement certifying your retirement income.
- Written undertaking of deposit to a financial institution in Belize.
- Original medical certificate or lab report of complete physical medical examination inclusive of HIV test results no older than three months are required for applicant and each dependent.
- Two passport photos—one recent notarized/certified passport photograph and one unnotarized/uncertified passport photograph of the same image for applicant and each dependent.

QRP Investor Application Requirements

A Qualified Retired Person who wishes to conduct business in Belize must apply in writing to the Belize Tourism Board for approval and send the following documents:

- A business plan (including provision for the employment of five Belizean citizens).
- Proof of investment capital—a minimum of BZ$1 million.
- Proof of residency by means of passport pages showing the applicant has resided in Belize for at least 90 non-consecutive days.

A Qualified Retired Person granted approval to carry on business in Belize shall...

- Employ a minimum of five Belizean citizens.
- Submit proof of employment of Belizeans to the BTB within 12 months of approval.
- Submit proof of business operation within 18 months of approval.
- Pay full duties and taxes on any business carried on in Belize.

From A Tourist Visa To Permanent Residency

The second option for obtaining residency in Belize is even more straightforward than the QRP program and gets you permanent residency. The only catch with this option is that, to qualify, you must remain in Belize for 12 months before you can apply.

On the upside, the main requirement is simply showing up.

When you enter Belize, immigration gives you a 30-day tourist stamp. At the end of those 30 days, you can go to the immigration office and renew your tourist status for another 30 days at a cost of BZ$200 (US$100). After 12 months, you can apply for permanent residency or continue to pay the monthly renewal cost.

During the 12 months you are renewing your tourist stamps, you can't leave Belize for more than 14 consecutive days. If you do, you have to start over the timeline to applying for permanent residency. The cost to apply for permanent residency is BZ$4,000 (US$2,000).

The benefits of permanent residency over QRP are that, with a permanent residency visa, you don't need a work permit to take a job and you are eligible to apply for citizenship after five years.

The path to citizenship in Belize is straightforward. Put five years of permanent residency under your belt (total of six years if you count the year it takes to get permanent residency), and you can apply for citizenship. The question is whether you'd want to do that or not.

If you're looking for a second passport so you can give up your current citizenship, then Belize may not be the best option. A Belize passport allows you to travel to but 102 countries without obtaining a visa and most of those countries are in the Americas and southern Africa.

However, holding a Belize passport does give you a leg up on residency and employment in any CARICOM country. CARICOM is a federation of Caribbean nations similar to the economic community formed in Europe in the 1950s that was the forerunner to the European Union.

If you are a Belize citizen, you can obtain residency and work permits much easier in the 20 CARICOM countries, which include the Bahamas, Jamaica, Barbados, Trinidad and Tobago, Grenada, and St. Lucia.

Another option is Belize's Temporary Investment Residency program designed for investors and entrepreneurs with investments in Belize valued at a minimum of BZ$500,000 (US$250,000). The threshold is typically met through a real estate purchase, but you could also invest in a business.

This program allows you to live and work in Belize and can be renewed each year provided you show proof that you have maintained your investment in Belize.

Asset Protection And Structures In Belize

Another flag you could plant in Belize could be an offshore structure.

I'll offer one caveat before reviewing the options for you: Before investing in any entity in Belize (or anywhere), make sure you understand your ultimate needs. Move too quickly, and you could end up investing in a structure you don't need and can't use.

Belize offers two classes of corporations—local corporations and International Business Corporations (IBC). The designations help to explain the different intended uses. Local corporations are for businesses operating in Belize that will pay taxes in Belize on profits. Belizean IBCs can't do business in Belize and therefore aren't taxed in Belize.

Most people go straight for an IBC because of the inherent tax-free status of the structure. However, a corporation is not always the best option... especially if you're an American. U.S. tax law treats passive income earned by a U.S.-controlled foreign corporation (CFC) punitively.

An American looking to use an entity to hold investments that generate passive income (essentially any non-business income) should use a pass-through entity, such as an LLC.

In 2011, Belize passed the International Limited Liability Company Act, which allows LLCs to be created in the country. The difference between an IBC and an LLC is that, in the eyes of the IRS, an LLC can be designated as a pass-through entity, meaning all income from the LLC flows through to the owner's personal tax return. This avoids the tax problems on the U.S. side that can arise from having passive income in a CFC.

Rounding out its entity options, Belize also offers trusts and foundations.

A trust can offer better asset protection than an IBC or LLC. A trust also allows better estate planning long-term.

Foundations are the civil law version of a trust and function 90% the same as trusts. However, foundations aren't defined under U.S. law and can be treated like a trust or a corporation depending on how the articles of formation are written. As assets in a foundation, like those in a trust, are generating passive income, you want to avoid the foundation being treated like a corporation for the same tax reasons that you don't want to use a corporation to hold passive income investments. Coordinate any foundation documentation with a U.S. attorney to ensure the foundation will be considered a trust by the IRS.

Belize entities can be a bit less expensive than comparable entities in other Caribbean offshore destinations, but I don't think price should be the ultimate determining factor for where to set up an offshore structure.

One benefit of setting up a Belize entity is that Belize also offers banking so you can typically set up both an entity and the related bank account at one of the international banks at the same time with ease.

Doing Business In Belize

The Belize government offers incentives to people who invest in different areas of the economy. Specifically, the government is interested in export and other businesses that either create a significant number of jobs or use technology new to Belize.

Through one of three incentive acts, if you receive proper approval in advance, your business can enjoy various tax holidays for income taxes, excise taxes, and import duties depending on the type of business and the incentive program the business qualifies for. The programs are Fiscal Incentive Program, Designated Processing Area, and Commercial Free Zones.

An exporting business could be your best option. Belize has a limited market, with its 430,000 people, making it difficult for any new business to do well locally. However, with the incentives available from the government for export businesses, you could operate in Belize, enjoying a low cost of employment and paying no taxes in Belize on your profits, even though you're "operating" locally.

In fact, you could establish your own Designated Processing Area (DPA) to benefit from the government incentives. A DPA can essentially be set up anywhere in the country your business plan is approved. This allows you to locate your business near the human or natural resources you need.

Alternatively, you could simply set up shop in one of the already established Commercial Free Zones (CFZ). The two CFZs in Belize are located near the Mexican border in the north and the

Guatemalan border to the west.

A CFZ differs from an DPA in that they don't have to be 100%-for-export businesses. However, any products introduced to Belize from a CFZ would be liable for the requisite import duties.

Beltraide (Belize Trade and Investment Development Service) a government arm established to help anyone interested in establishing a business in Belize, can help you navigate the application process required to have your business venture approved for the various government incentives on offer.

Additionally, Beltraide agents can make introductions to local suppliers and service providers.

Going Off-Grid In Belize

Neither Doomsday Prepper nor Wilderness Mountain Man need you be... but, with the right systems in place, living can be fully self-sustainable.

And Belize—specifically its inland Cayo District—is one of the best places on earth to embrace this lifestyle.

The reality TV vision of self-sufficiency is hairy rawhide-clad mountain men and women jumping into frigid rivers in the wilderness to wrestle salmon from giant grizzly bears. It's as comically ridiculous as it is unnecessary.

Self-sufficiency needn't be nearly so dramatic or exotic. It can be achieved from the comfort and convenience of your own home and garden, meaning you can reap all the benefits of a self-sufficient lifestyle while also continuing to enjoy all the comforts of our modern age.

Strictly speaking, self-sufficiency means being in the position of not requiring any aid, support, or interaction from anyone else. Being able to live comfortably completely on your own... should you need or want to.

You can take this to the extreme or you can start low-key by, say, planting a kitchen garden. Kathleen and I are not fully self-sufficient at Los Islotes, but we do grow herbs and vegetables and fruits in season. We're incorporating solar power in key points across the property. And we harvest trees for lumber that we use in the construction of houses and furniture. We're still on the grid, but we've got redundancies, and, if worse came to worst and global supply chains and support systems broke down, we'd be able to live comfortably on our own here indefinitely.

For us, that's the goal.

Friends in Belize are more serious in their pursuit of the self-sufficient life, wanting nothing to do with any government or third-party services. In Belize, they're in good and growing company.

Here are six reasons Cayo, Belize, specifically, can be the best choice for a self-sufficient, resilient, sustainable, neighborly, and fun life...

#1: Food Security

A key factor to a healthy lifestyle is access to quality, nutritious foods. In Cayo, you can grow your own food on your own land. Those things you choose not to produce yourself can be sourced very locally at the farmer's market in San Ignacio.

#2: Reliable Water Sources

No worries here about water shortages.

#3: Energy Independence

Living off-grid with solar and rain-catchment doesn't have to mean giving up the amenities of the modern world. In Cayo, you can have high-speed Internet, modern appliances, and an active lifestyle with neighbors. Today's technology allows you to embrace Cayo's abundant natural resources efficiently.

#4: Low Population Density

When there is a disruption in the supply chain, as we saw during the global pandemic, it's good to be a safe distance from big cities and high-density populations. Belize has a population density of just 37 people per square mile.

#5: Fertile Land

Everything grows well here.

#6: English Speaking

As a former English colony (and still a part of the English Commonwealth), Belize is the only officially English-speaking country in Central America.

Plus it's warm here year-round.

BELIZE

For The Cowboy Millionaire

Nearly two decades ago, gregarious Michigan native Phil Hahn conceived plans for a 98-acre inland residential community in Belize's Cayo District that he christened Carmelita Gardens.

Located on the mainland in western Belize, Cayo is a frontier of rivers and rain forest, the type of place where the burdens and concerns of the rest of the world feel far away and unimportant. The kind of place where a Cowboy Millionaire can thrive.

Carmelita Gardens lies beside the village of Santa Familia. It's seven miles past the bustling town of San Ignacio and seven miles before the modern Mennonite town of Spanish Lookout. It's in the sweet spot, halfway between San Ignacio and its social outlets and Spanish Lookout, a commercial and industrial center.

Spanish Lookout is like an American town, with car dealerships, auto part and hardware stores, churches, supermarkets, and everything else you might want, except for bars.

At the time, there was nothing in Carmelita Gardens except some roads and a hole in the ground that would become the foundations of the community's first cottage.

Today, thanks to Phil's pioneering spirit, what was once little more than a parcel of pasture land is now a thriving riverside village with residents of all ages and backgrounds and Phil's lifelong dream of a resilient and independent community is a reality.

Carmelita Gardens offers comfortable cottages, bungalows, and villas, as well as lots.

Every house comes with its own solar power system and backup generator, making this community the perfect bolt hole in times of social, political, or economic turmoil.

Being off-grid, you can easily become self-sufficient. Power cuts and electricity price spikes won't affect you there.

Rainwater harvesting systems and under-house cisterns to

see you through the dry season come with every house, too.

Each lot has enough space for a private garden, but there's also a large community garden if you aren't interested in growing for yourself.

The long-term vision is that Carmelita Gardens grows to be a vibrant small town with mom-and-pop shops in the town square, neighborhoods with independent off-grid homes, self-sufficient friendly residents, boutique riverfront resort and restaurant, civic buildings, parks and recreation areas, orchards, and gardens.

Carmelita and the wider Cayo District is a perfect place to enjoy the Cowboy Millionaire lifestyle. If I didn't have my own 225-acres in Panama, I'd likely be living in Phil's neighborhood. It's connected but off-grid, home to like-minded freedom-seekers, and a true escape from political squabbles and the chaos of our current world.

CHAPTER III

ARGENTINA

On The Cusp Of A New Golden Age

Argentina deserves the Cowboy Millionaire's attention as a top-tier "Plan B" option.

And it deserves your attention now, because it has begun a remarkable economic turnaround. If things continue as they're going, you'll be glad to have incorporated Argentina into your international diversification plan.

And you'll be glad you got in early.

The World Bank classifies Argentina as an Upper-Middle Income country. Despite the hard times it has and continues to endure, this country is ahead of the pack in the context of Latin American economies, with a high standard of living and good infrastructure.

The thing is, Argentina could and should be a much richer nation. Poor management for a century kept it from prospering as much as it's natural resources could have allowed.

Argentina has not kept economic pace with Uruguay or Chile, its regional first-world peers, but it has as many or more natural resources than both of those countries combined. Argentina has about 15% of the U.S. population in a land area that is about 30% of the U.S. In other words, about half the population density...and about a third of Argentina's population is in and around Buenos Aires.

In other words, the resources per capita in Argentina are much greater than in the United States and most other countries.

If only the Argentines could find a way to manage them better and consistently over time.

Perhaps, at last, they have... perhaps in the nick of time.

Argentina's debt has been an issue for at least a half century. Today's debt-to-GDP ratio is 83.3%, which is not hopeless... the world average is worse, at 93%.

The debt-to-GDP ratio in the United States is 123%, which likely is hopeless... but that's a different conversation.

Meantime, way down at the bottom of the earth, the Argentines have one Javier Milei on the case. They elected Milei to the office of president in December 2023.

When Milei was sworn into office, inflation was at 143% and about 57.4% of Argentines were living in poverty, according to a study by the Catholic University of Argentina.

The election of Javier Milei was a bottom... and a turning point.

Born in 1970 in Buenos Aires, President Milei is an economist and former professor who has earned two master's degrees and authored 11 books and more than 50 academic papers on economics. He is known for his right-wing populist and libertarian political stances.

When he assumed the presidency, Milei was relatively new to elected office, having served but one term in the Chamber of Deputies, Argentina's lower house of congress.

Before entering politics, President Milei became a popular figure in the media, often appearing on television and radio to discuss economic issues. There he gained a following for his outspoken and often controversial views.

Milei's presidency has been marked by a focus on deregulation and austerity measures aimed at addressing Argentina's economic crisis, including high inflation. He has also pursued a foreign policy that emphasizes closer ties with Israel and the United States while distancing himself from left-leaning governments in Latin America.

President Milei pioneered the use of a chainsaw (later adopted by President Trump and Elon Musk) to symbolize the slashing of government spending. At this point, he has been slashing long enough to see his policies beginning to have a positive effect on the economy.

Despite his austerity measures, President Milei has a decent approval rating, coming in higher than either of his previous two predecessors at this point in his presidency.

His programs are working. Argentines seem willing to put up with the pain of the withdrawal of huge social spending to be rid of record-setting inflation. So far.

With Milei at the helm, there's reason to believe that the next chapter for Argentina could lead to this country becoming the country it's always had the potential to be.

Economic issues notwithstanding, Argentina has a lot going for it...

- Buenos Aires is one of the world's best cities. It would draw people to the country even if it were the only city in Argentina.

- Entrepreneurs claim that it's a great place for hiring a workforce, with its skilled, highly educated population. (College education is free in Argentina.)

- Entrepreneurs also claim that Argentina is in the perfect time zone for doing business with the U.S. and Europe. At GMT-3, they're two hours ahead of New York and three hours behind London.

- Argentina is crypto-friendly, which has enjoyed a high adoption rate, wide acceptance, and legal recognition.

- If a second citizenship if one of your Cowboy Millionaire objectives, you'll be interested to hear that Argentina has a strong passport, with visa-free entry to most of the world's countries.

- Argentina is intrinsically beautiful, with an extremely diverse landscape from snow high in the Andes and world-class vineyards to high deserts in the north and several first-world, very livable cities… plus 2,900 miles of Atlantic coastline.

- Argentina has a strong European influence which sets it apart from other Latin American countries. The culture is predominantly Italian, with 62% of the population claiming Italian ancestry.

- If you're a wine lover, you'll find Argentina a paradise. I am… and I do. It produces some of the world's best wines, including my personal favorite (Malbec) and one of Kathleen's favorite sparkling wines (Chandon). We enjoy Argentine wines so much that we invested in the vineyard of a friend in Mendoza, where wine is a lifestyle.

Bottom line, Argentina offers a higher quality of life than you'll find anywhere else in Latin America, on par with life in Europe… for a fraction the cost.

Residency And Citizenship In Argentina

The rules for residency and citizenship in Argentina underwent a major overhaul in May 2025. The governing decree is *Decreto* 366/2025, and it has created some of the world's current best immigration opportunities.

The country offers three types of residency: Temporary, Permanent, and Transitory. The third is mostly relevant for medical tourists, students, and digital nomads.

An expat looking to become legally resident in Argentina starts off as a temporary resident, locally called *DNI Temporario*.

After three years, you can petition for permanent residency, called *DNI Permanente*. This status gives you all rights of an Argentine citizen except for the right to vote. Permanent residents also have the same access as Argentines to the (free) health care and education systems as Argentines.

Time-in-country requirements: As a permanent resident, you cannot be away from Argentina for more than one year. As a temporary resident, you can't leave the country for more than six months. If you lose your visa because you break these rules, the decision can be appealed. Time-in-country requirements are much stricter if you intend to apply for citizenship.

The Most Common Visas For Expats

Argentina offers many visa options. These are the most common for expats:

Rentista Visa: Intended for those with passive income from outside Argentina, you'll need an income of around $1,500 per month, per person (including children), to qualify. This visa does not apply to digital nomads. You must demonstrate that this amount is being transferred into Argentina, routinely, through normal banking channels. You'll need to lay the groundwork for this before applying, so you can show a history of transfers.

Pensionado Visa: This visa is intended for those who are receiving a stable pension. The required amount is around $1,500 per person per month. Although the threshold is the same as the Rentista Visa, a Pensionado Visa is easier to obtain approval for, because the income is guaranteed.

Note: The exact income requirement for both the Rentista and the Pensionado visa is five times the minimum wage in Argentine pesos and subject to exchange rate fluctuations.

Student Visa: This is for full- or part-time students enrolled in schools in Argentina. Under Decreto 366/2025, students are no longer automatically eligible for free public health care or tuition.

Family Unification rules allow an applicant who marries an Argentine citizen (or resident), has an Argentine parent, or has an Argentine child to obtain residency. As of mid-2025, you are no longer granted the same residency as your qualifying relative. Now you are given temporary residency for up to three years.

Digital Nomads can work in Argentina under the new law for up to one year. They will need to show a sustained income of a minimum of $2,500 when applying. The digital nomad visa does not give credit towards permanent residency or citizenship.

Document Authentication

Argentina is part of the Hague Apostille Convention, so you'll need to use the apostille process to certify any documents issued from outside Argentina. As of 2024, Canada is using the process along with former signatories such as the U.S., the U.K., Australia, and New Zealand.

Naturalization

To apply for citizenship, you'll need at least two years of uninterrupted legal residency. Unlike in most countries, all forms of residency—permanent, temporary, and transitory—other than the digital nomad visa qualify you for citizenship.

Note, however, that you must have been in Argentina, full-time, for the entire two years before applying. And, under the new law, the requirement for "continuous years" has no exceptions. As the law is interpreted now, you may not even leave Argentina for brief trips abroad during this time.

Aside from the time-in-country requirement, you'll also be

asked to re-verify much of the same information you provided to get residency in the first place, including showing the means to support yourself, a clean criminal record, your birth certificate, proof of residence, etc.

Argentina allows dual citizenship, so there's no need to renounce any previous citizenships you've acquired.

The Argentine passport is a high-quality travel document, with visa-free (or visa-on-arrival) access to more than 160 countries. What's more, you'll be part of the MERCOSUR trade block, which gives you the right to work or live in Brazil, Uruguay, and Paraguay, as well as the associate member countries of Chile, Colombia, Ecuador, Peru, and Bolivia.

Citizens also have access to Argentina's free health care system, as well as its education system.

Note that as a naturalized Argentine citizen, you are not eligible for fast-track Spanish citizenship. Only native-born citizens qualify.

There is no formal language test to become a citizen, but you will need to be proficient enough in Spanish to understand the process and get through the interviews.

Marrying an Argentine citizen (or having an Argentine child) used to put you on the fast-track for citizenship, but not anymore. As I mentioned above, it will get you temporary residency, but it won't shortcut citizenship.

Owing to the organizational changes in Decreto 366/2025, I believe the process of naturalization will be more efficient than it was previously. We'll see.

Citizenship By Investment

As this book goes to press, Argentina is in the process of approving a Citizenship By Investment program.

While this program does not have final approval, the plan is to grant citizenship to those making a $500,000 qualifying investment in the country. Allowable types of investments are not yet specified. You'll need a clean background check, and the government intends to perform due diligence on the source of the funds.

The program will require no minimum physical presence time in Argentina and no waiting period before obtaining citizenship.

Banking In Argentina

Here I'm rating the products and services offered by the banks in Argentina... not the stability of the currency or Argentina's monetary policy.

The critical point to understand is that, with the important exception of real estate, Argentina is not a good destination for storing wealth. In fact, most Argentines store the bulk of their wealth in U.S. dollars outside their own country.

That said, if you maintain a presence in Argentina—either as a resident, citizen, or landlord—you'll need a local bank account. There's no more efficient way to pay local bills, take care of expenses, pay HOA fees, or manage any interface with the local economy.

And the banks here—both the traditional and digital banks—offer a good selection of products and services.

The country's largest bank is Banco de la Nación Argentina. Founded in 1891, it is wholly owned by the government and acts as the government's financial agent. It's a solid bet for financial stability.

HSBC, a London-based bank, sold their assets to Grupo Financiero Galicia, an Argentine bank, in 2024 making Galicia the second-largest bank in Argentina and the country's largest domestically owned private bank.

Galicia offers both a traditional banking platform as well as digital.

BBVA, a Spanish-owned bank, is consistently rated as one of the best in Argentina.

Opening An Account

Using BBVA as an example, here's what you need to open a checking account:

- You must be over 18 years old.
- Proof of address (a utility bill or rental contract, for example).
- Official government ID (called INE).
- A tax ID number (called CUIT or CUIL).
- A signed affidavit attesting to your answers to the "know your client" questions... things like where the money came from, expected cash flow through the account, etc.

It's legal to open an account as a non-resident. You'll need your passport, and you *might* be asked for your foreigners' registration card or an address verification from the municipality where you live.

Many requirements are not cast in stone and vary from client to client and bank to bank. The best plan is to make an information-gathering trip to the bank where you'd like to open an account, with no expectation of success. Go to a specific bank branch, ask the agent what you'll need, and then return to the same individual when you've gathered everything.

Dollar Accounts

You can open an account in either pesos or U.S. dollars. If you are opening one in dollars, you will be asked to specify how much money will be passing through the account, and the bank could place a limit on how much can pass through the account monthly.

You'll have an easier time opening a dollar account if you have residency in Argentina.

I recommend getting a dollar account if you can. I find it useful when bringing money into the country, as you can control when the money gets exchanged into pesos. That way you can make the exchange when rates are most favorable to you. You can also use the dollar account to avoid local-currency volatility.

Good-To-Know Banking Services

- **Direct Debit** is widely available and often used for recurring payments like utilities.
- **DEBIN:** Standing for *Débito Inmediato*, this instant debit system allows financial institutions and other payment industry participants to debit funds from customer's bank accounts (with prior authorization). Transfers can be initiated by the recipient and are instant… unlike other forms of direct debit that run in batch.
- **Online Payment Options:** Services like *PagoMisCuentas* allow users to pay various bills, including utilities, through direct bank transfers.
- **Rapipago and Pago Fácil:** These networks remain popular for cash payments, especially for those who prefer not to use banks or credit cards. They allow consumers to pay utility bills, among other things, in cash at numerous locations across the country.

Taxes In Argentina

Tax Residency: If you are physically present in Argentina for more than 183 days in a calendar year—including non-consecutive days—you are considered tax-resident, regardless of your immigration status. Permanent Residents are generally considered tax-resident, regardless of days-in-country. Citizens living abroad for 13 months may be considered non-tax-resident.

Value Added Tax, locally called IVA: 21% standard rate, which is at the high end in South America, where Uruguay is highest at 22% and Paraguay lowest at 10%. Argentina's rate of 21% would be about average for Europe.

Income Tax: A progressive tax system with rates from 5% to 35%. Residents pay tax on worldwide income, while non-residents pay on Argentine-source income. Companies pay 25% to 35%.

Wealth Tax: This tax is in transition, and in 2026 the tax is .5% to 1% with the expectation of dropping to .25% in 2027. Deductions and exclusions apply, but the thresholds are relatively low except for properties that are your primary residence.

Property Taxes are levied at the provincial level but range between .75% and 1.5% of the cadastral value, which is generally much lower than actual value.

Inheritance Tax: Varies by province, with rates depending on one's relationship to the deceased.

Capital Gains Tax: A rate of 15% on most items, with some exemptions for non-residents.

Real Estate Opportunities In Argentina

Real estate has proven to be the most disaster-resistant commodity in Argentina and for my money is the safest bet for protection of wealth in this country, as anywhere.

Argentina does impose some limited restrictions on foreign ownership of real estate. The one to pay attention to is buying in a "security zone"—that is, close to a border with another country. That requires federal government authorization, which you're likely to get, but can delay the purchase and titling process.

Real estate prices in Argentina have come alive in recent years, gaining between 7% and 9% per year in dollar terms. The renewed momentum is driven by President Milei's economic reforms and deregulation efforts.

In Buenos Aires, investors are drawn to the high-end neighborhoods of Palermo and Puerto Madero, and these luxury segments of the market are seeing increased demand.

I bought in the Retiro and Recoleta neighborhoods back in 2002 after the financial crisis that Argentina suffered when it decoupled from its 1-to-1 peg with the U.S. dollar. It was a mostly a cash market then and it still is.

Friends and colleagues on the ground believe that when inflation is more under control and banks begin to loosen up lending, a growing mortgage market will lead to stronger real estate prices.

Doing Business In Argentina

Argentina has traditionally ranked among the world's worst places to do business. Last time the World Bank published their "Ease of Doing Business" report, Argentina came in at the sorry position of 141 out of the world's 190 economies. The country's mountain of regulations has historically made starting up a legitimate business here difficult.

Next time the "Ease of Doing Business" report is updated the ratings should be kinder to poor Argentina. I'd say it's reasonable to expect dramatic improvement in Argentina's business environment.

Argentina required considerable expertise to navigate the complexities of everything from getting permits to hooking up utilities, while dealing with Argentina's 18 government ministries.

So why be optimistic now?

President Milei has gotten rid of (or changed) over 300 laws and disbanded half of the country's ministries. Things are rapidly becoming more streamlined and efficient.

Business challenges that come with runaway inflation are diminishing, as inflation rates tumble. And trying to manage finances with several different exchange rates is becoming a concern of the past, as the official and black-market exchange rates converge. Argentina is seeing its first budget surplus in a decade.

Running a business here still has its challenges from strong labor unions and rigid labor laws to yet-to-be streamlined processes. But things are improving at a rapid pace, and there's more reason for optimism than I've seen in the past 30 years.

So why start an expat business in Argentina?

After all, you could go to the region's much more business-friendly places like Panama, Puerto Rico, or Colombia.

The reason to start a business in Argentina is because you want to be in Argentina. The lifestyle on offer in this country is special. It can't be matched anywhere else in the world. Starting a business is one way to access it.

What Expat Entrepreneurs Are Doing In Argentina

Tech-savvy expats are doing web design, web development, and working for digital marketing agencies. They're taking advantage of Argentina's well-educated workforce and lower costs. College is free in Argentina, so the workforce is highly-educated and free of student debt.

You'll also find many opportunities in tourism and travel. Expats are conducting cultural tours and adventure and ecotourism excursions. Special-interest tours are popular, especially to do with wine, food, and nature photography.

Friends have been successful building and operating boutique hotels and guesthouses, from Buenos Aires and Salta to Mendoza and Bariloche.

There is a demand for expertise in renewable energy, an industry still in its early stages in this country.

The best strategy for an expat entrepreneur anywhere can be a business to service the expat community. It's the market you know and understand.

And of course there's real estate. In my experience, there's no more-powerful combination than someone who brings a formula for success in North America and teams up with an Argentine who knows the local market and culture.

ARGENTINA

For The Cowboy Millionaire

In January 1994, I moved to Argentina. I was 25 years old.

By that time, I had already done short stints in Chad and Kazakhstan.

These aren't places known for their good living.

I contracted malaria within two weeks of arriving in Chad and was diagnosed with bronchitis after 48 hours on the ground in Kazakhstan. Everyone in Kazakhstan had bronchitis. Temperatures fell to minus 50 degrees each night.

Every night before falling asleep, I had to set my alarm to wake me so I could go outside to start my car at 3 a.m. Otherwise the battery wouldn't turn over the next morning.

In Chad I was the only white guy for miles in a village of mud huts.

Both moves were made on the directives of the international oil drilling company I was working for way back then.

Was I just a glutton for punishment? Not exactly.

I had an itch for adventure, yes... but, more than that, I realized, even at that age, the advantages of being an American offshore. I was a kid earning oil company wages that would be 100% tax free.

Then, New Year's 1994, that drilling firm sent me to Argentina.

Arriving in Buenos Aires for the first time, my initial reaction was...

This isn't Chad... this isn't Kazakhstan.

The international airport was busy but organized... orderly. The drive to the domestic airport to connect to my in-country flight to northern Salta Province, where I was being posted, took me through a metropolitan area that I later learned holds a third of the country's population.

But, again, this wasn't Third World Africa. The people were

well dressed, the men in suits, the women chic even... everyone going about their business.

This was before the Internet, and I didn't know I was going to Argentina until the day I left Kazakhstan, so I had had no time to study up on the country in advance of my arrival. I showed up and began trying to size up the situation as I experienced it.

At first I thought that the prosperity I was seeing was the result of the country's vast natural resources. After a couple of weeks, however, the local economics became clearer. Yes, Argentina was doing well... but not the typical Argentine on the street. They were struggling to make ends meet.

Stores didn't indicate sales prices on items but payment terms. Want to buy a shirt? You could make eight payments of $4. A television... that was 20 payments of $30.

Store owners were confused when I asked what the price would be if I paid in full. I was supplying a new office and camp for the drilling company. I had a lot of shopping to do, both immediately and ongoing. Paying over time would have been a nuisance. Plus I figured we should be able to get a nice discount by paying in full up front and indeed we did. With the discount, prices were more reasonable—not cheap but okay.

Then someone told me about shopping in Bolivia. The border was only an hour from the town in Salta where my operation was based, and prices in Bolivia were a fraction of prices in Argentina for, in many cases, the exact same products. So my assistant and I started traveling to Bolivia to do our shopping.

That got me thinking. Why was Bolivia so much cheaper than Argentina?

Locals would tell me stories about when the reverse had been true. They could remember, they said, when Bolivians came across the border to shop in Argentina, where prices were much lower.

What had changed?

The currency.

Argentina pegged its currency to the U.S. dollar in April 1990, eventually changing their currency from the austral to the peso and using a 1-to-1 peg between the Argentine peso and the U.S.

dollar.

Pesos or dollars... the average Argentine on the street didn't know the difference and didn't care.

However, the more sophisticated Argentines... the business people and the old-money families... they did understand the difference. And they wanted U.S. dollars.

In fact, they were accumulating them and hoarding them... in bank accounts outside the country.

They knew that the situation created by the artificial currency peg was unsustainable, so they were squirreling away everything they could and storing it outside the Argentine economy.

Prices for everything in Argentina rose and rose until, eventually, the country's manufacturing sector vanished. It became too expensive to produce anything in the country. Cheaper to import goods so that's what everyone did.

I left the drilling company after six months in Argentina, and it wasn't until eight years later that the economics of what I had lived through during those six months in 1994 became much clearer to me.

In December 2001, Argentina removed the peg between its peso and the U.S. dollar. The government converted all bank accounts from dollars to pesos in one fell swoop overnight. Same for debt. Whatever you owed was no longer repayable in U.S. dollars but now Argentine pesos. People with savings in banks woke up one morning to find that their account values had been decimated.

Meantime, farmers with mortgages on their properties got big breaks as the peso fell in the wake of the decoupling. In 2002, the exchange rate dropped from 1-to-1, where it'd been with the peg, to as low as 4-to-1.

Banks closed and real estate prices collapsed. It was a bona-fide crisis investing opportunity and perhaps the best chance of our lifetime to buy property in this country.

And I did. Friends and I purchased three downtown Buenos Aires apartments over the next six months. Those were some of the most successful buys of my career.

What surprised me during my property scouting trips and

then during the time I spent in the country over the next two years, while the local economy was trying to stabilize itself, was that most of the Argentine businessmen I met with didn't seem concerned. They weren't struggling financially. In fact, they were doing well.

What's going on here, I wondered. What do they know that I don't?

And then finally it began to sink in.

The businessmen and professionals I was speaking with were the ones who had been accumulating physical dollars and keeping as much of their wealth as possible outside their country. They could see the writing on the wall and had taken steps to prepare for the collapse they knew was inevitable.

Argentina's economic history is filled with dramatic ups and disastrous downs. Over generations of experience, Argentines, I realized, had learned to diversify their wealth outside their own country. It was simple—and effective—self-preservation.

That revelation in 2002 about the wisdom of keeping the bulk of your money outside your home country made a big impression on me. By this time, I'd already begun working to diversify my life and my investment portfolio, but watching this lesson play out in real life in Argentina compelled me to work harder and faster.

I wanted to be like the Argentine businessmen who were able to come through unfazed from what amounted to total economic collapse in their country.

I did not want to be like the average Argentine on the street struggling to pay his rent and buy groceries for his family because his life savings had literally disappeared overnight.

And, thanks to those Argentine businessmen, I understood in a real way the secret to making sure my family and I would be okay no matter what happened in the economy or markets of our home country... or of any other country for that matter.

For these Argentines, diversification was not a theoretical exercise. It was the key to survival.

The rest of us need to learn that lesson quick.

Argentina was once one of the wealthiest countries in world.

Bad management and politicians ruined this once-great economic powerhouse.

Sound familiar?

I wrote a decade ago that America "is on a path of self-destruction that it's probably too late now to avoid." The country's course has been set and will be very hard to change.

In an effort to maintain its position as the global leader as long as possible, the United States has put policies in place that run counter to the constitution and to good sense. And we are now well along this path.

The good news is that, just like those old-money Argentines, you can sidestep economic conditions on the ground and even "opt out" of the bad decisions made by the politicians in power by looking beyond your own borders... including and especially way down south to the land of the pampas.

Argentina has been through the ringer but now it looks like it could finally, truly be turning a corner. It makes more sense right now than ever for the Cowboy Millionaire to take a close look.

You'll have to ride out this new chapter and see where it leads. That will require a stomach for risk. The return could be a home run.

CHAPTER IV

★★★

PARAGUAY

Today's Wild West

A search of "Paraguay history" in Google returns a list of questions people ask about Paraguay, including: "What country is Paraguay in?"

For the record, Paraguay is its own country. It was wiped almost off the map by Brazil and Argentina during the Triple Alliance War.

Mid-19th century, Paraguay was a wealthy nation thanks to protectionist dictators who happily exported tea and wood to the outside world but taxed imports heavily, creating a self-sufficient, wealthy, and (unlike neighboring Brazil and Argentina) debt-free country.

In fact, at the time, Paraguay was flush enough to pay cash for technology that allowed it to own its railroad. Elsewhere in the region, it was the British who owned and profited from the railway operations.

That healthy economy inspired an attempt to interfere with Britain's tea monopoly in Europe, which led to the war of the Triple Alliance in 1864. Other stories about the start of this devastating conflict include that Paraguay was just trying to protect Uruguay's independence and got tricked into a much larger-scale conflict. Still others say the dictator at the time, Francisco Solano Lopez, was delusional enough to attempt to take over South America.

Whatever the reasons for the war, the results were disastrous for Paraguay. By the end of fighting in 1870, the country lost more than a quarter of its territory, as much as 90% of its male population was killed, and it was required to pay restitution for the cost of the war to Brazil and Argentina. Brazil occupied the country for six years.

A century-and-a-half later, Paraguay is still trying to get back on the path to prosperity.

In the live, travel, invest overseas world, Paraguay is an underdog. I like underdogs. However, there's a more compelling reason to be paying attention to this little-thought-of country right now.

Paraguay doesn't boast mega-tourist attractions, but it's got something that should catch your attention as a global investor—a burgeoning agricultural industry and oodles of fertile land.

Paraguay is a leading global producer and exporter of niche agricultural products including stevia, organic sugar, and chia. It's also a significant regional producer and exporter of soy, beef, corn, and cassava flour, contributing importantly to South American agricultural markets.

This country is also a competitive and tax-friendly investment hub. You pay no tax on yields earned from an investment in the Asunción stock exchange, and both the value-added (or sales) tax and the rate of corporate tax are 10%. This corporate tax rate compares nicely with those in Argentina (35%), Colombia and Brazil (34%), and Peru (30%).

At about 400,000 square kilometers, Paraguay is the size of California. It has a total population of 7 million (70% of which is younger than 30 years old), a working population of 3.1 million, and a GDP of US$26 billion. The guarani is the official currency.

Paraguay's capital, Asunción is located on the country's western edge alongside the Paraguay River (think Mississippi River) and serves as a regional hub. You can fly from Asunción to most anywhere you'd want to go in South America—Buenos Aires, Montevideo, Sao Paolo, La Paz—within two hours. The country beyond the capital is divided into 17 departments, and the country overall is natural disaster risk free.

GDP and GDP per capita are both expanding, and the 10% rate

of personal income tax is the lowest in the region. Elsewhere in South America, earners are paying 35% to 40%.

Paraguay qualifies as a "blue ocean" market, an investment arena awash with opportunity, including in my primary investment focus real estate. The very young population, as it matures, is going to need places to live, making the local housing market an interesting bet.

Perhaps the greatest appeal of this little-known country is the opportunity it offers for what could be considered the ultimate internationalization experience—disappearing.

It could be the thing the country is best known for historically. Folks on the lamb from far and wide have sought out this country because it has something people who don't want to be found appreciate: Super low population density, at least in parts.

Paraguay is divided in two by the Rio Paraguay. To the east of the river is the Oriente; to the west is the Chaco. Paraguay today is home to 6.9 million people. About 6.7 million of them live in the Oriente, leaving 200,000 for the Chaco, a region larger than the entire country of Uruguay. There is but one real road in the Chaco, the Ruta de Chaco, that travels from Asunción to the Mennonite town in the center of Chaco and then on to Bolivia.

Easy in a place like that to get lost never to be found again if you don't want to be. That reality has contributed to Paraguay's reputation as a global hide-out. I've met folks of all ages in the country who were attracted to this country initially for reasons that fall into this category.

Disappearing, dropping out, going off-grid, and living off the land isn't for everyone. If your global diversification plans are less extreme, Paraguay still has a lot to offer...

Residency In Paraguay

Planting a residency flag in Paraguay is about as straightforward as it gets. You don't need to make an investment or prove any amount of income. You simply apply for residency.

Okay, there's a little more to it than that.

You need a police report from your home country, showing you have a clean record... or at least a relatively clean record.

Small infractions or very old convictions may be overlooked by the Paraguayan authorities. Not that the Paraguayans are looking to attract criminals to their country, but they seem to use some common sense when reviewing residency cases where the applicant doesn't have a spotless record.

You can manage the residency application process on your own, but the bureaucracy in Paraguay, as in many countries, can be more than you might be up for. For those short on time or patience, using an expediter can make sense. That can be in the form of an attorney or simply one of the handful of people offering residency services. You can expect the process to take as little as 90 days.

Once you have your residency approved, you then need to get your *cedula* (the government-issued ID card used in most of Latin America). That's a difference process at a different office. The wait time on *cedula* applications is around 60 days.

Once approved, your temporary residency permit is valid for two years and can be renewed. To maintain its validity, you need to be in Paraguay at least once each year.

After completing two years of temporary residency, you are eligible to apply for permanent residency. Once you have permanent residency you only need to be in Paraguay once every three years to maintain it.

Paraguay also offers a retirement visa (Permanent Residency for Retirees and Pensioners) with no upper age limit. To qualify you need to show a consistent monthly income, often around $1,022 (or the equivalent of 100 times the current local minimum wage). This income can come from pensions (government, private, or military) or other stable sources.

Paraguay also offers fast-track permanent residency through SUACE (*Sistema Unificado de Apertura y Cierre de Empresas*), a special business-friendly governmental framework that accelerates applications for individuals setting up operations or businesses in the country. Fees in the region of $14,000 apply for the application, company formation, and registration.

Once in Paraguay, you must establish your company through an appointed representative from SUACE. The approval period for this process is around 45 days. The minimum investment amount is set at $70,000 payable over a 10-year period.

Citizenship In Paraguay

With such an easy residency program, it's not surprising that Paraguay also has one of the best citizenship options available anywhere.

After three years of permanent residency, you can apply for citizenship. You must be able to speak one of Paraguay's official languages—Paraguayan, Guarani, or Spanish—and have memorized the country's national anthem.

You also have to prove your assimilation into local society. In other words, to be approved for naturalization, you have to show you have a connection to the country.

While that should be easy enough if you move to Paraguay during the three-year residency requirement, it's harder if you get your residency but continue to live elsewhere. Simply put, to qualify for citizenship, you need to put some effort into creating some kind of life in Paraguay to help your case.

Buying property in Paraguay helps, as does having friends, speaking Spanish, and spending time in the country on a regular basis. The more support you can provide to show the effort you have made to establish a connection to Paraguay, the better.

While you are eligible to apply for naturalization after three years of legal residency, the approval process can take another 12 to 24 months, depending on the volume of applicants at the time of your application and the mood of the Supreme Court. All naturalization applications go through the court.

Even if it takes two years for your application to be approved, a total of five years to get your second citizenship (three years of residency and two years for the naturalization process) is no longer than the five years of residency requirement for most countries.

Paraguay recognizes dual citizenship, so you don't have to give up your current citizenship when you acquire Paraguayan citizenship.

A Paraguayan passport gets you visa-free or visa-on-arrival travel privileges in at least 114 countries, including most of Europe, making it a top-notch travel document.

Thanks to the short residency requirement, Paraguay is one of the quickest noneconomic citizenship options available. I give Paraguay five stars as a citizenship flag planting opportunity.

Banking In Paraguay

Banking in Paraguay can be a good option for holding cash. However, it's harder today than it has been for a foreigner to open a bank account in this country. Officially, you need a *cedula* to do it.

You get a *cedula* as part of your residency process. Get residency and you can easily get a bank account. However, what if you don't want residency in Paraguay. Can you still bank in Paraguay?

Yes. You'd need to use a fiduciary rather than a bank. To put it another way, you could open a brokerage account, not a bank account. And, in fact, a brokerage account could be a better option all around even with residency if you want to invest locally.

Interest rates in U.S. dollars are higher in Paraguay than in the United States, and interest rates in Paraguayan *guarani* are even higher. The higher interest rates on *guarani*-based corporate bonds have attracted foreign investors. Using a fiduciary account, you can easily access these bonds and other financial investments in Paraguay.

You can hold accounts in local banks in both U.S. dollars and *guarani*. Other currency options can be available in the fiduciaries or private banks.

Most of the big banks in Paraguay are subsidiaries of foreign banks. Two of the biggest are Itaú (Brazilian) and Banco GNB Paraguay (Colombia). HSBC has a presence, as well. Other significant foreign-owned banks include Citibank Paraguay (U.S. multinational) and *Banco de la Nación* Argentina (Argentina).

All in all, Paraguay is a reasonable place to park money, but I wouldn't recommend it for large sums or investment accounts. You have better options for that kind of banking.

Taxes In Paraguay

Paraguay taxes on a jurisdictional basis. Therefore, if you're a resident, income earned outside Paraguay isn't taxed in Paraguay.

For income earned in Paraguay, here's what you need to know:

Corporate income taxes, personal income taxes, and the national sales tax (IVA) are all imposed at the rate of 10%. That 10% rate on personal income is reduced to 8% if your income is less than 120 times the monthly minimum wage.

Another 5% is payable for corporate dividend income.

You get all kinds of deductions against personal income. Bottom line, the effective rate for anyone actually paying tax is less than 10%.

Foreign residents earning income in Paraguay are subject to withholding taxes based on the type of income.

For business income, Paraguay applies a 15% withholding tax on a presumptive tax base that varies by income type (typically 30%–100% of gross income). This means the effective tax rate on gross income ranges from 4.5% to 15%.

Interest, dividends, and royalties paid to non-residents are generally taxed at a 15% withholding rate. For related-party interest payments, the rate can be reduced to 6%.

Capital gains are taxed as income and therefore fall under the same rules as earned income—between 8% and 10%.

Property taxes are 1% of the cadastral value (the government's assessed value of the property). The cadastral value is generally much lower than the actual value of a property, meaning your effective property tax is well below 1% of whatever you paid for the property.

Further, Paraguay does not impose wealth tax, gift tax, or inheritance tax.

All that to say that, overall, Paraguay is a very low-tax jurisdiction, competitive with bona-fide tax havens worldwide.

The one tax that is not low in Paraguay is social security. If you're considering starting a business, know that employers pay 16.5% of the employee's gross salary in social security charges. Employees pay a further 9%. On the plus side, wages in Paraguay are low; the minimum wage is around $365 per month.

Real Estate Investing In Paraguay

Over the past decade, Paraguay's economy has averaged around 4.5% annual growth. Good, steady growth... and still plenty of upside.

About 70% of Paraguay's population is younger than 30 years old, many taking jobs with the growing number of foreign businesses setting up in this country and earning better than minimum wage. The middle-class is expanding.

One way to take advantage of this would be to invest in real estate in Asuncion and Ciudad del Este. Buying pre-construction apartments is probably the simplest option. It comes with leverage thanks to the typical progress-payment schedule.

While the country's currency is the *guarani*, real estate usually changes hands in U.S. dollars. Much of the property for sale and even many rental prices are quoted in U.S. dollars. That reduces currency risk for U.S. dollar buyers but means you won't get the currency diversification that you might be looking for.

The other real estate investment opportunity worth pursuing in Paraguay is agriculture. The options range from farmland in the east, where soy and corn are prevalent, to cattle land in the Chaco region, where you can buy raw land for as little as $500 per hectare.

The simplest agricultural investment would be to buy a large piece of undeveloped land in the Chaco and hold it for three to five years, speculating on potential land appreciation. Prices here have seen an average growth of 920% over the past decade.

You could fast track your land appreciation by developing it into a cattle ranch.

Paraguay is the eighth largest beef exporter in the world, and the sector has demonstrated robust growth, with a 21% increase in exports in early 2025 compared with the same period in 2024. Paraguay is the fastest-growing beef exporter in the MERCOSUR bloc.

Additionally, the average export price for Paraguayan beef hit $5,603 per ton in early 2025—a 17% increase from the previous year.

With the growing world population, raising cattle should be an increasingly profitable activity.

Of course, not everyone's up for becoming a cattle farmer. Therefore, you want to work with a local management company.

Despite the tremendous appreciation in value over the past 10 years, prices for farmland are cheaper than in neighboring Uruguay, and you could simply buy land and lease it to a farmer. You'd expect a net return on that kind of operation of maybe 4% to 5%. Take some risk with the farmer and get paid a portion of the proceeds of the crop and you could increase that yield to 7% to 9%.

Hire the farm operator yourself and capitalize the farming as well as the purchase of the land and you might see yields as high as 12%.

Of course, your risk goes up with each step away from simple landlord toward actual farmer.

Even just buying cattle land and sitting on it requires at least a

$500,000 investment. Smaller investors need to seek out groups that cater to individual investors, bringing them into their projects at levels of $50,000 to $100,000.

Doing Business In Paraguay

Paraguay's ease of company formation, favorable tax regime, and legal protections for foreign investors (Paraguayan law generally grants foreign investors the same rights and protections as domestic investors, with no restrictions on foreign ownership of companies or most real estate and unrestricted repatriation of capital and profits abroad) make it a business-friendly environment for U.S. expats, notably in services, agriculture, manufacturing, and export sectors.

And, remember, establishing a business can support your temporary or permanent residency application. Specific requirements (such as minimum investments and job creation) may apply depending on the visa category.

Common corporate structures such as the *Sociedad de Responsabilidad Limitada* (SRL) and the *Sociedad Anónima* (SA) allow 100% foreign ownership and limited liability, as well as branches or representative offices of foreign companies.

Registration typically involves reservation of a company name, filing incorporation documents with the Public Registry, obtaining a tax ID (RUC), and securing any necessary municipal licenses. While at least one director or legal representative often must reside in Paraguay, there is no minimum capital requirement in most cases, making entry relatively accessible.

PARAGUAY

For The Cowboy Millionaire

Paraguay is a solid match for the Cowboy Millionaire who prizes independence over hype. Residency is downright easy, and citizenship, too. The approach to taxation is as good as it gets; this is a bona-fide tax haven. Banking is functional and conservative, and real estate remains a bargain.

The big cherry on top is that this country does not overregulate your life or your ambitions. In Paraguay, you're left largely alone... and, for us Cowboy Millionaires, that is the country's greatest appeal.

Paraguay is for the pioneer, someone comfortable moving early, before the crowd shows up. The lifestyle isn't flashy. It's relaxed, affordable, and quietly resilient, prizing personal freedom, offering a rare chance in today's world to build a life on your own terms while positioning yourself for upside as the country slowly comes into focus.

CHAPTER V

★ ★ ★

URUGUAY

Cowboys Welcome

Can boring be good?

"May you live in interesting times" is an English expression with roots in a Chinese curse.

Thing is, "interesting times" are times of trouble... of war, drought, plague, famine... The periods in history that are interesting to historians.

It might also be a curse to live in an "interesting" country. The kinds of countries that make for interesting news stories in the mainstream media. They aren't necessarily the places where you'd want to spend time... or retire... or invest.

So, if a country doesn't make the news much... if it flies under the radar... that can be a good thing.

It means it doesn't have many problems. It's quietly going about its business. Life there must be good, making it perhaps just the kind of place I might take an interest in for residency or investment.

Perhaps the quintessential "boring" country—in this sense—is Uruguay.

A small nation sandwiched between two South American goliaths (Argentina and Brazil), it doesn't make world headlines much.

It's "boring" for all the right reasons: democratic, middle class, affluent. It's also full of rich, fertile farmland.

Nothing "exciting"—no wars or coups or mass killings or economic meltdowns—happening there.

Uruguay is the most democratic country in Latin America according to the Economist Intelligence Unit's annual Democracy Index. It's also the second wealthiest country in Latin America, with a GDP per capita about double the Latin American average.

Uruguay is, in many respects, a little piece of Europe in South America. Its populace is cultured and middle-class; and the country has a social safety net reminiscent of some European countries and Canada.

The European heritage is strong. The first European settlement on the *Rio De La Plata* (Plate River), where Uruguay's capital, Montevideo, sits today, was founded by an Italian (Venetian) explorer, Sebastiano Caboto, during the Great Age of Discovery, in 1527. Still today, almost half of Uruguay's population claims Italian descent... and 90,000 Italian citizens live in the country.

And it's known as the "Switzerland of South America" thanks not only to its high living standards but its reputation as a banking haven. It's also pro-business.

Uruguay is also known as the "Goldilocks of South America" because it gets things just right.

I'd like to add a third superlative designation to the list. Uruguay is also one of the world's top farming destinations. Specifically, it is the world's seventh-biggest exporter of beef and eighth-biggest exporter of soybeans.

For a country of just 3.5 million people, that's impressive.

Uruguay reminds me in so many ways of the American Midwest. A farming powerhouse. Vast open spaces. Strong communities. Safe and stable.

Unlike the Wild West that you find in many Latin American countries, where you can build a great life for yourself while also earning strong profits if you're willing to take some risk, Uruguay is genteel with a developed middle-class economy and a high standard of living.

You have at least three excellent lifestyle options. You could opt for cosmopolitan, European-style city living in the cultured capital, Montevideo, home to half the country's population.

You could enjoy upscale beach living in Punta del Este, just an hour from the capital. Punta del Este is the most luxurious beach resort on the continent, sought after by those with money from Argentina, Brazil, Chile, and beyond. Think Biarritz or Monaco.

Or you could settle into a quiet farm life in the interior of the country.

Unlike America's Midwest (sorry, Midwesterners), temperatures in Uruguay also fit into the Goldilocks category. Winter temperatures typically don't drop below 52 F, with summer temps in the 70s F.

If all of that doesn't persuade you to take a look at Uruguay, add easy residency to the equation.

Real estate transactions are done in U.S. dollars. So, that's easy too.

A Model For Internationalizing Your Life

Uruguay has risen and fallen in terms of expat and investor popularity over the past several decades.

This has always been a regional safe haven. Wealthy Argentinians have invested heavily in Uruguay to shield their wealth against Argentina's volatile currency and economy for generations.

North Americans and Europeans began to notice what Uruguay has to offer in the early 2000s. Their interest waned but is returning.

Live And Invest Overseas' Latin America Correspondent Lee Harrison first visited Uruguay in 2004.

"I was living in Ecuador at the time," Lee says, "and I had no desire to move. But a few weeks in Uruguay changed that."

Getting residency in Uruguay, Lee says, gave him "another place to call home, as well as a way to legally reduce my U.S. income tax burden significantly."

Uruguay provided "a model for internationalizing my life," Lee continues, "that I've taken with me as I've repositioned to other countries since then.

"Uruguay's banking system provided me with a safe alternative for keeping funds, earning interest, and diversifying outside the U.S. dollar.

"Best of all, I earned a good return on the country's solid real estate market."

Among the reasons Lee identified years ago to check out Uruguay, he cites the people, the solid financial system, the infrastructure, the non-intrusive government, and straightforward residency.

When I size up Uruguay in the context of the Cowboy Millionaire today, I see one of Latin America's First World countries, a country with one of the continent's highest standards of living, lowest levels of corruption, and best infrastructures.

Like Lee years ago, I'm attracted to the country's property market, specifically in Punta del Este.

Punta del Este, on Uruguay's southeastern coast, is South America's number one beach resort. The Punta del Este area includes about 15 miles of beachfront, with the town itself situated on a peninsula in the middle.

The area is a magnet for property investors. The huge flow of international traffic creates demand from around the world and a liquid market. People come by the hundreds of thousands to visit Punta del Este every year, and lots of them have an eye out for property. This results in thousands of real estate transactions every year.

As an added bonus, properties in Punta del Este are priced in dollars, as they are throughout Uruguay. This sits well with the international market, as it provides a way to invest in dollars while remaining geopolitically distant from the United States.

Notably, Uruguay attracts people concerned with individual sovereignty and international diversification.

It's one of the world's best locations for establishing a second residency, a second citizenship, and an offshore financial presence.

Taxes In Uruguay

Like other countries I'm spotlighting in these pages, Uruguay takes a jurisdictional approach to taxation. This can be a major benefit depending on where and how you earn your income.

For foreign residents, especially those earning income from abroad, Uruguay offers a blend of transparency and tax efficiency that is hard to match in the region.

One of the most compelling incentives for expats is the 10-year tax holiday on foreign passive income. Let's say an expat earns foreign income from shares, dividends, bonds, or similar investments—they're completely exempt from Uruguayan income tax on that income for the first 10 years of residency.

This exemption provides significant breathing room for retirees or investors who rely on global portfolios for income. After the initial 10 years, that same type of income is taxed at a flat 12% rate, and even then, expats are entitled to a credit for any tax they've already paid in the country of origin.

This double-tax relief mechanism ensures that expats are not taxed twice on the same income.

Beyond passive investment income, Uruguay's tax system is even more generous in other areas.

Pensions and foreign rental income are entirely exempt from income tax, no matter how long one resides in the country. This makes Uruguay particularly attractive to retirees and property investors living off overseas earnings.

Furthermore, Uruguay imposes no capital gains tax and no inheritance tax, making it a strong contender for those looking to plan their long-term estate or financial legacy without government intrusion.

Property taxes in Uruguay are also relatively low. For example, the annual property tax (*Contribución Inmobiliaria*) on a comfortable two-bedroom apartment in Pocitos, one of Montevideo's most desirable neighborhoods, is typically around $1,500 per year.

Plus, Uruguay's stable politics—and broad consensus between the major parties—means you have a lot of certainty that the tax situation won't change.

Overall, Uruguay offers a highly expat-friendly tax framework that supports financial freedom and long-term planning, making it a smart choice for those seeking a stable, low-tax environment in Latin America.

Residency And Citizenship In Uruguay

If you're looking for residency in another country as a backup plan if things go bad at home... or simply to internationalize your life... it doesn't get much more straightforward or simple than Uruguay.

If you enter the country as a tourist (visitors from the U.S. and Canada don't require a tourist visa and can stay for up to 90 days) you can apply for residency while you're there—in person at the country's National Migration Office or online.

The documents you'll need are:

- Passport and passport photos.
- Health card issued in Uruguay (you can get this by taking a medical exam at an authorized clinic in Uruguay).
- Clean criminal record.
- Your birth certificate.
- Marriage certificate (if applicable).
- Proof of income ($1,500 a month minimum requirement and this can include a pension or social security).
- Proof of address in Uruguay.

In addition to the above documentation, you will need to attend for an interview at an immigration office. If you're not a Spanish speaker you will need an interpreter to accompany you.

The process for residency takes about a year to 18 months. In the meantime, you'll be issued with a temporary residence card. Once it's approved, you'll receive your permanent residence card (*cedula*).

The benefit of having a *cedula* is that you are allowed the same luxuries and facilities available to any other national of the country.

The easy residency also allows you to import your household items before residency has even been granted.

Once you're a resident in the country you can apply for citizenship.

Citizenship is relatively easy to get when you move to Uruguay, given the low financial requirements for doing so (great for retirees).

It usually takes around three (for married couples) to five years (for a single person) to get approval for citizenship. You'll need to prove that you've integrated into your new life in Uruguay and that you can speak conversational Spanish.

There are some caveats to this easy residency and, later, citizenship. You must stay in the country more than 183 consecutive days in a given year. This is known as the Days Test.

However, if you have family ties in the country you can apply for residency. For example, if your spouse and children live there and your children go to school in Uruguay.

Or, if you make a business or real estate investment and stay in the country for at least 60 days in any given year, you can also apply.

The minimum real estate investment amount is $390,000. The minimum amount to invest in a business is $1.7 million.

Banking In Uruguay

Uruguay's banking system is a mix of domestic and international banks, regulated by the Central Bank of Uruguay (BCU). It's well-regarded for its stability, high level of digitalization, and focus on personal and corporate banking.

It's also notable thanks to its:

- Lack of exchange controls.
- Easy transfer of funds.
- Strict bank secrecy laws.
- Easy process for foreign nationals wanting to open an account.

The financial system of Uruguay relies heavily on banks, offshore banks, financial houses, and representative offices of foreign banks.

All of the above-mentioned institutions, however, require authorization and permission from Uruguay's Central Bank to operate within the country.

Uruguay has established itself as an important hub for trade and banking in Latin America. It is increasingly a platform for important financial transactions between countries in the region like Brazil and Argentina.

A foreign national can usually open an account with any bank in one day as long as you have an identity card, a local address, and, in some cases, a local introduction letter.

Minimums required to open an account are low--typically $2,500 to open a current account and $750 for a savings account.

But just because it's easy to open an account doesn't mean you sacrifice your privacy. Banks in Uruguay are subjected to some of the world's tightest banking secrecy laws. These laws forbid the banks to share any information about the account holder with any third party, including the government of the country.

However, they may be permitted to disclose certain information if the Family Court issues orders to assess an alimony case, if the Criminal Court requests so, granted they have sufficient evidence to back their plea, and in regard to money laundering cases.

Also, thanks to the U.S.'s FATCA legislation, many banks in Uruguay are compelled to report your new account to the IRS if you're an American.

So, while Uruguayan banks are not as private as they used to be, they still maintain more privacy than many of their South American and Central American counterparts.

Investing And Doing Business In Uruguay

One of Uruguay's most attractive features for North American investors is its monetary flexibility.

While the local currency is the Uruguayan peso, there is complete freedom of exchange, and the U.S. dollar plays an everyday role in the economy. Most locals maintain bank accounts in both U.S. dollars and pesos, using pesos for monthly expenses and saving in dollars to hedge against inflation.

In fact, real estate transactions, car purchases, and even some large business deals are routinely priced and conducted in U.S. dollars, making the country highly accessible and familiar for American investors in particular. This dual-currency system allows U.S. investors to operate comfortably without needing to constantly convert funds or worry about currency controls.

Additionally, Uruguay offers a number of financial and legal structures that are favorable to foreign investors. There are no restrictions on capital movement, profits can be freely repatriated, and foreigners enjoy the same property rights as locals.

The banking system is modern and efficient, with relatively easy processes for foreigners to open accounts once residency is in progress.

Combined with Uruguay's low property taxes, strong consumer protections, and the absence of capital gains or inheritance taxes, these factors create a uniquely favorable environment for American investors seeking a stable offshore option.

Whether investing in real estate, business ventures, or simply preserving wealth abroad, Uruguay stands out as a low-risk, high-comfort destination.

URUGUAY

For The Cowboy Millionaire

Whatever about millionaire, if you want to be a literal cowboy, Uruguay is the place.

The old real estate investment adage recommends buying beachfront because they're not making any more of it. There's a limited supply of farmland, too, and a fast-growing demand. Farmland, therefore, is and will continue to be the world's best possible store of value. It is the world's oldest asset class, and its appeal is growing further still as the world's population continues to expand.

About 95% of the land in Uruguay is farmable.

Until the start of this century, most of Uruguay's land was used for cattle. When farmers began to recognize the implications of the coming global population crisis, they switched from cows to soybeans and other crops. Because Uruguayans haven't farmed their land for 200 years, it's virgin. There's been no soil degradation as in more recognized global breadbaskets.

In Uruguay, turnkey farmland investments, where the land is farmed and managed for you, are available to foreign investors just as they are to locals. As a foreign investor, you face no restrictions on ownership and no currency controls, unlike in other Latin American locations.

The chacra (CHA-kra) in Uruguay is a piece of land smaller than 100 hectares. It can be as small as a half-hectare. Bigger than 100 hectares or so (247 acres), and a chacra becomes an estancia in this part of South America.

A chacra is sometimes used for agriculture but is more often enjoyed by Uruguayans as a country vacation property. Many families spend holidays and weekends at their chacras, tending gardens, barbequing, and simply enjoying the open spaces. Often people own horses on their chacras or do a bit of "gentleman farming."

For anyone who wants to establish an international presence in Uruguay, a chacra holds other advantages.

First, they can often be self-sustaining. Most chacras start at about five hectares (12+ acres), so even the smaller ones can be used for agriculture. I know expats who own chacras. While the land may not feed the family now, the expats in question made the purchase counting on the fact that it could, if they wanted or needed it to.

Chacras also provide a nice buffer of privacy, for those who like to be off on their own.

While a chacra can serve as a vacation home for the time being or even a full-time residence, they can often be set up to operate off the grid, for those looking for that level of independence.

Finally, chacras generally cost less, as they are often found away from the more expensive beach areas.

Shopping for a chacra in Uruguay, you'll find that the most expensive ones are often part of a development, rather than off on their own. Both approaches offer advantages.

With the developed version, a chacra typically comes with electricity and a maintained road, as well as a front gate. But they can also be high end (usually near the coast) with elegant club houses, restaurants, and pools. I've seen 5-hectare chacras go for $55,000... but I've also seen them priced at $350,000.

The best land buy in Uruguay is agricultural land. Before you go shopping for it, you need to understand CONEAT. You want to know a piece of land's productivity rating to be sure you're paying a fair price. Details of this below.

Meantime, regarding buying property in Uruguay in general, note that the country has an excellent system of property registry and a well-organized process for property purchase. Buying here is low risk.

Every property transaction is processed by an escribano, who is a hybrid of a real estate attorney and a notary. The escribano's role is defined by law and includes title verification prior to closing. It's a level of built-in due diligence. However, you must understand that the escribano is only verifying that the transaction is safe and sound, not that the property you've chosen is necessarily the best for your intended purpose.

The Uruguayan government categorizes all land in the country according to its productive capability. The rating system is called CONEAT, and it assigns a numerical rating. You can check the rating of any piece of land anywhere in Uruguay by looking it up on the government's CONEAT rating map.

Ratings range from 0 to 263; the national average is 100. Pastureland is typically rated at 90 or below, while agricultural land is typically 90 to 120 or higher. A good agronomist or agro-land broker can tell you specifically which kinds of crops will thrive under any given rating.

As you might guess, land with a higher CONEAT rating costs more than land with a lower rating. Unless you're near the ocean, when your proximity to the beach trumps the land's productive value.

Remember, if you are buying land that's destined for recreational, development, or personal use (rather than growing crops), then you do not necessarily care about a high CONEAT rating. If the rating is high, the land could be unnecessarily expensive for your intended purpose.

When seeking to diversify your life internationally, owning a chacra in Uruguay could fit the bill perfectly. The cost of entry can be as low as $39,000. In high-demand production zones expect to pay closer to $60,000.

For that price, you could have a vacation property now that's capable of serving as a sustainable, off-the-grid escape hatch in the future, if and when you need it.

Most important, a chacra is an easy way to gain a foothold in Uruguay. With its easy residency and second citizenship, this is a country that gets top marks for freedom and individual sovereignty. It's also one of the best places in the world to live thanks to its refreshing lack of corruption and culture that respects personal autonomy.

PART II

THE MILLIONAIRE NEXT DOOR

CHAPTER VI

★ ★ ★

FRANCE

Rich Living In La Lumière

The food, the wine, the art, the shopping, the history... France is home to arguably the most beautiful city on earth and also offers the best of country living and dramatic Mediterranean and Atlantic coasts.

France also boasts excellent health care, infrastructure, schools, and, in some regions, almost zero crime. And, in some parts of the country, the very good life can be very affordable, as well.

The lifestyle here is among the world's most sought-after. From the romance of Paris to rustic living in the countryside, France is where you can enjoy Old-World living at its best. It truly is the good life defined.

Foodies and wine lovers know that to live in France is to be at the center of the universe. Whether it's *pâté de campagne* and a rustic Beaujolais, grilled salmon with a *rosé d'Anjou*, or caviar and a fine champagne, the French are masters at pairing wine with food. After all, they've been doing this since the Middle Ages.

For the culturally minded, life in France is rich indeed. In Paris alone you can find over 130 museums, including the world-famous Louvre, the *Musée d'Orsay*, and the National Museum of Modern Art at the Centre Pompidou. The number of galleries showcasing fresh, new works is almost bewildering, and since the days of the Renaissance, French philosophers, authors, and playwrights have enriched all our lives.

France would never feature on a list of the world's bargain destinations; still, outside Paris, this country can be much more affordable than you might imagine... and even Paris doesn't have to be hyper-expensive. Plus, you have to remember what you're buying...

Paris is, in our opinion, the most beautiful and romantic place on earth. And Paris is only the beginning of this story. There's a reason, after all, why more tourists seek out France each year than any other country on earth.

Paris is also a lifestyle play that can double as a solid investment, since apartment values in some *arrondissements* continue steadily up. A piece of Paris real estate is a hard asset worth holding. In addition, beyond Paris, it can be possible still to indulge your French farmhouse renovation fantasies for as little as €50,000 (plus renovation costs).

France's rich history and culture provide visitors and retirees with endless opportunities for enjoyment, in Paris and around the country. The variety of lifestyle options available here is tremendous, from medieval walled villages to the City of Light, plus the best of country living and dramatic Mediterranean and Atlantic coasts, retiring in France means you'll never be bored.

France has arguably the world's best health care, and if you qualify for French Social Security, the cost is minimal. The World Health Organization routinely awards France top honors, bestowing it the title of "Best Health Care System in the World." In fact, life expectancy in France exceeds that in the United States.

In addition to top-notch medical resources, the French lifestyle values leisure, with the average person receiving five weeks of vacation per year—compared to the standard two in North America. The infrastructure is also among the best in the world and less expensive than in many U.S. cities.

Residency And Citizenship

France doesn't offer a retirement visa, a golden visa, or a digital nomad visa, yet establishing residency here is fairly straightforward.

Like most European countries, France will grant residency if you can prove you can support yourself without undertaking paid work. The basic requirement is proof of monthly income of €1,400 for an individual and €2,100 for a couple (although the final amount required is always at the discretion of immigration officers). This grants you a residence permit that's valid for one year and renewable.

The type of visa required depends largely on the amount of time you intend to spend in France and what you intend to do there. The visas broadly divide into two options: the short-stay/ Schengen visa, and the long-stay visa, of which there are two main types—up to one year and more than a year.

Americans don't need a visa for short stays but still have to follow the Schengen rules of no more than 90 days in the Schengen zone in a rolling 180-day period. In simple terms, you can be in France for up to 90 days at a time, but then have to leave not only France, but the entirety of the Schengen zone for 90 days.

For stays longer than 90 days you must apply for a long-stay visa. Most people start with a "*Visa Visiteur*" which is for financially independent people or those with income sources outside of France. The income threshold to be financially independent is around €22,000 annually.

After your first year as a visitor, you can convert to a *Carte Sejour* and then apply for a 10-year residency permit.

However, after five years of legal residence, individuals can apply for French citizenship through naturalization.

Banking

Many banks in France have regional English-language websites, and many banks in cities and larger towns have English-speaking staff.

There are two main banking options for non-French customers: a resident's bank account or *compte bancaire* (if you plan to be in France for more than three months a year) and a non-resident account or *compte non-residente* (if you plan to be in France for less than three months a year).

First of all, to save your jaw from dropping, it's worth knowing ahead of time that free banking does not exist in France. Different banks make different charges, and some are very obscure.

An EU commission set up to study banking charges had to return to France for a second explanation, and even then they could not understand the charging system. So the best idea is to shop around and ask upfront if you can have a list of known charges.

It is also worth noting that even the big international banks in France operate a local system. This means that your local branch is your main point of operation.

You will be able to make transactions within the department where you live, but, for example, you may find it difficult or impossible to deposit checks outside your department.

The upside of this is that you actually have a real-life bank manager and will get to know him or her and the staff at your bank instead of an ATM.

To open a French resident's bank account you will need to provide:

- Proof of identity. EU citizens: a valid passport or ID card. Non-EU citizens: proof of residence (*carte de séjour*).
- Proof of a French address: a utility bill, rental agreement, or property deeds.
- Proof of earnings or your status: employment contract, proof of earnings, proof of status (e.g. retired with a pension, student).
- Reference from your current other bank.
- Birth certificate (only in some cases, but better to have it and a copy, just in case).
- A witnessed signature (not always needed but better to have it). If you open a French bank account you can choose between a current account (*compte courant*) and a savings account (*compte d'épargne*).

Some of the larger French banks allow you to open an account remotely (e.g. in the United States with BNP Paribas). Your own bank at home may also have an agreement with a French bank. If this is the case, go ahead and do it—it will save you a lot of hassle and time when you get to France.

Credit Agricole Normandie has a banking service called Britline (www.britline.com) providing a banking service in English to clients resident in France, the U.K., and Ireland, and it has an easy-to-understand website which details bank charges.

To open a non-resident account: Not all banks offer this service but those that do will require proof of a residential address (a recent utility bill) and proof of identity.

Note: If you open a joint account, be careful about the wording on the contract. You need to have Mr. or Mrs. Smith, not Mr. and Mrs. Smith (that is "*M. ou Mme. Smith*").

The reason is that if one partner passes away and the words "Mr. and Mrs. Smith" are on the contract, the account will be frozen.

If the word "or (*ou*)" is on the contract, either partner can make transactions without the other partner's permission.

Taxes In France

France is a high-tax country... but this doesn't really matter for U.S. retirees thanks to the U.S.-France tax treaty.

Basically, if you're not working, you're not taxed on anything that isn't earned in France. The tax treaty gives you a "deemed" tax credit for the total tax amount in France for any income taxable in the U.S. If all your income is passive, you're not taxed in France at all as an American.

The U.S.-France tax treaty is so advantageous that my French tax specialist calls it the bee's knees for American retirees.

Earned income is a different story, but there are still ways to reduce your taxes in France using the treaty.

If your tax domicile is in France, you're subject to income tax on your worldwide income. A surtax of 3% applies to income that exceeds €250,000.

Social surcharges (on employment income, rental income, interest, dividends, and capital gains) of 7% to 9% also apply.

Different types of capital gains are taxed differently in France. For real estate sales, if the home sold is your principal residence, it's exempt from capital gains tax. Tax treatment on real estate sales varies depending on the situation, so it's important to consult a real estate tax specialist.

France imposes an inheritance tax of up to 60%, but it does not apply if the inheritance is between spouses or brothers and sisters living together under specific conditions. Between direct dependents, progressive rates apply after a rebate on €100,000.

It also imposes a net wealth tax of 0.5% to 1.5% on worldwide real estate assets that exceed €1.3 million.

Income Tax: 0% to 45%

Inheritance and Estate Taxes: 0% to 60%

Property Tax: Variable

Capital Gains Tax: 0% if real estate is your primary residence. 36.2% for non-primary residence real estate (19% capital gains tax and 17.2% social charges). However, there are reductions to the capital gains taxes on real estate starting in the sixth year you own the property and eventually becoming zero for the capital gains tax after owning for 22 years and zero for the social charges after owning for 30 years. 30% (for financial assets e.g. stocks, crypto, etc.).

Determining Fiscal Residency

Fiscal residency depends upon the location of your principal residence, where your principal professional activities are carried out, and where your center of economic interest is. The 183-

day rule per calendar year assists in the determination of your tax residency but is not the only criteria considered.

If you are a French tax resident you are liable to pay French income tax on your worldwide income.

If you are not a French tax resident you are only liable to pay French income tax on income earned in France.

Article 24 of the French-U.S. Tax Treaty in conjunction with other articles provides special treatment to U.S. citizens and offers a credit (against the French taxes) of an amount equal to the French taxes on U.S.-sourced interest, dividends, capital gains, pensions, and rental income received by U.S. citizens.

This income is therefore only subject to U.S. income tax for U.S. Citizens.

There is also a tax treaty between France and Canada. It prevents double taxation on income earned in either country and outlines how tax residency, pensions, business profits, and capital gains are taxed.

It also allows tax credits or exemptions in one country for taxes paid in the other, and includes provisions to prevent tax evasion and resolve disputes between tax authorities.

France Form 3916

French tax residents must also declare their foreign bank accounts and capitalization or investment contracts of the same kind, as life insurance contracts, underwritten abroad.

Real Estate Investing In France

France has no restriction on foreigners owning property. As one of the most visited countries on earth, it's one of the safest real estate investment markets in the world. You can buy and collect guaranteed returns every year or live in France part-time and cash the rent checks while you're away.

Paris, in particular, is perhaps the world's most proven rental market. If you're considering a real estate purchase in the French capital, think about a place you could use yourself from time to time... and then rent out when you're elsewhere.

Paris, obviously, is the highest-priced property market in France (and one of the highest priced in the world). The good news is that not all of France is nearly as costly a place to call home.

Outside of Paris, property prices drop dramatically, sometimes to bargain levels. And, of course, not all neighborhoods in Paris are as expensive as one another. Paris divides into 20 districts, or *arrondissements*, numbered in an outward spiral starting in the center of the city on the right (or northern) bank of the River Seine.

The most sought-after of these, the best in terms of typical Parisian experience, are the 1st, 4th, 5th, 6th, and 7th. They are all near the river in the heart of the city... and all at the top of the property pricing scale.

The lowest property prices in Paris are in the 10th, 13th, 18th, 19th, and 20th *arrondissements*. Every *arrondissement* is distinct, a village or small town unto itself, with its own character.

The purchase of a house in France is usually straightforward and regulated. Generally speaking, problems only arise because the buyer has not understood the procedure or the property documentation.

If you are not a French speaker it is essential to find either a bilingual agent you trust and/or a bilingual notary.

If you are buying a house, always examine the cadastral plan of the property you intend to buy and the land around your plot. The last thing you want is to buy a property only to find a chicken farm is setting up just upwind of your new dream home. The cadastral records of all new or planned buildings are available in the mayor's office and online.

The purchase involves the signing of two contracts: the preliminary sales agreement (*compromis de vente*) and the formal deed of sale (*acte authentique*).

The preliminary sales agreement, drawn up by a notary or the sales agent, is an important step, and you may need advice from your bank or independent notary (if your agent is drawing it up) to make sure the wording is correct.

If the property is being financed with a mortgage, the preliminary sales agreement should contain a condition stating that if your application for a mortgage is not successful, your deposit will be refunded.

There are three main types of preliminary sales agreements, depending on whether you are purchasing a house that is already built, a house that is off-plan, or a plot of land where you are going to build a house.

Purchasing A House That's Already Built

When the buyer and seller have agreed on the property and the price, both parties commit to the sale by signing the compromise de vent. Once signed, the buyer deposits 10% (this may vary slightly) of the purchase price with the notary or agent or realtor. The deposit (called a payment on account) will be deducted from the purchase price when the deed of sale is completed, or it may be given to the seller if the agreement is broken.

Before signing the *compromis de vente* consider carefully whether you want to add any conditional clauses (*clauses suspensives*). You can add as many clauses as you like, but, of course, the seller has to accept them.

Typical clauses include the bank's acceptance of the mortgage (the *notaire* should automatically include this), whether or not planning permission is obtainable (e.g. for renovations or minor building work), potential plans for undesirable development of land adjacent to the property, and a satisfactory survey provided by the seller.

Once you have signed your *compromis de vente*, you have a seven-day cooling-off period, during which time you can withdraw from the sale without penalty but the seller can't.

After the seven days, you could return home, safe in the knowledge that the road to owning a property in France is well underway and should not be interrupted.

A word of caution: I read about a couple who bought a home and then decided during the cooling-off period that they had made a mistake. They tried to contact the *notaire* and then the agent on the last day of the cooling-off period only to find that it was a national holiday and both offices were closed. The sale went through. Moral of the story: Make absolutely sure the *notaire* will be available during the cooling-off period.

The deposit, or payment on account, system works like this:

- If the buyer does not wish to proceed he or she forfeits the deposit.
- If any conditions of sale included in the *compromis de vente* are not fulfilled (for reasons beyond the buyer's control) the deposit will be refunded to the buyer.
- If the seller withdraws, he or she may have to pay a penalty to the buyer.
- The *compromis de vente* will include a date when it is expected that you will sign the final formal deed of sale (this is a target date and not legally binding).

Acte Authentique: The Signing Of The Final Sales Document

Your agent or *notaire* will let you know the proposed date to sign the full contract. It is preferable that you be present, but you can arrange a power of attorney to act for you. It is advisable that you (or your power of attorney) see the property on the day of signing to check that you are buying the property "as seen on signing date." In other words, make sure that the beautiful wooden doors or floor tiles you fell in love with are still there.

The whole sales process should take between three and four months.

Purchasing A Home That Has Not Yet Been Built: Off Plan

A contract called the *vente en l'état future d'achèvement* (or VEFA) will be drawn up. Your funds will be released in installments to the owner.

Both parties also sign a reservation contract (*contrat de reservation*). This states the price of the home when built, technical specs, as well as the methods and dates of payment. The off-plan buyer usually pays a deposit of 5% of the price (deductible from the final sale price).

At the signing of the final deed of sale you become the owner of the property, irrespective of the phase of building.

Purchasing A Plot Of Land To Build On

After finding your plot of land, you must contact the local *mairie* to find out about planning permission. Once you are certain that planning permission will be granted, you enter the same sales process as outlined in "Purchasing A House That Is Already Built."

Separate contracts must be drawn up with a fully qualified and registered (in France) builder in order to obtain a French mortgage.

Notes For Buyers: When you choose an agent or realtor, check that he or she belongs to a government-regulated body such as FNAIM, SNPI, or UNPI. The agent should have this clearly visible in his or her office.

Always meet an agent at their office first. It is common for an agent to ask you to sign a *Bon de visite*—a simple form confirming that that specific agent showed you the property. This is done to prevent agent conflicts, as most properties have multiple listings.

To draw up the agreements you have to provide your passport, marriage papers, divorce papers, and paperwork showing details of any loans.

There is a tax credit scheme for ecofriendly home improvements including solar panels, insulation, and double glazing. The equipment and installation must be from and carried out by a reputable seller with accreditation. Ask your local *mairie* for providers.

Why Do I Need A Notary (*Le Notaire*)?

In France, the whole business of buying and selling properties is dealt with by a notary. A French notary is a public official responsible for ensuring that all deeds are authentic and can't be contested. They are responsible for drawing up the final deed of sale and often the preliminary sales agreement (*compromis de vent*).

Notaries must act impartially and therefore generally act for both parties. However, if the seller's notary does not speak English, you can employ your own bilingual notary.

If two notaries are used, the fees (which are set by French law) will be shared equally between them. The notary fees are paid by the buyer.

What are generally referred to as notary fees includes both the cost of the notary itself as well as the transfer tax on real estate in France and any other registration fees. For properties older than five years the total amounts to about 7% of the total purchase price. For new properties, the transfer tax is reduced significantly bringing the total in at 2% to 3%.

The transfer tax is the bulk of the fees for older properties at 5.7% to 6.2% depending on the *department* (province).

What Are The Agent's Fees?

An agent will usually charge between 5% and 10% of the purchase price. Sometimes the fees are included in the purchase price and are paid by the seller, in which case you will see FAI after the sales price. If a property is sold and bought privately (*de particulier à particulier*), these fees are not payable.

The best thing is to ask upfront which fees are included and then to ask for an estimate of any extra fees, remembering to add 20% to the estimate to cover sales tax.

What Is A Valuation Appraisal?

If you are applying for a loan to buy a property, the bank will send an assessor to make an appraisal of the property.

An assessor is not a qualified surveyor—he or she will not identify structural defects. The purpose of the appraisal is only for loan assessment. You will not be privy to the information.

If you want to carry out your own structural survey, you will need to contact a growing band of expat surveyors located throughout France.

Surveys: There's no such thing as a property surveyor in France instead the seller will provide a technical diagnostic file (*dossier de diagnostic technique*). This should include a report on gas, electricity, lead, asbestos, and termites (termites only for certain areas of France). If the property has a pool, the report should also include the safety features of the pool.

Can I Get A Mortgage In France?

Yes. The simplest way to finance the purchase of a property is through a French mortgage provider with a mortgage (*prêt immobilier*) in euros. Shop around—low interest rates make the business of lending very competitive.

French interest rates are based on the Euro Interbank Offered Rate (the Euribor) and are usually linked to a Euribor variant.

The French tend to prefer fixed-rate (*taux fixe*) mortgages more than variable rate (*taux variable*). Life insurance linked to the loan is required. Once you have chosen a mortgage lender, that company must send a contract by mail, detailing the repayment timetable and the agreed-upon interest rates.

Once you receive these documents, you must wait at least 10 days (but no more than 30 days) before signing and returning them.

The 10 days are known as the period of reflection. Once signed, there is no backing out of the contract (unless any conditions of sale of the property for which you are purchasing a mortgage, included in the *compromis de vente*, are not fulfilled).

You will also need to purchase insurance for your mortgage. In the past you had to buy the insurance from the lending bank. That has changed and you are free to shop around for your insurance, though some banks may still try to insist that they will only accept their insurance. If they refuse your chosen insurance, they must put their objections to you in writing.

Documents needed to take out a mortgage include:

- Your last two tax returns.
- Your last three pay slips or proof of pension income and your last three bank statements.
- Original passport.
- Proof of current residence (e.g. a utility bill or phone contract).
- A *compromis de vente* if you already have one.

Finding a mortgage lender and taking out a mortgage is not something you want to do in French, unless you are fluent and understand the language and cultural differences. If you do not speak French, contact an English-speaking agent, bank, or realtor.

FRANCE

For The Millionaire Next Door

If I could only live in one place for the rest of my life, it would be Paris. When I can no longer get on a plane anymore, that's where you'll find me.

For now, Kathleen and I divide our time between France and Panama and it often shocks people when I tell them that our day to day expenses in Paris are lower than they are in Panama City.

In Paris, we don't need a car. We walk or take the metro everywhere we want to go and most everything we need is close by in our neighborhood. Our utilities are cheaper, too... no air conditioning bills in Paris and heating bills are low. Food is fresh and local, dining out is inexpensive, and wine is cheaper than soda.

Of course, buying a home here isn't cheap but our Paris apartment has only risen in value and I look upon it as a legacy investment.

For us, Paris offers culture, convenience, and a lifestyle that can't be beat. Here, you can enjoy a low-key, upscale life and know that your real estate is helping to grow your nest egg with every passing day. For the Millionaire Next Door, it's the perfect place to diversify and savor the good life.

CHAPTER VII

THE DOMINICAN REPUBLIC

The Pearl Of The Caribbean

The Dominican Republic first came onto my radar in 2005. It was the country's undervalued beachfront property that got my attention back then.

I was among the first to shine a light on this country for American property investors, but its miles and miles of soft-sand beaches had been attracting foreign tourists and European investors for decades before that.

Now that I've gotten to know it as well as I have, I believe this island nation is as close to perfect as an offshore destination gets. It checks nearly every box on my flag-planting list.

For the past few years, the Dominican Republic's economy has been the fastest growing in the Americas. Pre-pandemic—between 2015 and 2019—the country enjoyed average growth rates of 6.1% per year.

The economy rebounded strongly following the pandemic—after a sharp contraction in 2020 it returned to high growth, achieving 4.9% in 2022 and 5.1% in 2024. Growth is expected to remain solid—with projections among the highest in Latin America and the Caribbean.

The country's infrastructure has improved dramatically since my first visit. Today new highways connect most of the resort and beach areas. The colonial zone in Santo Domingo is enjoying a facelift.

New roads and sidewalks are being built, and utility cables are being buried underground.

Increased flight options from the United States make the island more accessible—you can quickly and easily get to Santo Domingo International Airport (SDQ) from Canada and the U.S.

The flight time from Miami (MIA) is two hours and 20 minutes; from New York (JFK) it's three hours and 25 minutes; from Boston (BOS), three hours and 47 minutes; from Toronto (YYZ): four hours and eight minutes; and from Montreal (YUL): seven hours and 44 minutes.

Major international hotel chains are targeting the DR, specifically Santo Domingo, for new properties.

Nowadays, you can find five-star hotels such as JW Marriott, Embassy Suites by Hilton, InterContinental, and Hard Rock Hotel & Casino, to name a few.

Meantime, Santo Domingo and Puerto Plata's cruise docks regularly host Royal Caribbean, MSC, Norwegian Cruise Line, Virgin Voyages, Disney, Celebrity, and more.

The DR sees about 6 million tourists per year; about 60% of these are from North America.

Beyond tourism, the Dominican Republic's economy relies on agriculture (bananas, coffee, and cocoa) and mining.

That's the country's big picture. Here's how it stacks up as an offshore haven, flag by flag.

One Of The World's Best Residency-For-Citizenship Option

Gaining a second citizenship takes time or money. If you don't have or aren't willing to spend the money to purchase a second citizenship, you have to put in the time.

Most countries require at least five years as a legal resident before you become eligible for naturalization.

The Dominican Republic requires only three years of residency... and that can be fast-tracked.

The Dominican Republic offers ordinary and fast-track residency options. The fast-track includes residency through investment as well as a program for retirees who can prove $1,500 a month in pension income.

Obtain residency under a fast-track option, and your naturalization process is fast-tracked as well. You can start the application process for naturalization after just six months rather than waiting the full three years of residency. This means that you can complete the naturalization process in 12 to 18 months from the time you obtain your residency... and the speed of residency processing continues to improve, as more staff are added to the department.

You can't count on this in every case, but it can be possible to have your residency card in as little as 30 days.

The invest-for-residency option in the Dominican Republic requires a minimum investment of $200,000, which can be made in a Dominican company, real estate, or approved financial assets such as term deposits.

To qualify for the invest-for-residency option, you could put your money in approved assets such as Dominican government bonds or bank term deposits. Some government bonds may offer tax-exempt interest, local bank CDs yield around 7% to 10% annually in Dominican pesos, though rates vary depending on the currency and terms.

Alternatively, you could set up a company to start a business... or you could set up a company to manage a real estate investment (that is, a rental property).

The regulations, requirements, and opportunities associated with qualifying for residency and a passport in the Dominican Republic are changing in real time as the government is working aggressively to attract more foreign investment and more expats and retirees interested in living in the country.

Bottom line, this playing field is continually changing for the better.

An additional benefit of qualifying for a fast-track residency in the Dominican Republic is that you are granted permanent residency immediately upon your first application. As a fast-track resident, you are required to renew your residency (assuming you don't opt for citizenship) within a year the first time, then every two years. If you decide to opt for citizenship, you should renew it after two years of permanent residency status under the investment category.

You don't actually have to be present in the country at all during those years to maintain your residency status. Just return for your renewal. However, if you can't return to renew your residency card, you could provide a Power Of Attorney to the Migration Office so that your attorney can handle the renewal process for you.

If you miss a renewal deadline, our contacts in the country recommend to not show your expired residency card while entering the DR, as the Immigration authorities will hold your card, adding another process aside from renewal, plus expenses to recover your card. You will have to pay penalties when you do return to the DR to renew your residency card. For some, though, the small fines (around $23) are worth the flexibility of not having to return to the country according to a specific timeline.

Note that a Dominican Republic passport won't give you the visa-free travel options that you get with a U.S., Canadian, or EU passport. In fact, a DR passport is among the worst travel documents in the world in this regard.

Banking In The DR: Strong, Stable, And Growing

The DR shines as a residency-for-citizenship option... and for banking, too.

DR banks are FATCA-compliant, meaning an American opening

an account with a DR bank must complete a W-9 form just as you would when opening an account in the United States.

Other paperwork requirements are standard. You'll need a copy of your passport, maybe a second ID, a reference letter from your current bank (which can be waived if you are able to obtain an introduction locally), and, increasingly, proof of income.

Panama with its more than 50 banks qualifies as a banking center. The DR does not. You'll find less than 20 commercial banks operating in the country. I recommend sticking with the biggest and best-known among these—Scotiabank, Banco Popular, Citibank, or BanReservas.

Account options are similar to those in the United States, including checking, savings, and CDs. You can hold deposits in U.S. dollars or Dominican Republic pesos. CD rates for U.S. dollar deposits run in the 2.5% range. Peso CD rates are higher as local interest rates remain high compared with the rest of the world.

Local banks will lend to foreigners—whether you hold residency or not—for the purchase of real estate. The terms will depend on the source of your income. You'll be required to make a bigger downpayment if your qualifying income is coming from outside the DR. Expect a loan to value of no more than 80% and probably no more than 70%, depending on your personal financial statements.

Interest rates are higher than the low rates currently available in the U.S. and Europe. Expect a rate in the 8% to 10% range, with terms of maybe 15 to 20 years. Additionally, most banks won't give you a mortgage beyond the age of 75.

The DR doesn't rate as strong as other jurisdictions for investment banking. The country has a small bond market and no stock market. Some banks offer private banking, but, really, the DR is an option for holding some money in another jurisdiction in the form of liquid investments—cash, CDs, or bonds. Banks that trade in local company and government bonds help "make the market" so their clients have liquidity.

Taxes In The Dominican Republic

The DR takes a jurisdictional approach to taxation, meaning it taxes residents only on income earned within the country… except for foreign residents, who are technically liable for tax on their foreign-sourced income from their third taxable year as a resident.

You're considered a resident for tax purposes if you spend 183 days or more in the country in any given year. However, obtain citizenship, and you're no longer a foreign resident for tax purposes… you're a citizen.

If you are earning income in the DR, you'll be liable for income tax on a scaled basis according to these four tax bands—0%, 15%, 20%, and 25%. The zero rate applies up to 416,220 DR pesos, (around $7k). The 25% bracket kicks in at 867,123 DR pesos (about $15k).

Run a business in the DR and basically every expense you can prove with a factura fiscal is deductible.

The bad news regarding taxes in the DR is capital gains which are taxed at 27% for companies and 25% for individuals. If you invest in real estate and sell it for a profit, you'll have a tax on the gains in the DR. Of course, if you're an American, any tax paid in the DR can be used to offset your tax due on the U.S. side.

Real estate is exempt from property taxes up to a value of 8,138,353 DR pesos (around $143k as of this writing). Property taxes are 1% of the amount over the exemption. If you're living in the DR as a *pensionado*, you have a 50% exemption in property taxes.

The final tax to be aware of in the DR is the inheritance tax, which is 3% of the value of the inherited estate.

All in all, the DR is a favorable tax jurisdiction, with the exception of the capital gains tax, which is higher than in many countries. For Americans, again, though, this tax isn't the end of the world, as you'll be liable for taxes on any DR capital gains in the United States anyway.

One Of The World's Top Real Estate Investment Markets

Real estate was a great bargain in the Dominican Republic in 2005. Then came 2008/2009, when the bottom fell out of global property markets around the world. The DR wasn't immune to the dramatic down cycle.

Prices have moved up in the past half-dozen years and are moving up more sharply right now (thanks to the strong local economy and expanding tourism, both local and international) but remain a good value in most areas.

Pre-pandemic, rental yields ran to the high end of the 5% to 8% range you should expect generally in any market. With some work, you can find opportunities to push net yields into the double digits. Well-priced ocean-view properties in prime tourist areas are the sweet spot.

In Santo Domingo, a burst of new high-rise (a high-rise by DR standards means up to 30 stories tall) buildings means pre-construction opportunities. Developers give the best prices when they launch a building so they can get construction going. Expect prices to increase as much as 10% or more during construction.

Flipping upon completion is one option with a pre-construction buy. However, in Santo Domingo, you could improve your long-term return by holding onto a unit and renting it out on the furnished short-term business-traveler market.

Santo Domingo also offers one of the biggest Spanish colonial zones in all the Americas. The government has been improving the infrastructure in this area, which has become a central tourism zone for both land based travelers and cruise-goers. I've noticed more restaurants, museums, boutique hotels, and shops catering to tourists in this area each time I've returned in the last few years.

While much of the Spanish-colonial has been renovated already, you can still find buildings available for fixing up. You have to be careful when shopping in this zone to make sure you're paying a fair price. The historic properties for sale are controlled by one or two real estate agencies that price them on request, depending on who's inquiring. Make inquiries through a local contact if possible.

One property I looked at a couple years ago was listed on an agency website for $1.2 million. No way this building was worth that price, but I was interested in the property so I asked my attorney to see what she could do.

My attorney was able to make contact with the owner of the building, who said he's asking $250,000. My attorney thought the building could be bought for $200,000.

THE DOMINICAN REPUBLIC

For The Millionaire Next Door

The Dominican Republic offers strong flag-planting options across the board. It's the best quick residency-for-citizenship option—although other jurisdictions offer lower income and investment requirement levels for residency.

Banking is easy and interest rates are good.

A jurisdictional approach to taxation is the best possible option in today's world, and that's what the DR offers. However, the country taxes capital gains from any local investment at a rate of 27%.

Real estate opportunities abound. This country has been on my shortlist of property investment markets for the past decade.

Bottom line, the DR is as close to perfect as an offshore destination gets.

CHAPTER VIII

MEXICO

Geoarbitrage Made Easy

There's nothing like a good, solid Plan B.

Nothing will prepare you better for whatever happens in the world, whether it's a natural disaster, civil unrest, or even a war. A well-designed Plan B can enable you to pick up almost where you left off at a place of your choosing.

But there's one crucial element of a Plan B that many people only realized they had overlooked when the pandemic hit: A Plan B location is of very limited value if you can't get there.

And that's probably the biggest advantage to Mexico... its proximity. If necessary, you can access Mexico easily, with convenient flights or by land.

An estimated 1.5 million Americans and a half-million Canadians live in Mexico, making it the most-popular destination for North American expats in the world.

Here are a few reasons for this:

They're a culturally familiar neighbor. This shows up in many small ways... from the amazing food to the TV shows they watch, to the big, American SUVs they drive.

You can drive there. Many of Mexico's most-popular expat areas are an easy drive from the U.S. border. This can make both moving and seasonal visiting easy by eliminating the air travel.

Affordability. Exchange rates play a major role in day-to-day costs, and during periods of dollar strength, expenses like dining out, groceries, transportation, and household goods are generally significantly cheaper than in the U.S. Even when the dollar softens, many everyday prices in Mexico remain comparatively reasonable by North American standards.

There are lots of English-speaking expats and service providers (depending on where you settle). If you're weak on Spanish, then you'll appreciate Mexico's wealth of English-speakers.

Easy and fast immigration or long, six-month tourist stays make it simple to become a resident, or to maintain a second home here without even bothering with residency. More on this later...

Inexpensive and fast relocation from the U.S. and Canada. Little can compare with the ease of moving to Mexico. And, you can import your household effects duty-free as a new resident.

You can return easily to use Medicare in the U.S. You'll appreciate this one if you are nearing (or over) age 65. You can get good medical care in Mexico but if you'd rather have a more-familiar setting (and let Medicare pay for it), then you're only a drive or a quick flight away from the U.S.

Mexico is large, broad, and diverse, with hundreds of good living options. Whatever your preference for climate, you'll find it in Mexico. Throughout the mountains, you'll discover beautiful colonial cities like San Miguel de Allende, Ajijic, Guanajuato, or Oaxaca... places that enjoy mild climates without extreme heat or cold.

But Mexico also offers thousands of miles of beautiful beaches, from temperate to tropical, on both its Atlantic and Pacific coasts. Places like Tulum and Playa del Carmen... Mazatlán and Puerto Vallarta... and Los Cabos and Ensenada, all continue to be popular with expats.

The Mexican government is a stable democracy, with executive, legislative, and judicial branches functioning in a similar way to those in the U.S.

It's a civil law country, so you can forget the threats (and expense) of protecting yourself from frivolous lawsuits or personal injury lawyers.

Mexico ranks well for "individual sovereignty" through international diversification.

By *individual sovereignty*, I'm referring to the concept that an individual can themselves be sovereign, rather than being exclusively and irrevocably tied to a single sovereign nation.

And the best way to achieve individual sovereignty is through *international diversification*; that is, by not having all of your eggs in the basket of a single sovereign nation.

Here's how Mexico stacks up as an offshore haven, flag by flag.

Residency And Citizenship In Mexico

Overall, Mexico offers one of the easiest residencies available. The process is simple, straightforward, and fast.

My friend Lee Harrison, a Mexico resident, shares his first-hand experience:

"All it took to get my residency visa was a single consular visit, where I was helped by an English-speaking agent. And even better, they accepted my English-language documents at the consulate with no translations.

"I also didn't need apostille certifications of my income, social security, or banking information... although if a couple applies as a family unit (my wife and I applied as separate individuals) they will require that you apostille your marriage or birth certificate.

"Best of all, *there's no lawyer required*... although if you do not speak English or Spanish, you'll need to bring a translator.

"The biggest thing that stands out about Mexico is that they allow you to use savings in lieu of income when qualifying for a visa. This is great for people who have savings (like a 401k) but don't have a formal pension.

"Finally, Mexico is the last place that I know of that does not require a criminal background check."

An Outline Of The Process

Generally, Mexico's visa regime has you start out as a temporary resident. You can hold a temporary resident's visa for four years, after which you convert to a permanent resident.

If you follow this option, you do not need to provide any additional income verification to advance to permanent residency.

But you also have the option of jumping right to a permanent resident visa—without serving the normal four years as a temporary resident—by having somewhat more income or savings.

Qualification thresholds have become high, at least for now. This is because income requirements are based on multiples of the Mexican minimum wage, which has gone up dramatically in recent years. There are plans to correct this calculation, so that thresholds are more reasonable... but no timetable as to when it will happen.

Since consulates differ in pricing, understandably, many people are consulate-shopping. The cheapest consulate as of this writing is in Raleigh, NC. They require the following:

- Temporary Residency: $3,100 (income) or $51,800 (savings)
- Permanent Residency: $5,180 (income) or $207,240 (savings)

Other American consulates that charge less than their peers are San Francisco, McAllen (TX), and New Orleans. The most-expensive consulate in the U.S. at this writing is Seattle, which requires $5,000 per month for temporary residency.

The average of all U.S. consulates is:

- Temporary Residency: $4,295 (income) or $71,375 (savings)
- Permanent Residency: $7,075 (income) or $284,089 (savings)

In Canada, consulates require the following:

- Temporary Residency: CA$6,160 (income) or CA$102,617 (savings)
- Permanent Residency: CA$10,672 (income) or CA$410,685 (savings)

These amounts are slightly less in Toronto.

Here's What Most People Really Do...

Most people choose to qualify with savings, using an IRA or a 401(k). Then they switch to permanent residency after four years, with no required proof of income.

No minimum stay time is required to maintain your visa. You do not need to live in Mexico to maintain residency, however you do need to be there to renew your residency if you have a residency that expires.

Of course you may not even need residency in Mexico, thanks to their liberal tourist-entry policies. You get an automatic 180-day stay when you enter the country, which is usually enough for a part-year resident. And if you leave Mexico during your stay, you get another 180 days when you return.

You can import your household effects duty-free as a new resident. The nearest consulate will give you the permit upon request.

Becoming A Citizen Of Mexico

Mexico offers a clear path to citizenship, after either two years or five years of residency.

If you were born in Mexico, or born to a Mexican citizen outside of Mexico, then you already qualify for citizenship (Mexico recognizes dual-citizenship). Just grab your parents' birth certificates and head to immigration to begin the process.

If you have been a resident for five years, you can apply for naturalization. All time as a resident counts, including time as a temporary resident.

If you are married to a Mexican citizen, then the required residency is only two years.

Likewise, if you are the descendant of a Mexican citizen by birth, have a Mexican child, or are a citizen of a Latin American country (or the Iberian Peninsula), the required residency is also two years.

As part of the naturalization process you must take an exam on Mexican history, and prove that you can speak functional Spanish. The history test can be waived if you are over 60 or under 18... there is no waiver for the Spanish test. They offer a study guide to help you pass the history test.

Investing In Mexico

From an investment perspective, Mexico looks stable.

Under President Claudia Sheinbaum, elected in 2024, Mexico is positioning itself as a key nearshoring destination, emphasizing infrastructure and industrial expansion under the pan national "Plan México" framework, which aims to attract up to $277 billion in investment by 2030, create 1.5 million jobs, and increase domestic content in exports.

Here are the recently affirmed sovereign ratings:

- Moody's Baa2 (outlook negative)
- S&P BBB+ (outlook stable)
- Fitch BBB- (outlook stable)

In late 2024, Moody's downgraded Mexico's outlook from "stable" to "negative" citing weakening judicial independence and the elimination of independent regulators as factors.

That said, the OECD, a club of mostly rich countries, holds with the "stable" theme. They mentioned that after a slow recovery from the pandemic, the Mexican economy has done a good job *"...of navigating the global environment of tightening financial conditions and heightened uncertainty. Fiscal policy has a robust track record in attaining fiscal targets and keeping public debt low."*

Public debt is, again, stable. Mexico's debt to GDP ratio is 49%... not exactly world-class, but neither is it out of control, as in the U.S. (at over 124%).

The Mexican peso is one of the world's most-traded currencies. And the exchange rates are quite favorable against both U.S. and Canadian dollars, making the cost of living in Mexico very inexpensive for holders of these currencies.

The USD and CAD hit their peaks just after the 2016 U.S. elections. They've since pulled back from their high points, but the exchange rates remain very favorable.

Real estate investments represent a good opportunity right now. Properties in Mexico trade in U.S. dollars or Mexican pesos.

Mexican coastal properties are generally well below average by international standards, so it's a great country to shop for a beach property, and several markets are producing good rental returns... places like Puerto Vallarta, Mazatlán, and Playa del Carmen are currently among those performing well. Here are the 2026 benchmarks per square meter:

- Mazatlán $2,718 (beachfront)
- Playa del Carmen $3,997 (all properties)
- Puerto Vallarta $5,720 (all properties)

Mazatlán's property prices have gone up 51.6% over the past three years, yet they are still reasonable, even by Mexican standards.

Of course the best part about investing in real estate in Mexico is that it's easily accessible to the U.S. and Canada, if you're using the property yourself.

Your Tax Picture In Mexico

Mexico has a good tax treaty with their USMCA brothers in the U.S. and Canada, as well as a lax policy for categorizing you as a "tax-resident".

Mexico has the lowest tax burden among all OECD countries (a group of the world's 35 wealthiest nations).

You are a tax-resident of Mexico if you have established your primary home or center of business there. Unlike most jurisdictions, they do not use time-in-country to determine tax residency.

Non-tax-residents are subject to tax on their Mexican-source income only, paying zero, 15%, or 30%, depending on your income. Capital gains for non-tax-residents are taxed at either 25% of the sale, or 30% of the gain (the highest tax bracket), whichever is less.

Tax-residents are subject to tax on their worldwide income, although much of your income may be exempt for various reasons. (For example, any income that had tax withheld is considered final, and not declared on a Mexican return.) Also, Mexico has tax treaties with the U.S. and Canada, designed to prevent double taxation.

Otherwise, tax brackets run from zero to 35%. Capital gains for tax-residents are taxed as ordinary income.

There is no inheritance tax or wealth tax in Mexico.

Doing Business In Mexico

Mexico has long been attractive to large businesses wanting to set up outside the U.S. This is mostly due to the world-class trade agreement with the U.S. and Canada called the USMCA (the US/Mexico/Canada Trade Agreement) which took the place of the NAFTA trade agreement in 2020.

And recently, it's become a haven for small business startups as well, thanks to new startup incentives and (some) reductions in red tape. For example, Mexico's Special Economic Zones provide incentives for developing a business in underdeveloped parts of the country. And their Free Trade Zones allow goods shipped to foreign markets to leave Mexico duty-free.

Mexico's expanding middle-class has provided a wide range of opportunities for U.S. and Canadian entrepreneurs, as it provides an entrepreneurial outlet that complements America's shrinking middle-class.

Thanks to the USMCA, there are very few restrictions on your ability to own and operate a Mexican business... you don't even need to be a resident.

Also thanks to the USMCA, those who engage in an import-export business can do so with a large degree of tariff immunity, giving them an advantage over almost every other country in the world.

Who Should Consider A Business In Mexico?

The advantages of running a business in Mexico are many, including a great employee work ethic, easy and inexpensive access to the U.S. and Canada, and friendly trade regulations. You'll also benefit from a workforce that includes a large percentage of English-speakers, if your business requires it.

There are more small businesses than you can count operated by Americans in Mexico.

Corruption

One disadvantage of doing business in Mexico is corruption. In the latest *Transparency International Corruption Perception*

Index, Mexico scored poorly.

The index ranks the world's countries from the least corrupt (Denmark) to the most corrupt (Somalia), with Mexico falling unimpressively at position 126 out of 180 countries. In the region, Mexico falls behind Panama and Ecuador, but is better than Paraguay or Nicaragua. The least corrupt country in Latin America, in 16th place, is Uruguay... which ranks higher than the first world countries of the U.S., France, Spain, or the U.K.

This corruption means that it's more likely you'll encounter bribery, dishonest business relationships, and dishonest employees, when compared to countries that scored higher.

Employee Development

Culturally, most workers don't believe they're paid to think, and their cultures have made it unlikely that they can ever cross the line between a worker and a decision-maker... so there's little incentive to step up and take on responsibility. You'll find yourself called on to make frequent minor decisions that you'd otherwise expect an employee to make on their own.

Inept Legal Support

Many lawyers are incompetent... and even those who know what they're doing will rarely work on your behalf unless you're constantly supervising them and holding them to account. You cannot simply agree to a task and expect it to be finished in your absence.

Managing a lawyer requires that you be super-clear on the task, agree on interim milestones, and follow up frequently to see that the milestones are being met.

The one exception to this rule is a property purchase, where notaries can make great money for what's normally a routine task. They need no encouragement to keep a property closure on track.

Ease Of Doing Business

Mexico is rated #1 in the region (Latin America and Caribbean) by the World Bank's *Ease of Doing Business* report. In the world, Mexico is a better-than-average 60, among the 180 countries in the survey.

Among our popular expat destinations, Ireland (24), Spain (30), France (32), and Portugal (39) are all ranked higher than Mexico. The #1 spot in the world goes to New Zealand... the U.S. comes in at #6, with Canada at #23.

Mexico's strongest rating was for arranging credit—they're ranked 11th in the world. One of their weakest areas is getting electricity.

Banking In Mexico

Mexico is a good place for banking, offering good account services, state-of-the-art online account management, and good interest rates. Mexican peso accounts come with the risks and rewards associated with exchange rates, as is the case with any foreign-currency account.

Many banks will require that you have at least temporary residency in order to open an account.

Given that residency is so easy to obtain, you can open a local account in about an hour, and likely won't need a bank reference letter, tax returns, etc.

Don't forget the exchange rates for accounts denominated in pesos. Depending on where it's running your account value could go up or down.

The central bank will do what it will when it comes to interest rates. The best you can do is "stock up" when you think pesos are a good deal... knowing that you won't always be right.

Regarding discriminatory banking practices directed at U.S. citizens, the playing field is level for all applicants.

Earn Over 10% With High-Interest T-Bills

The Mexican government has a program that allows anyone with five bucks to buy treasury certificates directly from them… commission-free. (The minimum investment is low to encourage people of modest means to have a savings account.) The instrument is known as a CETE (pronounced SEH teh).

The CETE is just like an American Treasury Bill (T-Bill). It doesn't pay interest, per se. Instead, you buy CETEs at a discount to their face value, and redeem them at their face value… like a U.S. Savings Bond. You can invest any odd amount you want.

You can buy a CETE with as short a term as one month… or as long as two years. The interest rates vary but you can check them online.

You can order CETEs at any time online, but they only issue them once per week, on Wednesdays.

CETEs are secure, much like buying a U.S. Treasury bond. Some expats consider them more secure than keeping money in the bank in Mexico.

The major risk of buying a CETE, which is denominated in pesos, is that the exchange rate will turn against you.

You need a residency card to participate… but if you're using Mexico as a Plan B location, having a stash of CETEs should be high on your list of preparations.

The main downside you'll likely find with respect to banking in Mexico is the lack of English-speaking agents but if you shop around you should find adequate support at one of the banks.

Diversion

This is a category where Mexico leads the pack for a couple of reasons. One is that you can stay for six months every time you enter the country as a tourist, with no cumulative annual stay-time restrictions. So you can plant the "diversion" flag—spending significant time enjoying Mexico—without establishing residency, or planting any other flag.

The other reason is that Mexico is geographically and culturally diverse, so there's literally something for everyone.

You can enjoy a number of climates, from spring-like temperatures in the mountains, to tropical weather on the coasts. You can explore beautiful, 16th century colonial cities, or walk for miles on unspoiled sandy beaches.

You can have small villages or sophisticated cities... some of which rarely see a tourist.

Mexico also has a rich indigenous presence with cultures like the ancient Mayan people and Aztecs still showing their influence today.

And what's more, you can get to Mexico easily, by car, boat or plane. So even if you only have a few days to spend, you can easily spend them in Mexico.

Mexico also offers excellent transportation options for getting around. The country offers very inexpensive air travel, so exploring the regions won't bust the budget. They also offer a good, first-class bus system, with direct services to several U.S. cities. Throughout most of the country, taxis are plentiful and inexpensive.

Best of all, at current exchange rates, everything in Mexico is essentially going at a significant discount for USD holders.

MEXICO

For The Millionaire Next Door

Mexico is a star when it comes to residency, which is easy to obtain, and has no required in-country stay time. The current financial requirements are restrictive for some but being able to use savings to qualify can offset this problem.

Its banking system is convenient, with no discrimination against American citizens.

As a business base, Mexico is a unique haven, thanks to its easy geographic access to the U.S. and its easy access to U.S. markets due to the USMCA.

And best of all, Mexico is simply a great place to live. It will be a valuable stop in your quest for international diversification.

CHAPTER IX

★ ★ ★

THE PHILIPPINES

Low Cost Luxury

Expat life in the Philippines offers Americans a blend of English-speaking convenience, quality private health care at affordable prices, a fairly easy visa process, and locals that will welcome you into the community and make you feel at home.

The Philippines is an attractive retirement destination due to its incredible natural beauty spread over 7,500 islands, otherworldly landscapes of tropical beaches and crystal-clear waters, vibrant culture, low cost of living, rich history, and diverse experiences for everyone.

The Philippines is known for its vibrant nightlife and casino culture, particularly in entertainment hubs like Manila's Entertainment City and Cebu City, where ritzy resorts offer high-end gaming, gourmet restaurants, and luxury hotels.

These areas provide expats with a cosmopolitan lifestyle similar to other major Southeast Asian cities, while still offering local cultural touches and a generally lower cost of living compared to say, Hong Kong or Singapore.

Golf enthusiasts will find plenty to enjoy, with private and semi-private country clubs offering championship courses, clubhouses, and social events. Clubs like The Manila Polo Club, Sta. Elena Golf & Country Club in Laguna, and Apo Golf and Country Club in Davao are popular choices.

Many of these clubs also include tennis courts, swimming

pools, and dining facilities, creating a well-rounded lifestyle destination where business and leisure often intersect.

Yachting and sailing are equally popular in coastal regions; Subic Bay, Batangas, and Cebu all host marinas and yacht clubs that organize regattas, private charters, and sailing lessons.

Outside the cities, resorts along the coast or in mountain destinations like Tagaytay combine privacy with luxury amenities, from spa services to fine dining.

Retirees on a budget also benefit from the low cost of living you can enjoy in the Philippines. In fact, a couple could live comfortably here from as little as $1,000 a month. For $2,300 per month, you could enjoy a luxurious lifestyle.

In terms of residency, the Philippines offers specific, easy to attain programs to incentivize expats to move.

One such option is the Special Resident Retiree's Visa (SRRV), a non-immigrant visa that allows multiple entries and indefinite stay in the Philippines.

The SRRV offers other special benefits, which allow you to work, study, or invest in the country, and also grants discounts from the Philippine Retirement Authority partners.

The Philippines offers a wide variety of lifestyle options, too, from laidback coastal towns to buzzing city centers. Here are three of the best places to retire to in the country...

Manila

The capital of the Philippines, Manila is located on the eastern shore of Manila Bay on the island of Luzon. You can travel to Manila from the United States on direct flights from major hubs like Los Angeles, New York, and Miami.

Retirees choose it because it provides easy access to top hospitals, embassies, shopping malls, and international restaurants.

For leisure, Manila offers a mix of cultural, historical, and gastronomic experiences that are highly appealing to retirees. Intramuros, the walled city of Manila, is the oldest district in the city.

Here you can explore Fort Santiago and the UNESCO World Heritage Site of San Agustin Church. There's also the National Museum Complex, home to the museums of Fine Arts, Anthropology, and Natural History.

In the Cultural Center of the Philippines, you'll enjoy regular performances of ballet, classical concerts, and traditional Filipino shows.

If you're looking to connect with other expats, the American Association of the Philippines and other social clubs host events, talks, and mixers throughout the city.

In terms of health care, Manila has some fantastic options. You'll find English-speaking doctors, many who have trained in the U.S. Out-of-pocket costs for doctor visits and procedures can be much lower than in North America and Europe, with specialist consultations priced at about $20 to $50. The St. Luke's Medical Center is considered a world-class hospital and has international accreditation.

Overall monthly expenses for a couple are from $1,400 to $2,300—that's for a comfortable, middle-class lifestyle.

Cebu

About 350 miles southeast of Manila, the city of Cebu is located in central Philippines, on the eastern coast of Cebu Island. There's an international airport, and although no direct flights are available from the U.S., you can easily get here from a stop in any major Asian or Middle Eastern hub.

Retirees are drawn to Cebu for its coastal lifestyle, strong expat community, good health care, urban conveniences, and beach escapes. This city is more laidback than Manila but remains vibrant, with surrounding areas offering plenty of natural beauty.

For cultural and historical attractions, explore the Basilica Minore del Santo Niño, the oldest Catholic church in the country or the Casa Gorordo Museum, located in a well-preserved colonial mansion.

In expat and retirement communities, senior-friendly yoga and tai chi classes are commonly available. From Cebu you can island hop to nearby Pandanon or Nalusuan, and also take easy nature trips and day tours.

Health care access in Cebu is great for retirees. It's not as extensive as in Manila, but this city has several high-quality hospitals, modern clinics, and English-speaking health professionals. The Chong Hua Hospital is one of the top private hospitals in the area with modern equipment and international standards. Out-of-pocket fees for consultations usually range between $15 and $30.

A couple can live a comfortable lifestyle in Cebu City for about $1,300 to $2,200 per month.

Dumaguete

Dumaguete is on Negros Island, south of Cebu Island, which you can see across the water. It has its own airport, and you can get here through a connection from Manila or Cebu City.

This area is known as a retirement haven because of its affordability, walkability, laidback environment, and growing expat population.

Retirees seeking a low-stress life will thrive in Dumaguete.

If you're looking for a slower pace, friendly locals, and low costs without choosing a completely rural location, this could be your idyll. It's a perfect blend of seaside living and small-town charm with plenty of access to nature.

Rizal Boulevard is a popular spot for walks. It's a seaside boardwalk with views of Siquijor Island and the best place to watch Dumaguete's sunsets. It's lined with cafés, bakeries, and plenty of benches to enjoy the view.

Silliman University has an anthropology museum and historic building for those looking to learn about the area, and it also offers cultural events, exhibits, and classes. For those seeking peaceful outdoor adventures, you can find lakes, waterfalls, and hot springs to spend the day in. Island hopping is also fun, easy, and affordable.

The expat community of Dumaguete has weekly meetups and clubs for activities like chess, reading, and volunteering, making it easier to make new connections. You can start talking with your new community even before arriving by joining online groups like the Foreigners And Expat Families Living In Dumaguete Facebook group.

Because the Philippines has designated Dumaguete as one of the top five areas in the country that are retirement hubs, medical care here is excellent. Silliman Medical Center is considered one of the most modern in the country and offers emergency services and modern diagnostic units. A consultation here costs only about $9. Various private clinics in the fields of surgery, dentistry, cardiology, and geriatrics are available, as well as senior-friendly services.

A couple can live comfortably in Dumaguete for about $1,000 to $1,800 a month.

Residency And Citizenship

U.S. citizens may enter the Philippines without a visa and remain in the country as a tourist for a maximum of 30 days per trip provided the visitor's passport has at least six months validity and an ongoing ticket has been purchased.

If you wish to stay longer than 30 days, you can seek permission to remain in the country once you arrive or you can apply for a 59-day visa at the Philippine embassy nearest you before leaving home.

The Philippine government offers one of the best retirement programs for foreigners that comes with more benefits than any other country in the region and one of the easiest paths to permanent residency in Southeast Asia.

The SRRV: Special Resident Retiree's Visa

The Philippines offers a retiree-specific resident permit, the Special Resident Retiree's Visa (SRRV), which makes it easy to set up life here. This is a non-immigrant visa that allows multiple entries and indefinite stays in the Philippines

.

The SRRV offers special benefits like:

- Multiple entry privileges.
- A lifetime visa exempt from Bureau of Immigration requirements.
- Allows holders to work, study, or invest in the country.
- Discounts from the Philippine Retirement Authority partners.
- Free assistance with government agency transactions.
- Access to Philippines Health Insurance benefits and privileges.

The Classic SRRV is designed for active and healthy principal retirees who wish to use their visa deposit for approved investments such as purchasing condominium units or securing a long-term lease of a house and lot.

The required visa deposit depends on your age and pension status.

For applicants aged 40 to 49 that takes the form of a $50,000 deposit—a pension is not required.

For applicants aged 50 and above with a qualifying pension the deposit amount is $15,000. For those 50 and above without a pension, that deposit amount rises to $30,000.

To qualify as a pensioner, applicants must show proof of a lifetime pension of at least $800 per month for a single applicant or $1,000 per month for applicants with dependents.

The deposit can later be converted into eligible investments, such as a condo purchase or long-term residential lease, in accordance with the Philippines Retirement Authority rules.

The SIRV: Special Investor Resident Visa

The Philippines offers a specialized residency program for foreign investors known as the Special Investor Resident Visa (SIRV) which is designed to encourage long-term investment in the country.

This visa is a non-immigrant, multiple-entry permit that allows holders to reside in the Philippines indefinitely while actively managing or overseeing their investments. It provides a streamlined path for investors who want both security and flexibility in living and conducting business locally.

The SIRV comes with a variety of benefits including:

- Multiple-entry privileges for easy travel in and out of the Philippines.
- A permanent visa that exempts holders from standard immigration requirements.
- The ability to invest in Philippine businesses, hold property through corporate structures, and participate in approved economic activities.
- Assistance with government transactions, such as business registration or permits.
- Access to banking, tax, and financial services designed for foreign investors.
- Eligibility for certain economic incentives offered to registered foreign investors.

The visa has specific investment thresholds depending on the type of business or investment undertaken. Typically, applicants are required to invest a minimum of $75,000 in a Philippine-registered company or government-approved project, although higher amounts may provide additional privileges or faster processing.

Investments can include establishing a corporation, purchasing shares in a local business, or contributing to sectors designated as priority industries by the Philippine Economic Zone Authority (PEZA) or other government agencies.

The SIRV is ideal for investors who want to combine business opportunities with long-term residency in the Philippines. It allows for active involvement in ventures while providing legal security and access to local financial and administrative systems.

By meeting the investment requirements and complying with relevant regulations, foreign investors can enjoy a lifestyle that combines the Philippines' economic potential with the comfort and convenience of permanent residency.

DNV: Digital Nomad Visa

The Philippines offers a Digital Nomad Visa (DNV) for foreign nationals who want to live in the country while working remotely. This non-immigrant visa allows holders to stay in the Philippines for up to one year, with the option to renew for an additional year.

The DNV comes with several practical benefits including:

- Legal residency in the Philippines for up to one year, with a possible one-year extension.
- Multiple-entry privileges, allowing nomads to travel in and out of the country freely.
- Permission to live in the Philippines without requiring a local work visa or sponsorship.
- The opportunity to explore local culture, leisure, and lifestyle while maintaining full-time employment or freelance work remotely.

To qualify for the Digital Nomad Visa, applicants must meet several requirements. They must be at least 18 years old, provide evidence of remote employment or freelance work conducted digitally, and demonstrate sufficient income generated outside the Philippines to support themselves while living in the country—

the amount is not set in law but around $2,000 a month is the generally accepted figure.

Proof of income can include contracts, invoices, or bank statements, while remote work may involve online meetings, digital project submissions, or other verifiable tasks performed over the internet.

Applicants are also required to present a clean criminal record.

The Digital Nomad Visa offers an attractive option for those seeking a combination of work flexibility and lifestyle benefits. Many nomads take advantage of this visa to live in cosmopolitan cities like Manila and Cebu, or in more relaxed coastal and island destinations such as Palawan, Siargao, and Boracay, where modern amenities, co-working spaces, and vibrant expat communities make it easy to balance productivity and leisure.

Citizenship

Obtaining Philippine citizenship is possible but not automatic. Most foreigners need to go through naturalization, a legal process that involves applying to a Philippine court.

To qualify, you generally must be at least 21 years old, of good moral character, and have lived in the Philippines continuously for around 10 years. That residency requirement can drop to five years in certain cases, such as being married to a Filipino, having Filipino children, or contributing significantly to the country through business or work.

You'll also need to show some proficiency in a Philippine language or English and demonstrate integration into local society. The process involves submitting a petition, attending court hearings, and publishing your intention publicly before citizenship is granted.

Marriage to a Filipino citizen or having a Filipino parent can make a significant difference. While marriage does not instantly confer citizenship, it can shorten the required residency period and strengthen your naturalization petition.

Similarly, if you were born to a Filipino parent, you may already be considered a Filipino citizen by birth and simply need to have your citizenship recognized by the authorities. This recognition process allows you to enjoy the rights of a Filipino, including the ability to get a Philippine passport, without going through the full naturalization process.

The Philippines permits dual citizenship. If you are a natural-born Filipino who later became a U.S. citizen, you can take an oath of allegiance to regain your Philippine citizenship while keeping your U.S. passport.

Taxes In The Philippines

The Philippines has tax treaties with the U.S. and Canada, which reduces the risk of double taxation. Because of the Foreign Earned Income Exclusion and Foreign Tax Credit, American expats usually pay little or no U.S. taxes, especially if you're not planning on earning much abroad. However, you still do need to file your U.S. taxes and report your worldwide income.

If you have a foreign bank account with over $10,000, you must file FBAR annually.

Income taxes are moderate, ranging from 0% to 35%. Capital gains tax on the sale of property is fixed at 6% of the sales price. There is no inheritance tax in the Philippines.

You can still receive your Social Security benefits while living in the Philippines, as the United States and the Philippines have an agreement, and they can be deposited directly to a Filipino bank account or a U.S. account that you can access from abroad. You'll need to stay in touch with the local U.S. embassy or SSA office in Manila to report you're alive and eligible to receive your SS benefits.

Banking In The Philippines

Banking in the Philippines is generally reliable and well-regulated, with oversight from the *Bangko Sentral ng Pilipinas* (the central bank).

Expats will find a wide network of commercial banks offering standard services such as savings and checking accounts, debit cards, online banking, and foreign-currency deposits.

While day-to-day banking is straightforward once an account is open, the initial set-up can feel laborious and document-heavy. Opening an account usually requires an in-person visit to a local branch. Most banks ask for a valid passport, proof of a local address such as a lease agreement, and a minimum opening deposit.

Expats who stay longer than a short visit are typically required to present an Alien Certificate of Registration (ACR I-Card), which serves as the primary form of local identification for foreigners.

Some banks may also request additional documents or conduct a brief interview, especially if the account will be used for salary deposits or regular international transfers.

The ease of opening an account often depends on your visa type and length of stay. Expats on work visas, retiree visas, or other long-term permits usually face fewer obstacles, while tourists and short-term visitors may be limited to basic peso or foreign-currency savings accounts, or may be declined altogether.

Requirements can vary not just by bank, but by branch, so it's a good idea to confirm expectations ahead of time and be prepared for some flexibility in the process.

Among the more expat-friendly banks, large Philippine institutions such as BDO Unibank, Bank of the Philippine Islands (BPI), and Metrobank are popular due to their extensive branch networks, English-speaking staff, and functional online banking platforms.

International banks like HSBC Philippines and Citibank (which operates mainly through wealth and corporate services) are also used by expats who want global account integration and foreign-currency services.

Choosing a bank with strong digital tools and accessible branches can make your everyday life in the Philippines much easier.

Real Estate

Many expats choose to live in modern condos or gated communities in cities like Manila, Makati, and Bonifacio Global City, where high-rise towers offer amenities like pools, gyms, and 24-hour security.

For those seeking a coastal lifestyle, Cebu, Palawan, and Subic Bay offer ocean views, marinas, and waterfront residences.

The real estate market caters well to foreigners, with condos available for freehold ownership, while gated subdivisions offer spacious houses with landscaped gardens and modern amenities.

That said, legal restrictions make outright real estate ownership difficult for non-citizens. Under the country's constitution, only Filipino citizens or corporations at least 60% owned by Filipinos may hold title to private land—a rule which is strictly enforced.

For foreign buyers, the most straightforward way to legally own real estate is to purchase a condo. The Condominium Act allows non-citizens to hold title to a condo unit in their name, provided that foreign ownership in the entire project does not exceed 40%.

Foreigners cannot generally own land outright. Even if you are married to a Filipino the land title must remain in the name of your spouse or a qualifying Filipino-controlled entity.

To have long-term rights to land, foreigners typically use lease arrangements instead of ownership. Historically, the Investors' Lease Act allowed long-term leases of private land for up to 50 years with a one-time renewal of 25 years (75 years in total) for approved investment projects.

Recent legal changes have expanded these options for foreign investors: under Republic Act 12252 (signed in 2025) qualified foreign investors with registered investment projects can now enter into long-term land leases of up to 99 years. This extended lease regime is aimed at providing greater stability and long-term security for investment use, replacing the older 75-year model for eligible cases.

For foreigners who are not engaging in registered investment projects, the older lease rules under Presidential Decree 471 still apply, typically allowing an initial lease of up to 25 years, renewable for another 25 years (50 years total).

Under either lease regime, the foreigner does not own the land itself; they hold leasehold rights for the agreed period and may construct buildings or homes on the leased land.

Doing Business In The Philippines

Doing business in the Philippines as a foreigner can be both rewarding and complex, thanks to a combination of growing markets, strategic location, and regulatory requirements.

Expats interested in establishing a business typically start by understanding the types of visas available, with the most common being the Special Investor Resident Visa (SIRV). Bear in mind, certain business activities may require additional permits from local or national authorities.

While foreigners are generally restricted from owning land outright, they can establish a company and own up to 100% of a corporation in certain sectors under the Foreign Investments Act.

Other industries, such as retail, mass media, or natural resource extraction, are subject to ownership limits or require a Filipino partner. Many expats structure their ventures through corporations, often with a minimum of five shareholders, to comply with legal requirements.

Business registration, licensing, and tax compliance are well-defined, but navigating bureaucracy can take time, so hiring a local lawyer or consultant is highly recommended.

Opportunities for expat entrepreneurs are abundant, particularly in real estate, tourism, IT and outsourcing, health care, and retail. The Philippines' young, English-speaking workforce and growing middle-class provide both labor and a consumer base for diverse industries.

Cities like Makati, BGC, Cebu, and Davao are popular hubs for startups and foreign-owned companies, while tourism-heavy regions offer niche opportunities in hospitality, food and beverage, and lifestyle services.

While regulations can be strict in some sectors, the country's open economy, favorable tax incentives for registered foreign investors, and strategic position in Southeast Asia make it an attractive place for long-term business.

THE PHILIPPINES

For The Millionaire Next Door

If you dream of living the high life without breaking the bank, the Philippines offers a combination of luxury, natural beauty, and affordability that's hard to match.

High-end villas and stylish condos with 5-star resort-style amenities are surprisingly affordable and offer the chance to enjoy upscale living with sweeping ocean or city views. Services that would feel extravagant in the U.S. such as personal chefs, drivers, housekeepers, and private fitness instructors are accessible here on a modest budget.

World-class golf courses, serene yoga retreats, private beach clubs, and ritzy restaurants are within reach and budget here, along with rich opportunity for adventure... think diving in turquoise waters, exploring hidden islands, and hiking misty mountains...

Residency options make settling in easy for retirees. The Special Resident Retiree's Visa allows long-term or even indefinite stay with benefits like tax perks, easier access to property ownership, and hassle-free travel in and out of the country.

Across Asia, older people are generally treated with respect and warmth, and the Philippines is no exception—Filipino culture places a high value on family, community, and hospitality. Expats are welcomed into neighborhoods, social clubs, and local networks.

For a retiree who wants to live big without draining a lifetime of savings, the Philippines makes perfect sense.

CHAPTER X

★ ★ ★

CYPRUS

The Mediterranean's Offshore Vault

Located in the far eastern Mediterranean, Cyprus is an enigmatic but opportunity rich island...

It offers excellent residency and citizenship options and its investment potential is significant.

The British have been coming here since they took control of the island in 1878... and they've never stopped. (The island owes many of its idiosyncrasies to the former British presence—driving on the left, for example, along with no shortage of roundabouts).

For decades, the U.K. has been exporting tourists to Cyprus, who revel in the sun and beaches. Cyprus claims the longest summer in Europe, the season beginning in March and lasting to October, even November, with over 300 days of sunshine.

The beaches here are a mixed bag, which I find more interesting than, say, a Caribbean haven with a uniform beach all around. On Cyprus, from one mile to the next, the coast could be fine sand to cliffside, to rocky, to easy pebbles. The waters around the island on all sides are clear and clean.

Again, the U.K. tourist traffic to this ancient island has been constant, and word seems to have spread west to Scandinavia from there, because this is the next biggest market of individual investors in many regions.

When you factor in neighboring Turkey and Israel's tourists, the Russians, for whom this is the closest Mediterranean destination, and the more recent African contingent, the demand on this island is about as high as it can get—and the industry caters to all these nationalities equally. Casinos, spas, and water parks abound, particularly in the north.

Short-term lets are in high demand on every coast, with condos and villas, plus apart-hotels seeing consistently high occupancy rates for seven or more months a year.

The island is home to over 20 universities (three of which are British, one American), attracting students from Central and Eastern Europe, Africa, Greece, and the Middle East. A couple of these institutions are currently expanding, and student housing is a growing market for several of these universities' campuses.

Plus, there's a significant and growing medical tourism market. Between the ultra-affordable health care and the pleasant climate, people come from around the world to have both elective and lifesaving procedures.

Factor in the highly affordable estate inventory especially in the north, and this all adds up to a remarkably robust investor's market.

First, some background...

The third-largest and third-most populous island in the Mediterranean and sitting at its far eastern edge, with Egypt to the south and Turkey to the north, Cyprus is divided from east to west...

The southern two-thirds of the island is called the Republic of Cyprus, and the northern third is officially called the Turkish Republic of Northern Cyprus... yet Turkey doesn't actually govern it. It's more commonly known simply as Northern Cyprus.

The island's official languages are Greek and Turkish, but English, though not an official language, is the *lingua franca* between these and it's very rare to meet someone who doesn't speak it. Over 80% of Cypriots are said to be proficient in English.

English was the official language from 1878 to 1960, during British rule, and continued to be used in courts until 1989 and in legislation until 1996. Not only is it widely spoken, even among locals, but much of the signage and advertisements are also in English.

That's not to say Cyprus feels Westernized, though... when you're here, you know you're at the edge of Europe, on the cusp of the Middle East.

When it comes to doing business, the island attracts companies of all sizes for its low corporate tax rates and ease of administration. Plus, it's located between multiple continents, making it an ideal location for multi-national headquarters.

While the complicated recent history and politics of the island are sure to dominate any thinking about investing here, I assure you that they don't pose any threat to foreign investors or their assets on Cyprus.

Most Americans may not have heard much about Cyprus yet, but the rest of the world has been investing here for decades.

In fact, it's come to be known as the "Plan B Country" in that part of the world... Russians, Chinese, and other nationalities who don't entirely trust their government have been coming to Cyprus for residency, citizenship, and investment for years already.

They aren't coming for the lifestyle, enviable though it may be, they are coming simply to have a backup. To have another country to bail out to should politics in their own country become untenable.

In any case, you've got to get familiar with the island's thorny history and politics in order to understand what the island has to offer, which is, effectively, two jurisdictions—therefore, double the opportunities to choose from—on one island.

A Brief History

Cyprus has been an active player on the world stage since the 2nd millennium B.C. when it was settled by Mycenean Greeks.

An incredibly strategic location, over the centuries the island was ruled by the Assyrians, Egyptians, Persians, Alexander the Great, Ptolemaic Egypt, Rome, the Eastern Roman Empire, Arab caliphates, the French Lusignan dynasty, the Venetians, and the Ottomans...

In 1878, the British took over the island, developing it heavily before and during WWI.

Over the following decades, tensions bubbled between the two ethnic groups that made up the island: Greek Cypriots and Turkish Cypriots. The Greeks wanted the island to become Greek. The Turkish didn't, and at first were happy to remain under British rule instead... then decided to push back. They demanded that their own Turkish state be created by partitioning the island.

The island was a powder keg in the 1950s, with nationalist violence leading to the Cypriot War of Independence with Britain from 1955 to 1959. The army that was formed to fight the British was right-wing Greek... and if they won, they'd have had the power to bring the island into Greece's fold, taking any voice from the Turkish population who might oppose.

In response, Turkish Cypriots formed a resistance army, also fighting the British, yes, but for partition of the island instead of unification with Greece.

The war ended with a treaty that granted Cyprus independence from Britain in 1960 and forbade Britain, Greece, or Turkey from trying to influence the island in any way. Over the next 13 years, violence between the two communities flared up regularly to the point that by the 70s much of the Turkish population lived in enclaves and Turkish representation in the Republic ended.

During the immediate post-independence period, the country was catapulted into the 20th century. Before 1960, most of the island had no electricity. In the 1960s, power stations, telecom stations, energy centers, and refineries were installed all over the island, including on valuable beachfront real estate.

In 1974, Greek Cypriots attempted a *coup d'état* with the aim to unite with Greece, which prompted Turkish invasions. Northern Cyprus (36% of the island) was thus taken by Turkey, with the ceasefire line drawing the border, called the Green Line, between the two sides.

In 1983 Turkey declared the north a Turkish Cypriot State,

to universal international condemnation… the state still isn't acknowledged by any other country. Turkey is the only nation to recognize the Turkish Cypriot State, and they are inextricably linked in many ways, but Turkey has no actual authority over the territory.

In 2004, Cyprus as a whole was admitted to the EU, with legislation on hold in the north until resolution of the conflict. The north doesn't benefit from EU accession, but individuals who can prove their Cypriot ancestry can. North Cypriots who travel to the south with documentation will be granted Republic of Cyprus passports and can thus gain access to the EU and the benefits offered in its member nations.

With admission to the EU, Cyprus was told to clean up its energy act… all the energy stations on coasts had to be moved to safer areas. The coasts were slated for sanitation. This is currently having a huge impact on some of the affected coastlines, Larnaca's, for example, that is being cleaned up and redeveloped with an idea of becoming a mini-Barcelona (more on this anon).

The Republic of Cyprus joined the eurozone in 2008, and uses the euro for all transactions, including real estate. Northern Cyprus officially uses the Turkish lira, with euros, pounds, or dollars sometimes accepted instead. Real estate in the north is typically priced in British pounds, occasionally in euros depending on the developer.

Over the decades since the Turkish invasions, there have been several attempts at resolution, some coming closer to fruition than others, but none ever accepted by both sides…

The latest closest they came was in 2015, when both sides came to the table for reunification talks. These failed by 2017.

Cyprus Today

Today, feelings on the island are varied and variously impassioned or indifferent…

When business reigns, things are sanguine. Those working

in the same industry are polite and respectful, often introducing someone from the other side as a brother or sister from the north or south.

On an individual level, though, there can be tension. One waiter who served my family turned on his heel when we told him we'd be visiting the north. A developer I spoke with in the south said that he had to fight against prejudice taking hold in his seven-year-old daughter who was picking up at school that the north was a bad place, and those in it bad people.

On the other hand, most Turkish Cypriots who were involved in the drama of the last century have been succeeded by the second generation, many of whom have cut all ties with their Turkish heritage and consider themselves purely Cypriot.

When it comes to speaking about the island's history, though, it seems as though all Cypriots, regardless of side, hold a resentment against the British and their role in Cyprus' history...

Americans, for once, come off unscathed here. In fact, Cypriots are currently eager for American (or Canadian) attention—be it political or individual. They've never really had much to do with us, nor us them, but there's a mutual interest being nurtured right now, and my takeaway was that Cypriots are very glad to have North Americans in their country.

There may not be many Americans living here yet, but there are plenty of foreigners... It's estimated that there are over 110,000 (out of 1.2 million) foreign residents on Cyprus, the largest groups being Greek, British, Romanian, and Bulgarian.

Politics are still dominated by the events of 1974, and "resolution," as any potential solution is simply referred to, precedes discussion of anything. So much is dependent on a possible reunification, that virtually every conversation is prefaced with some reference to resolution.

There was a serious effort at increasing intra-island freedoms over the last couple of decades. In 2003, the north eased border restrictions, allowing Cypriots to cross the Green Line for the first time in 30 years. In 2008, two walls came down: one that had separated the UN buffer zone from the Republic, and another that had separated north from south in the capital city of Nicosia.

Practically speaking, the politics aren't as fraught as they once were, and the two sides often come to agreement when it comes to helping out in an emergency. When the south suffers a drought, the north sells some of its water (brought in via massive underwater pipe from Turkey). When the north has a power shortage, the south helps out. And regardless of emergency, the south is fed in large part by the north, the breadbasket of the island.

With oil having just been discovered off the island's coasts in 2019, there's a big new variable at play in resolution negotiations... the south has control of all the island's exclusive economic zones, so all that wealth would theoretically only benefit the south.

Cyprus has historically suffered from droughts, which have become more extreme in the last couple of decades.

In 2015, the Northern Cyprus Water Supply Project was completed, which brings massive amounts of water for drinking and irrigation from Turkey to Northern Cyprus via underwater pipe.

While the individual homes you'll see around Northern Cyprus still have big tanks on the roofs for water storage, they are obsolete these days.

The island is not yet connected to the European network for electricity, but the world's longest submarine power cable is currently under construction, set to connect Cyprus' grid to Greece and Israel's by 2029.

While this is said to be the fourth most religious country in Europe, religion is seemingly an afterthought to the arguments for separation between the Greek Orthodox south and the Sunni Muslim north.

Education is a top priority here, with 7% of the GDP spent on education (third-highest rate in the EU, after Denmark and Sweden). The majority of Cypriots have a degree of some sort, having studied at Greek, British, Turkish, or other European or Northern American universities. In fact, at 30%,

Cyprus has the highest percentage of working age citizens with higher education in the EU. For the 25 to 34 age group, 47%

have a tertiary education, again, the highest rate in the EU.

Government And Law

The Republic of Cyprus is a presidential republic; the current president is Nikos Christodoulides, elected in 2023 for a five-year term.

According to the constitution of 1960, a careful balance of power was supposed to be maintained in the government: a Greek-Cypriot president, a Turkish Cypriot vice president, each with equal veto power.

However, since the violence of the 1960s, the Turkish seats have been left empty.

In 1985, Northern Cyprus, which had unilaterally declared independence in '83, adopted a constitution and held elections... The south still holds sovereignty over the entire island and is the only internationally recognized government on the island, but its effective control ends at the Green Line.

The north holds independent, democratic elections. While Northern Cyprus is in many ways an independent state, it has been shunned by the international community since its inception, so it depends heavily on Turkey for access to the rest of the world—import and export is all via Turkey, for example, as no country will use any of its ports, and Turkey contributes significantly to their annual budget.

As a former British colony, the local law is closely aligned to the common law system with some influence from civil law.

The Economy

Tourism, financial services, and shipping are the main sources of Cyprus' income. The island is seen as a bridge between east and west and acts as a financial and shipping hub in the region.

In 2012, the island began to suffer from the eurozone financial crisis that had already taken down so many European economies.

It was heavily impacted by the exposure of its three largest banks to the Greek financial crisis.

With a €7.3-billion bailout from the troika (the European Commission, the IMF, and the European Central Bank), the country righted itself, not before getting a slap on the wrist for letting themselves become a tax haven for Russian millionaires, which resulted in the end of the country's CIP program.

The three-year recession ended in 2015, and the economy had been growing steadily until 2020, when, as with most countries in the world, the COVID-19 recession struck Cyprus, which rebounded in 2021. It's been steady for the last couple of years, with 3.4% growth observed in 2024 and a similar figure for 2025.

Cyprus' 2025 GDP ranked 19th highest in Europe.

In the 2023 Legatum Prosperity Index, Cyprus came in 34th out of 167, and its Human Development Index ranking for 2025 was 32 out of 189 countries.

These indices are seen as indicating the level of wealth in both economies and populations of a country, and Cyprus comes out very well in both, speaking to the island's overall financial wellbeing.

The Island

Nicosia, the capital city, is located more or less dead center of the island. This is the administrative and governmental hub of the island but, by all accounts, there's little reason to spend time there unless you work there.

In the south, Larnaca and Limassol are the two port cities, both located on the southern coast, servicing cargo, passenger, and cruise ships. Limassol is the second-largest city on the island, Larnaca the third.

In the north, the cities of importance are Kyrenia and Famagusta (fifth and seventh largest cities on the island), also port cities, but whose ports are underused these days. Both of these cities were the go-to beach destinations on the island until the separation in 1974.

Once the border closed, it forced towns in the south to fill the void.

Generally speaking, the southern coast is flat and the northern coast is backed by mountains, making it more visually (and practically) interesting. Inland, the west is dominated by the Troodos mountains, but the western coast, around Paphos, is as flat as the south.

These flat coasts make for good beaches, and therefore prime locations for resorts, which is why they've already been largely developed. To the north, there's a lot more virgin coastline, leading to the exciting investment opportunities.

Larnaca

Larnaca, the oldest city in Cyprus and birthplace to ancient Stoic philosopher Zeno, is now leading the island into the future. Home to the main international airport, the city is the entry point for the majority of visitors to Cyprus, and it is currently undergoing a renaissance.

Larnaca is known for its seafront. It's got the requisite sand, sea, and palm trees... but when Cyprus was divided, the city lobbied to become the island's oil and gas supply base—and therefore never became a tourist hub. The industrialized harbor that resulted is today a rusting eyesore.

The enormous makeover now underway along Larnaca's coast will transform it within the decade, though, and the city is primed to become the island's next tourist hub.

Larnaca is also home to several universities.

Limassol

Limassol is the other port city of the Republic, and this city has been well looked after.

Unlike many cities on the island, Limassol was never neglected. From the start, it was chosen as a favorite city by British colonizers, and enjoyed improvements from day one of British rule. Roads were repaired and cleaned, animals removed from the city center, landscaping added, lanterns installed, and docks constructed.

Boasting a post and telegraph office, hospital, printing press, and hotels, Limassol was the cosmopolitan capital of the country at the end of the 19th century and the start of the 20th.

The city is the base for much of the island's wine companies, but its main industry comes from its port, the busiest in the country.

Like Larnaca, Limassol's coast is undergoing an update... the construction boom started in 2013 and from 2018 to 2021, 12 buildings with more than 26 floors were constructed on the island—11 of them in Limassol.

The major construction boom here, as well as on all of Cyprus' coasts, was catapulted by the Golden Visa program that brought in so much capital before being tightened up.

Today, the market here is stagnant, with few sales and sky-high rents compared to other cities.

Paphos

Paphos, the legendary birthplace of Aphrodite, is one of the big tourist draws in the Republic, with historical sites, beach resorts, and tourists to occupy them. This is where the Republic's second airport is, but the city has only recently come back to prominence.

Once an important city due to the pilgrims who came to worship Aphrodite at her temple here, when Nicosia was founded in the 10th century, traffic dried up.

During the British Colonial period, the region became even less of value, and many residents moved elsewhere. It was the most underdeveloped part of the island until 1974.

In 1980, Paphos was granted UNESCO World Heritage Status

for its ancient architecture, mosaics, and ancient religious importance. It was a European Capital of Culture in 2017.

Since the 1980s, the city has garnered much attention from developers, and the coast here is now highly developed, home to a string of large-scale resorts.

Troodos

The green heart of the island, the Troodos Mountain range in the west is a major tourist draw among locals, with year-round attractions—it's the cool retreat in the summer and the only snowy destination in winter.

The mountains offer hiking in the foothills, skiing from the peaks, Byzantine churches, and old wine villages... and lots of country house hideaways.

Kyrenia

Said to have been founded by two veterans of the Trojan War, Kyrenia is the tourism capital of Northern Cyprus, offering spas, casinos, and beach resorts for all demographics.

With its old harbor and seafront castle, the old town itself is worth visiting, but it's the residential developments outside of town that are currently where the interesting opportunity lies.

Several development companies are working up and down this coast, offering everything from studios to 10-bedroom beachfront villas.

Famagusta

Famagusta is a walled city that dates to the Medieval era and gained wealth over the centuries to that point that by 1300 it was one of the richest cities in Christendom. By the mid-14th century, Famagusta was said to have the richest citizens in the world.

Back then, wealth was measured by the number of churches you had, so the city built churches.

Sometimes called the city of 365 churches, legend has it that at the city's height, it had a church for every day of the year. To this day the old town is known as the church district.

Famagusta owes its historic wealth to having the deepest harbor in the region, one of the reasons the British singled the city out during their reign, as well. From the start, it had been targeted for development with the Famagusta Development Act, and after WWI, the city's shipping traffic had increased and it began to rival Larnaca.

By 1974, it was contributing over 10% to the country's economy and accounted for a major portion of tourism. It was taken in the Turkish invasion, and a suburb of the city, Varosha, was kept fenced off from the public until 2020. It's now open to tourists, and it's worth a walk through the ghost town... it brings a new level of reality to the historical conflict.

The city is now the most important port in Northern Cyprus, accounting for much of its shipping and travel, as well as a significant amount of tourism.

Buying Real Estate In Cyprus

For the most part, the property purchase process is the same in the north and the south. The most obvious difference is the currencies...

Prices for real estate transactions are quoted in British pounds in North Cyprus—but always double-check the currency being used in the contract.

In the south, the currency is euros, and property is priced in euros.

While there are attractive opportunities in both the north and the south, the north is where the bargain-basement prices can be found. Between the cost of the property and the fees associated, prices in the south will consistently be about 20% more than in the north.

Cyprus inheritance laws would allocate your local assets equally among your spouse and children, so it's important to make a will here if you'd like things to be distributed otherwise.

The Buying Process

Briefly, the process is completed in the following steps:

1. Reservation agreement signed;
2. Sales contract drawn up and signed;
3. Registering the sale with the land office;
4. Application for purchase permission submitted to government;
5. Title deed transfer.

Some vendors offer longer payment plans than the completion period for the property. In this case, you can receive the keys—either to move in personally or start generating returns through rentals—without having to pay off the property in full.

If you're buying in a development, there may be a maintenance agreement for care of any shared common areas, and these fees are payable monthly or annually (essentially HOA fees). Make sure you are clear on what these are or are projected to be before signing your contract.

An agreed amount of deposit per the agreement might be paid at the time of entering into the contract, usually at the time of key handover.

Buying For Investment

From an investment perspective, keep in mind that rental income from the north would be in British pounds, but in the south the income would be in euros.

If you're buying for investment with the idea of renting out your property, you will, of course, want to employ the services of property and rental management representatives. Finding third parties to provide these services is difficult all over the island, so if your goal is pure investment, make sure the developer you buy from provides these services, as you won't feasibly be able to rent anything out without them.

Buying from a developer is a much more secure way to pursue a purchase in Cyprus. Buying resale can be risky because of the various titles that have existed over the years on the island. If you go the resale route, make sure you work with an experienced attorney so the title can be cleared.

A local lawyer can handle several aspects of the real estate purchase process for you, from simply signing the sales contract in your stead, to filing your permission to purchase application, or applying for permanent residency on your behalf once you've made your purchase.

To make sure you're making a secure purchase, your lawyer should do an in-depth search on the property to find any liens, charges, or encumbrances; check building permits and approvals; draft up a sales contract where responsibilities of both parties and default penalties and compensation clauses are clearly stated; and handle and/or assist with procedures at local government offices.

Most developers offer furniture packages. If you'd avail of one, you'll choose based on style and price.

Property advertised as unfurnished usually comes with fitted tiles, kitchen cabinets, fitted sink, toilet and shower, and air conditioning infrastructure.

Always check what is included in the purchase price and make sure it's in written form attached to the sales contract.

Cyprus' Property Titles

One of the issues the complex history of Northern Cyprus

brings with it is questions about title. There are four types...

Pre-1974 Turkish Cypriot or foreign ownership. These titles are straightforward and have no potential problems.

Pre-1974 Greek Cypriot Exchange Land. This land was titled to Turkish Cypriots by the Northern Cyprus government in exchange for land lost in the south by the Turkish Cypriots.

These titles are considered rectified by the 1983 Northern Cyprus constitution and are freely transferable to foreigners.

Tahsis (TMD) Deed. This is land owned by Greek Cypriots pre-1974 that was titled to a Turkish Cypriot refugee from the south or to a Turkish mainland settler. Stay clear of this kind of title.

Leasehold. These are properties owned by the Northern Cyprus government that they grant a long-term lease for 49 years.

Leasehold is common in many countries, but North Americans aren't generally familiar or comfortable with this type of property.

The pre-1974 Greek Cypriot title can be fine, but ask questions. Many Greek Cypriots have been compensated already for their land.

Others are still waiting. This is one of the contentious items that needs to be resolved for reunification.

The One Property Rule

Per the 2025 Northern Cyprus Property Laws, foreign nationals can own only one residential property, no larger than 2,500 square meters, in Northern Cyprus.

In the Republic of Cyprus, non EU nationals are generally allowed to purchase up to two residential units or one property plus limited commercial space providing those units are for personal use only and council approval is granted.

Not Taking Title In Your Own Name

Some investors choose not to transfer the title deed of their property in their name, generally because they intend to resell within five to 10 years and it's not worth the cost and hassle—in fact, several owners in a row can do this. (If there's a long line of previous owners who never took the title to their own name, it will take longer to finalize the purchase.)

If you decide to go this route, you'll receive ownership rights when the contract of sale is registered to the government. It costs around 0.5% of the purchase price in stamp duty fees.

The title deed transferring process incurs a further 3% (on your first purchase) to 6% (for subsequent purchases) of the sale price in transfer taxes.

When buying directly from a developer, you'll need to confirm that they allow the option, but if you're buying for pure investment it can make sense to reduce your buying costs by not taking title in your own name but using one of the vehicles outlined above. This strategy does not affect your ownership, inheritance, or residency rights and is commonly done.

The title deed is held by the developer for as long as you'd like; at any point you can transfer the deed to your name. If the developer goes bankrupt or dissolves for any reason, your registered contract of sale will grant you the title deed of the property in court, but you'll have to pay the transfer fees. Just make sure to register the sale with the District Land Office (or that your lawyer has done this for you).

Buying On-Site

You'll need your passport to initiate the process, and the first thing you'll do is sign a reservation contract. This comes at a small fee ranging between $1,000 and $5,000 which goes towards the down payment.

Following this, a sales contract is drawn up between the developer and the buyer. The contract is signed in person by the buyer and the developer's representative; two witnesses will be required, and the contract must be signed in blue ink.

Assuming you're using an attorney, they will check that the developer representative has a valid POA or is the director of the development company.

The contract of sale is then registered to the District Land's Office.

Buying Remotely

In terms of administration, you'll want to have a rental and property manager in place ahead of time, as well as make sure any outstanding furnishings can be dealt with.

You also want to be sure you're working with a trusted attorney, and be sure the deed of the property is clean.

As with buying in person, once you find a place of interest, you can make your offer. When both parties have agreed, you'll sign a reservation contract with a fee ($1k to $5k) acting towards the down payment.

In exchange, you'll receive a reservation contract and a receipt. The payment can be made through a wire transfer or via credit card using a mail order form. You'll also provide a copy of your passport and some basic personal details.

The next step is the contract of sale, which must include all the agreement details, including the payment terms, late delivery penalty clause, title deed copy, site plan copy, etc.

If you weren't already working with a local lawyer, you should at this stage to make sure your rights are protected—of course, this should be an independent lawyer who was not referred by the developer. Work from recommendations from expats who have already bought if possible.

When buying a property remotely, you'll likely use a trust company or sign a Power of Attorney (POA). With both of these methods, your local lawyer acts as your nominee and signs everything on your behalf.

This is a common process you're likely familiar with if you've bought property remotely in the past... the complication with Northern Cyprus is that you may not be able to access a North Cyprus Representative Office... There are two TRNC Representative Offices in the United States, one in D.C. and one in New York; in Canada the only office is in Ontario. If you're not near enough to any of those, you'll have to work with your nearest Turkish Embassy.

If buying in the south, you'll go to a Republic of Cyprus embassy; there are 12 in the States and three in Canada.

For purchase through a trust, you simply send an email approval for the contract of sale between the trust company and the seller. Later, a trust agreement is signed separately between the buyer and the trust company.

Trusts come at a cost of £350 for the first 18 months, with annual fees of £1,000 thereafter.

Once either a trust or a power of attorney is obtained, and the details of the contract are agreed by buyer and seller, the contract is signed.

Registering Contract Of Sale

When the sales contract is signed, the buyer typically pays 30% to 60% of the sales price as the down payment, depending on the stage of construction of the property. These payments can be made to the developer, real estate agent, or your lawyer to avoid the need for a local bank account.

If the property is a resale or ready for key-handover at the time of signing, then the full sale price is paid at the time of title deed transfer.

The sales contract should be registered with the District Land's Office within 21 days of signing. At this stage, stamp duty of 0.5% is also paid to the government. Registering the sales contract secures the property in your name and is legally binding; it ensures that you are protected from the property being sold or transferred to a third party and from any subsequent liens being placed on the property.

If the property is complete, you don't have to wait until the purchase permission application is finalized to take possession; you can as soon as the sale is registered.

Permission To Purchase Application

Non-Cypriot citizens must request permission to acquire property on the island and, bizarrely, this is applied for after the purchase has already been completed.

You'll need to submit a criminal background check and bank reference letters.

Really, though, this step is a formality... The only reason permission would be denied would be to a serious criminal. Small infractions and/or minor crimes committed many years prior are likely to be overlooked. And in the rare event that the request is denied, you can reapply.

Your lawyer can make the application for a purchase permit on your behalf and follow it up until the completion. It can take up to a year to complete the process, but you can use the property as you wish in the meantime, and the status does not affect residency and/or inheritance rights.

Purchase permission is not a requisite for re-selling property; if you wish to sell before permission is granted, you can.

Title Deed Transfer

Separation of title deeds for individual properties when a pre-construction unit is bought can take up to two years after the date of completion. Following this, it's a simple process to transfer the Title Deed.

Your lawyer can help you with the application, and the transfer is usually completed the same day.

Closing Costs And Maintenance Fees

In both the North and the South, legal fees will range from £1,000 to £5,000 depending on the services performed.

If working with an agent for a sale, the commission is payable by the seller.

In The North...

In the North, first-time sellers are exempt from paying capital gains tax; from the second sale onward, you'll be subject to capital gains of 4.7% of the value of the property.

Stamp duty is 0.5% of the purchase price due at the time of registry of the Contract of Sale. This one-time fee applies only to resales. It's typically paid by the buyer, but can sometimes be negotiated to be split or paid by the seller.

VAT on new property is 5% of the sale price and is due when the title is transferred or the keys are handed over (not at the time of signing).

The title deed transfer fee is 3% of the purchase, payable at the time of title deed transfer for the first purchase of the buyer.

When a buyer purchases second or more properties, title deed transfer is 6%. If you're planning to flip the purchase within a few years, you can avoid paying the transfer fee by not taking title in your own name.

Infrastructure contribution and utility connection fees are paid by the first owner of a property, in some cases, the contract might stipulate that the vendor covers these costs. They range between £1,000 and £3,000.

Home Ownership Tax (HOT) is three Turkish liras per square meter (HOT is paid annually) for properties up to 120 square meters. Larger properties may have the upper portion of area taxed at 2 Turkish liras per square meter.

If you earn rental yields from your property, a capital gains tax of 10% of the revenue is due. This is also called the Stoppage tax and is paid annually.

Americans and Canadians would not be subject to double-taxation.

When selling the property, the capital gains tax (stopaj) is payable to the tax office by the vendor, although this can always be varied by an express clause in the contract of sale.

Your foreign pension is not taxed in North Cyprus. You are only taxed on the earnings made in the country.

In The South...

Transfer fees will be between 3% and 8%. It's 3% for properties up to €85,000, 5% for properties between €85,000 and €170,000, and 8% for properties above €170,000.

Stamp duty is 0.15% to 0.20%, and legal fees range from 0.10% to 1.00%.

VAT is typically 19%, but first-time buyers purchasing or constructing less than 250 square meters are eligible for a 5% rate. This may also apply if the property is used as a primary and permanent residency for the next 10 years.

If you own a property that's earning rent locally and it's titled in your name, standard income tax rates apply. If titled to an entity, the corporate flat tax rate of 12.5% applies.

Capital gains are taxed at 20%, with a lifetime exemption of €85,430 if the property was owner-occupied for at least five years.

Financing

While it is possible for foreigners to get mortgages here up to the age of 70 to 75, it's not necessarily worth it. The maximum term would be 15 years and you'd have to put 60% down and you need life insurance to be eligible, which would likely be a monthly cost of over €200 a month.

Residency In Cyprus

No matter which side of the island you move to, residency is just about as easy as it gets in Cyprus.

The Republic's Category F Permit

In the south, the easiest residency route is the Category F Permit, which is renewable annually, but it's slow—it can take up to two years to be approved (during this time you can leave the country without penalty). This is what we commonly refer to as the "self-sufficiency option." As long as you can prove an income that will support you in the country, you'll be given residency.

You don't need to apply for this visa in advance of arriving in Cyprus, you can simply land in the country on your tourist visa and extend it for up to a year while you apply.

To apply, you'll need to open a bank account, make a deposit of €9,000 (which can be moved back out once your application is approved), and either purchase a property or sign a rental contract of at least one year. You'll also need to prove that you have a steady income; the number isn't specified, but generally €1,000 a month will suffice.

This is an immediate permanent residency. You may be asked to reprove your qualifications after a few years, but it is essentially without expiration.

You cannot work with this visa, and you only need to visit the country once every two years to maintain the status.

The Fast-Track Program

If you don't want to wait the two years, you can fast-track your residency by purchasing property worth a minimum of €300,000 (plus tax), which can be split between two properties.

You'll also need to make a fixed-term deposit in a Cypriot bank of at least €30,000 for three years.

You must prove an annual foreign income of at least €30,000, plus €5,000 for each dependent child and €8,000 for each adult dependent (spouse and parents).

The attorney fees for the fast-track visa will be about double those for the Category F visa, but the process only takes two months.

Alternative Investment Funds

If you're not comfortable making such a big investment alone, but want to take advantage of the fast-track option, you could join a qualifying fund. Once you've invested, you can apply for the fast-track visa, come to Cyprus and live for a while to see if you like it before making the financial commitment that the fast-track requires. This also gets you around the VAT of buying a new property.

After two-and-a-half years, you can take the money out and put it into a personal property if you want, or cash out altogether.

Again, this is immediate permanent residency, doesn't confer a work permit, and you must visit every two years.

Nomad Or Nothing

Unless you're able to snag a digital nomad visa, you're unlikely to be able to work in Cyprus. Work permits are only granted if your employer can prove that your job can't be completed by a Cypriot or other EU national.

The Republic's Digital Nomad Visa

Launched in October 2021, this visa option offers 500 annual permits to individuals with an income of €3,500 a month. To apply, you need to provide a letter from your foreign employer, rent a property in the south, and get local insurance.

Residency Permit Through Property Purchase In The North

Once you've initiated the purchase of a property in Northern Cyprus, you are eligible to apply for residency and reside in the country while it is processed.

The property in question does not need to be in your own name, nor does it need to be fully paid off. Eligible dependents include your children under the age of 18, and your spouse (gay marriage is not yet legally recognized in either the North or South). Other family members would only be entitled to apply if their name appears on the contract and they have some rights to the property.

The application is straightforward, you can live in the country while it's being processed, and you can reapply as needed.

Requirements For Permanent Residency:

- You must be present at the time of application;
- Passport original and photocopy;
- Owning a property/land in Cyprus (contract of sale deposited to the District Land Registry) or in the case of a resale, the title deed of the property;
- Proof of sufficient funds to support yourself. Before application, you must open up a local bank account and deposit £8,000 as proof of sufficient funds to support yourself for two years.
- Health tests obtained from licensed clinics or state hospital;
- Proof of address obtained in writing (*Ikametgah belgesi*) from the local Muhtar (village chief);
- Clean background check obtained from your local police department.

You'll need to resubmit all of this annually to renew, except for the health check.

The residency permit that comes with property purchase is simply that: a permit to reside. It does not give you the right to work or set up a business locally.

Children under the age of 18 years do not require residency permits; families moving to North Cyprus only need to apply for residency for the adult members of the family.

Citizenship In Cyprus

While a passport from the Republic of Cyprus would be a useful one to have, being an EU nation, a passport from the north has virtually no value.

While residence-based citizenship is possible in Northern Cyprus it is not automatic and remains discretionary dependent on a decision by the Council of Ministers. Applications can be made after five years of residency.

Having a passport from the Republic of Cyprus, however, would be hugely valuable, as it's an EU travel document.

Beware, though, that Cyprus is not part of the Schengen Area, so while you can travel throughout the EU visa-free, you still need to go through immigration and you're still bound by the 90-days-in-180 limit.

In the south, on any type of residency visa, you are eligible for citizenship after just four years of residency if you are able to speak Greek, or after five years if you don't. You must be living in the country for at least the last 12 months to qualify.

What's especially interesting here is that the naturalization "clock" begins ticking as soon as you enter the country—while you're still technically on a tourist visa, you can be earning time to count towards an eventual passport.

Naturalization is generally granted easily; there is no language requirement, but there is an interview about Cyprus culture.

There is also a military duty demanded in Cyprus, but it doesn't apply to naturalized citizens or their descendants, only to those of Cypriot origin.

Banking In Cyprus

Opening an account is easy here—even for Americans.

All you really need is a proof of address...

If applying for residency, you'll need a local bank account.

Having a bank account isn't a prerequisite for purchasing property, though. If you don't intend to live in Cyprus and you prefer not to open a local account, you can simply use the client accounts of the lawyers, developers, and rental teams to handle local transactions and use a wire transfer to access the accounts.

Many banks here advertise "Expat Banking," so working with foreigners is nothing new to bankers here. Accounts can be opened in different currencies, including Turkish lira, U.S. dollars, euros, and pounds sterling.

In the south, all you need to open an account is a proof of address, and ideally it should be your tax base.

In the north, it's even simpler: Proof of address and ID can be fulfilled by just your driver's license, and the process takes about 20 minutes.

Taxes In Cyprus

You're a tax resident in Cyprus if you spend more than 183 days a year there.

VAT: Sales tax is generally 19% in both the north and the south; 5% on property.

Income Tax: Residents of Cyprus will be taxed on worldwide income, but there's no chance of paying tax both back home and in Cyprus, as the island has tax treaties preventing double taxation with the United States, Canada, all EU member nations, and about 50 other countries.

In any case, a unilateral tax credit is granted for any tax paid abroad, regardless of the existence of a treaty.

Foreign pensions are taxed at a flat rate of 5%, with an annual exemption of €3,420.

Individual Income Tax Rate

Up to €19,500: 0%
€19,501 to €28,000: 20%
€28,001 to €36,300: 25%
€36,301 to €60,000: 30%
Over €60,000: 35%

Inheritance Taxes: Different taxes are applicable where the transfer is made by way of a donation (gift):

- To a child from parents: 0.2%
- To a spouse: 0.4%
- To a grandchild: 0.4%

Taxes When Selling Property: In the north, first-time sellers don't have to pay capital gains tax; from the second sale onward, you'll be subject to pay 4% of the value of the property.

In the south, capital gains is 20%, with a single lifetime exemption possibility:

- An individual selling a private residence owned for five or more years: €85,430;
- A farmer selling agricultural land: €25,629;
- Any other property disposal: €17,086.

Spending Time

With over 12,000 years of history, plus arts, golf, beaches, villages, resorts, and fantastic cuisine, Cyprus is worth a visit for further exploration—if you decide not to invest, you can do worse than spending a vacation week on a Mediterranean island...

Getting To Cyprus

Flying into North Cyprus, you'll land at Ercan International Airport in Nicosia and be asked to fill out a form which acts as your visa.

If flying into the south, either Larnaca or Paphos Airport will be your entry point and no form is required.

Tourist visas are granted for 90 days; to stay longer, you'll need to apply for residency.

Getting Around In Cyprus

You'll need a car to get around on the island, even within cities. Cyprus has a disproportionately high car ownership rate, due largely to the heat.

Roads are good quality and well maintained across the island, but traffic in the main cities can get bad.

The standard of driving on the island is generally low compared to North America or the rest of Europe, so be wary of other drivers here.

Don't forget that they drive on the left, and brush up on roundabout etiquette—they're abundant.

Crossing The Border

Crossing the North-South border is easy and fairly fast, with

10 to 15 minute wait times on average. There are nine border crossings on the island, and they're all open 24 hours a day. You need your passport to cross, as well as insurance if you're driving. You can cross as many times as you like, and you don't have to return through the same checkpoint as you arrived from.

North-South Border Cross Points:

1. Ledra Palace, Nicosia (pedestrians only)
2. Ledra Street, Nicosia (pedestrians only)
3. Agios Dhometios, Nicosia
4. Pergamos
5. Strovilia
6. Astromeritis / Zodhia
7. Kato Pyrgos / Karavostasi / Yesilirmak
8. Lefka / Apliki Kato
9. Deryneia

The Local Languages

While few foreign investors or holiday homeowners are eager to try to learn either Turkish or Greek to partake in the island's lifestyle—nor do they need to, it's wholly unnecessary—it's worth noting that the dialects of Cypriot Turkish and Cypriot Greek vary from the standards significantly. (So if you do try to learn them, be warned that Duolingo's versions, for example, won't match up with what's used on the island.)

When speaking in English, though, bear in mind that the American (or Canadian) accent is not well known to most Cypriots, who are much more familiar with the British or even Australian accent. Speak slowly and be patient if you feel you're not being understood, it's likely that your accent is the hurdle.

CYPRUS

For The Millionaire Next Door

Cyprus' unique geographical position at the crossroads of Europe, Asia, and the Middle East, makes it a compelling choice for those looking to diversify overseas. Here, you get all the perks of a Mediterranean lifestyle but at a much more attractive price. Plus, English is widely spoken and the legal and business environment is familiar and stable.

For my money, Northern Cyprus has all the right ingredients for a dream retirement and fantastic investment opportunities.

It's arguably the most beautiful area of the island, boasting incredible castles, colonial villages, and miles of sandy beaches. Plus, a favorable climate.

As well as attracting sun worshippers, it has a strong casino industry (hence its reputation as the "Las Vegas of the Mediterranean") and a burgeoning medical tourism sector. All of this means an increase in demand for tourist accommodation.

For the Millionaire Next Door seeking a retirement destination, a second home, or property investment, Northern Cyprus is a strong contender.

PART III

THE JET-SET MILLIONAIRE

CHAPTER XI

GREECE

The Elite Escape

As home to the longest coastline in the Mediterranean Basin, Greece's reputation as a bona fide beach destination is well-founded.

It's not just about beaches, though. Greece offers mountains, thousands of picturesque islands, olive groves, vineyards, and an untouched inland wilderness, as well as a bounty of ancient and wonderfully scenic villages.

Plus, Greek people are warm and welcoming, the food is some of the best in the world, and the cost of living is low, especially for Europe.

Greece is a culturally fascinating place—the cradle of Western civilization with foundational concepts like democracy, western philosophy, political science, and literature originating here.

Sites of cultural and historical importance, some dating back thousands of years, are found all over the country, making Greece a must-visit for history buffs.

Greek's worldwide influence is hugely down to its location. At the southernmost point of the Balkan peninsula, Greece is at the crossroads of Asia, Africa, and Europe, resulting in a diverse cultural mix. Greece has also had a colorful history, undergoing the ruling of several empires, contributing to its cultural influence on the world.

The 2008 global recession hit Greece particularly hard, triggering a prolonged debt crisis and years of austerity. By the late

2010s, the country was slowly regaining its footing before the pandemic disrupted global economies in 2020.

Today, Greece's economy is on an upward trajectory once again, supported by growth in tourism, shipping, renewable energy, and foreign investment. While challenges remain, the overall outlook is far more stable than a decade ago, and many investors see now as an attractive window to explore opportunities in Greece's growing economy.

Greece's advantage over its European counterparts is its laid-back version of life on the Continent. One in which you can eat delicious local produce, live in a safe, welcoming environment, and enjoy a Mediterranean lifestyle at a low cost.

Greek Residency And Citizenship

Greece offers several paths to residency, although technically, it doesn't offer a retiree-specific visa. The residence permit that most retirees use to live here long-term is an independent means visa called the Financially Independent Person (FIP) Permit.

The basic requirement to qualify for the FIP visa is showing that you receive enough income to support yourself while living in Greece. You need to show that you receive €3,500 (about $4k) per month. This residency permit is available for three years and is renewable.

Greece also offers a digital nomad visa which has the same financial threshold as the FIP—this increases by 20% for a spouse and by 15% for each child included. When granted, it permits holders to live in Greece for up to 12 months, with the option to extend for an additional two years through a residence permit.

Greece's Golden Visa Program

Greece offers a Golden Visa program that can lead to citizenship within seven years.

Greece Golden Visa Investment Options

Launched in 2013, Greece's Golden Visa program is one of the last remaining in Europe.

A €250,000 investment in Greek property makes you eligible for a Golden Visa in this EU member state however at that level you are restricted to specialized real estate investments whereby industrial buildings are converted for residential use or historical restoration projects.

For those wishing to make a more straightforward real estate purchase, the entry point rises to a minimum of €400,000 with restrictions on the property size and location imposed. If you wish to buy a qualifying property in Greece's most sought-after areas such as Athens, Thessaloniki, Mykonos, and Santorini, for example, the minimum investment amount increases further to €800,000.

A Greek Golden Visa is renewable every five years, so long as you maintain the required investment.

There is no minimum in-country requirement to qualify or to renew the visa, and your spouse and children under 21 can join you.

You must have a clean criminal record and health insurance valid in Greece to be eligible to apply.

Continued residency leads to eligibility for citizenship after seven years, but you must learn Greek which effectively excludes most candidates for a Greek passport.

Lawyer's fees, stamp duty, and government fees will cost you about €15,000 for the minimum-priced investment.

Alternative Greek Golden Visa investment pathways include putting funds into local companies, securities, or bonds. For Government bonds the required investment is €500,000, for investment funds it's €350,000.

Greece has also launched a five-year residence-by-investment program for investments in the startup sector. Investments can be made through a Greek legal entity (whereby sole ownership required) or a foreign legal entity (which can have up to three shareholders, each holding at least 33% of shares). Permit holders cannot control more than 33% of the company's shares or voting rights.

Applicants must invest a minimum of €250,000 in shares or equity in a Greek startup registered on the national registry, Elevate Greece. At least two new jobs must be created within the first year of the investment and maintained for five years.

Greek Citizenship

After seven years of permanent and legal residency you can apply for Greek citizenship by naturalization. That reduces to three years if you're married to a Greek citizen or are the parent of a Greek citizen.

Key requirements for a successful citizenship application are:

- **Residency:** You must hold a valid residence permit and have lived in Greece for a minimum of 183 days per year for seven consecutive years.
- **Knowledge:** You will need to pass the Citizenship Knowledge Test covering Greek language, history, geography, and culture.
- **Integrity:** You will need to hold a clean criminal record from both Greece and your country of origin.
- **Economic Stability:** You will need to show proof of sufficient income and tax compliance.

For those with Greek ancestry, the process becomes much faster and cheaper.

Greeks believe in bloodlines. You're eligible for Greek citizenship if you have at least one biological parent or grandparent of Greek origin, i.e., born in Greece.

The name of the game is "Find As Many Supporting Documents As You Can"—birth, marriage, and death certificates; baptismal records, IDs, passports, even college records... extra points for a Greek municipality certificate certifying your ancestor's birth and municipality number.

Along with the family supporting documents, you'll need to provide a clean police report.

You can apply in Greece at a registry office in Athens, or you can apply at the Greek consulate in your home country.

A common concern with Greek citizenship is military service. Males aged 19 to 45 can circumvent the requirement by maintaining foreign resident status (possible as a Greek national), which permits up to six months of residency in Greece per year. Anything beyond six months automatically renders the citizen a permanent resident and may require up to 15 months of military service.

Taxes In Greece

Greece offers significant tax breaks for foreign retirees, the very wealthy, and entrepreneurs.

Ordinary tax residents will face relatively high marginal tax rates (from 9% to 44%). The standard progressive system ramps up quickly to 44% for income of €40,000 and above.

Residents of Greece are taxed on their worldwide income, and income tax rates are relatively high... But Greece offers a tax abatement program called the Non-Dom Regime for Retirees. It allows for a 7% flat tax on many types of passive income (including pensions) for 15 years.

Also, the tax treaties in place between Greece and the United States and Canada help residents avoid double taxation.

Qualifiers for tax residency in Greece are being physically present on Greek territory for 183 days or more in any 365-day period; having a "residence" in Greece (habitual abode); and/or Greece being the principal center of your economic or social interests.

Inheritance tax applies to the current value of property in Greece. It kicks in on properties worth €150,000 ($174k) or more.

Greek Property Tax is 3.09%; Capital Gains Tax is 15%; and Inheritance and Estate Taxes run from 1% to 40%. Immediate family inherit tax free up to €150,000.

Greece's Flat Tax Regime For High Net Worth Individuals

Greece's Flat Tax regime is aimed at High Net Worth Individuals (HNWIs), offering them the option to pay a flat rate of income tax on all foreign income. Any Greek-sourced income, however, remains taxed at the regular Greek progressive rate.

Under the Greek Flat Tax regime, you pay a fixed flat rate of €100,000 per annum. Family members can also be added for an additional €20,000 per person, per year.

This rate applies to foreign-sourced income only. Greek-sourced income will continue to be taxed at normal rates, while the flat tax applies to all your foreign-sourced income, regardless of how much foreign income you earn.

You also enjoy exemption from inheritance and gift tax on foreign assets.

As it's a flat tax, no foreign tax credits are available, so paying taxes abroad won't offset the lump sum amount, which remains fixed for the duration.

You can avail of the flat tax for up to a maximum duration of 15 tax years, after which time you will revert to the standard progressive rate of income tax. It's worth pointing out that it takes less than half that time to naturalize, after which time you are free to live anywhere in the EU that you choose. Before you do that, however, you need to first understand why the Greek Flat Tax regime is also often referred to as the "regime for investors."

Greek Flat Tax: How To Qualify

To qualify for the Greek Flat Tax, you must not have been a

Greek resident for seven out of the preceding eight years before moving to Greece. You are also required to make a minimum investment of €500,000 in real estate, a Greek-based business or state-approved funds/bonds.

Keep in mind, also, that this investment can also be the foundation of a Greek golden visa application, giving you full Schengen area access.

Regardless of which option you chose, you have three years from the date of your application to make your investment. Once successful, you can take advantage of the special tax regime for a maximum of 15 years, after which point the standard progressive tax rate applies.

This rate also applies to all your Greek-sourced income, which naturally includes the investments you make within Greece, so it's worth exploring that next.

Greek Income Tax Structure

Under the special Greek Flat Tax regime, investors can take advantage of a €100,000 tax exemption on all foreign-sourced income for a period of 15 years.

For locally sourced income and income generally once the 15-year period ends, Greece's standard progressive income tax rates will apply and, as with the majority of older EU member countries, the rates ramp up dramatically for high earners.

Banking In Greece

Banking in Greece can feel a little old-school at first, especially for North Americans, but it's generally straightforward once you know what to expect.

The Greek banking system is fully integrated into the EU so things like SEPA transfers, debit cards, and online banking are standard. That said, paperwork is taken seriously: opening an account usually means an in-person visit and documents like your passport and a Greek tax number (AFM) will be required.

The good news is that most major banks now offer online and mobile banking in English, and digital services have improved a lot in recent years.

For expats, having a local bank account makes everyday life much easier— paying rent, utilities, or getting paid locally is often simpler with a Greek IBAN.

While branch experiences can vary depending on the location and staff, the big banks are used to working with foreigners and generally have English-speaking support available. Many expats find that using a Greek bank account in combination with an international service like Wise or Revolut helps smooth out currency exchanges and transfers back to the U.S.

Piraeus Bank, Alpha Bank, Eurobank, and the National Bank of Greece (NBG) are the main players and are commonly used by expats.

Piraeus and Eurobank offer solid English-language apps and services, while Alpha Bank and NBG are well-regarded for their reliability and wide branch networks.

While Greek banking may not feel quite as fast or automated as services back home, it's dependable, increasingly expat-aware, and perfectly workable once you're set up.

Real Estate In Greece

Non-EU citizens face a couple restrictions when it comes to buying property in Greece. These restrictions apply to agricultural land and areas that are close to international borders. You'll need to apply for a license to buy or sell property in one of these areas.

Athens: Europe's Best Value Capital For Property Investors

Athens is one of the world's most iconic cities. Named after Athena, goddess of wisdom, it's one of the oldest cities with a recorded history that stretches back 3,400 years. An ancient center for democracy, the arts, education, and philosophy, it's considered the cradle of Western civilization.

But Athens's importance isn't stuck in the past. Today, this cosmopolitan metropolis of 3.6 million people remains the economic, financial, and cultural hub of Greece and one of Southeast Europe's most important economic zones. It hosts a major financial sector, a thriving port, and an increasingly globalized economy.

Tourism keeps breaking records. Athens now welcomes around 6 million visitors a year who come to see the Acropolis and Parthenon as well as modern attractions: award-winning gastronomy, buzzing café culture, a thriving contemporary art scene, live music, performances, and shopping.

This blend of global appeal and modern growth is fueling a property market that has quickly risen to the top of international investors' watchlists.

Thanks to strong domestic demand, a surge of foreign buyers, and favorable economic conditions, Athens real estate has been on a steady climb. Prices are rising in all of the city's main areas.

From Q2 2024 to 2025, Athens Center prices rose by over 13%, reaching €2,400 per square meter. The most expensive area is Athens South, where prices hit €4,052 per square meter, an 8% increase year-on-year.

These are low prices compared to Europe's other capitals. For comparison, the price per square meter in Rome is about €3,600; in Madrid, it's €6,000; and in Paris, it's €9,600.

Even with recent growth, Athens remains one of Europe's best-value capital cities—a major draw for yield-focused investors looking for upside.

The Best Income Play In Athens

Beyond residency and tax incentives, Athens offers another compelling angle for investors: short-term rentals (STRs).

With millions of visitors every year, Athens is an active tourism destination where demand for short-term accommodation is steady and growing. For investors, that translates to high occupancy rates during peak tourist seasons and above-average yields.

The renter base is well-diversified, from tourists to business travelers to digital nomads. A smart strategy could be a city-center apartment near attractions or properties in coastal districts.

There are two caveats to this strategy to be aware of:

- Golden Visa properties can't be used for STRs. For investors who aren't pursuing residency and are instead focused on cash flow, an STR in a historic tourism destination like Athens is one of the strongest methods of generating foreign-sourced income.

- Regulations related to STRs around the world are subject to change. This is something for investors to keep an eye on in Athens.

Why Athens Belongs On Your Radar

No market is without risk. In Athens, potential headwinds include global economic and geopolitical shocks, imbalances between supply and demand that could cause changes to investment policies, and strains on domestic demand caused by rising prices.

Even so, the fundamentals are sound:

- Affordable entry point by European standards.
- Growing international buyer base.

- Strong domestic and international demand.
- Europe's most popular golden visa program.
- Attractive tax incentives for investors and retirees.

As of 2026, Athens is in a sweet spot—still undervalued relative to its peers yet supported by strong fundamentals and growing foreign demand. For savvy investors, the timing couldn't be better to get positioned.

Crete: Europe's Most Undervalued Island Market

In the Mediterranean, few places offer as much value as Crete, Greece's largest island and one of Europe's fastest evolving real estate markets. Tourism here is booming—more than 7 million visitors a year—yet property prices remain 30% to 60% below comparable destinations like Mallorca or the Côte d'Azur.

The island's €3.5 billion infrastructure plan includes a new international airport, upgraded highways, and expanded cruise terminals—all catalysts for rising property values.

These are the sweet spots:

Chania: The investment nucleus, with strong short-term rental demand and €2,500 to €4,000 per square meter pricing.

Rethymno: Affordable charm, liquid resale market, and yields in the 3% to 5% range.

Maleme and Nopigia: West of Chania, these coastal towns offer Blue Flag beaches, modern developments, and "path-of-progress" potential.

Greece's visa and tax incentives, including the 7% flat tax for retirees, further boost its appeal. Strict development rules preserve long-term value, keeping the island authentic and unspoiled.

Doing Business In Greece

Greece has become increasingly proactive about attracting foreign entrepreneurs, investors, and remote professionals through a range of visa options and incentives. The Golden Visa program, residence permits for financially independent individuals, and visas for self-employed professionals and digital nomads have made it easier for non-EU nationals to live and operate in Greece legally.

In most sectors, there are no major restrictions on foreign ownership of businesses, and non-EU citizens can fully own Greek companies, though certain regulated industries may require additional approvals.

From a practical standpoint, Greece offers several advantages for expat entrepreneurs and investors.

As a member of the European Union, it provides access to the broader EU market, a stable legal framework, and incentives aimed at attracting foreign investment.

Key sectors like tourism, real estate, shipping, renewable energy, technology, and agribusiness continue to draw international interest. Expats often find opportunities by combining local demand with foreign expertise, whether that's introducing new services, modernizing operations, or catering to international clients and visitors.

That said, doing business in Greece does require patience and good local support. Bureaucracy can be slower and more complex than what many North Americans are used to, so working with a knowledgeable accountant and lawyer is essential.

Tax registration, licensing, and compliance are manageable, but they're not areas to navigate alone. Expats who succeed tend to be those who adapt to the pace, invest time in relationships, and stay flexible.

With the right mindset and team in place, Greece can be a surprisingly welcoming and strategically positioned base for doing business in Europe.

GREECE

For The Jet-Set Millionaire

Greece has long been associated with a jet-set lifestyle and for good reason. Few countries offer such a seamless blend of natural beauty, cultural depth, and effortless glamor. From the whitewashed cliffs of the Cyclades to the cosmopolitan energy of Athens and the refined elegance of the Athenian Riviera, Greece delivers a lifestyle that feels both luxurious and authentic.

A global sailing and yachting hub, with calm waters and well-developed marinas, in this part of the world island-hopping can be a way of life.

For golfers, high-end courses such as Costa Navarino attract international players and host major tournaments, while tennis academies, equestrian centers, diving, and wellness retreats abound.

Whether it's private beach clubs, summer festivals, international art fairs, world-class dining, or yacht-side soirées, the social calendar here caters to a well-heeled crowd.

Greece also offers enticing opportunities for business-minded folk. The country's real estate market is attracting growing international interest and you can take your pick from luxury villas on the islands to income-generating apartments in Athens.

For entrepreneurs, Greece allows full foreign ownership in most sectors, and strategic locations make it an ideal base for tourism, hospitality, or lifestyle-oriented businesses.

CHAPTER XII

★ ★ ★

THAILAND

A Millionaire's Playground

For many years, Thailand has been a popular destination for retirees and expats. It boasts some of the best beaches in the world, lush mountains and jungles, a laidback, welcoming culture, and a foreigner-friendly infrastructure. Thailand also offers a raft of fun and luxurious entertainment and lifestyle options.

Tens of thousands of foreigners have settled down throughout the country: in world-renowned resorts such as Koh Samui, Koh Lanta, and Phuket; cities including Bangkok, Pattaya, Chiang Mai, and Chiang Rai; and the smaller towns of Hua Hin, Cha-am, and Pai. It's rare to find any town in Thailand that doesn't have at least a few foreign residents.

Here are some of your best choices for enjoying a jet-set lifestyle in the Land of Smiles...

Koh Samui

Koh Samui is situated 23 miles off the east coast of Southern Thailand, with the closest large cities being Surat Thani and Nakhon Si Thammarat. It is Thailand's second largest island blessed with white sand beaches, towering mountains, lush jungles, and crashing waterfalls.

Some 70,000 people inhabit Samui, with about 8,000 being expats from all over the world.

Samui's expat demographics are different to other parts of Thailand. The average age of expats is much lower than in other tourism hubs like Pattaya or Phuket. While there are a fair number of retirees and retired couples, there's also a growing group of digital nomads and online entrepreneurs calling Samui home. Thirty and 40-something couples are common.

Along the northeastern shore of Samui, you'll find its most famous beach and the epicenter of nightlife and tourism: Chaweng Beach. This seven-kilometer crescent-shaped beach is framed by a rocky headland at each end.

It offers great swimming and plenty of water sports, as well as dining and accommodation options. It has a fun, holiday atmosphere during Samui's high seasons, with sun worshippers and families enjoying the clean beach and calm water.

It's not the most secluded or peaceful of Samui's beaches, but everything you'd want is within a few meters of your sun bed, such as cold drinks, snacks, and massages. The beach is most often accessed through hotels or restaurants that have paths leading there from the main road that runs parallel to Chaweng beach.

Chaweng beach is the liveliest community on the island and caters to a younger crowd. You'll find some of Samui's best nightclubs both on the beach and behind it on the Soi Green Mango Entertainment Street, which is a series of streets in a square shape that feature bars, clubs, and restaurants.

Heading north along the east coast of the island, you'll come to a long outcrop of land that juts out from Samui that some call the horn of Samui. The beach community on the eastern side is called Choeng Mon.

Since it sits on a secluded bay, the water is calm and shielded from high winds. The beach is lined with all kinds of interesting places to eat and drink but even more awaits a little further inland on Choeng Mon's main street.

The people living in this part of Samui are a little higher on the socioeconomic ladder than most on the island. Owning or renting big luxury villas and enjoying life at a slower speed is the order of the day for residents here.

Continuing around the horn, you run into Big Buddha Beach and the community of Bophut. The area further inland west of the airport is known as Bangrak. This part of the island is quickly becoming home to the newer wave of expats who want to be close to everything but still have a little private strip of beach life.

The main attraction in this part of the island is Fisherman's Village, a stretch of shops and restaurants along Bophut Beach with a walking street and a famous night market.

This area attracts a mellow crowd of families, couples, and older expats. Bophut isn't a place you go to party but somewhere to relax, have a glass of wine, and watch the sun go down. Some of the best restaurants on the island can be found at Fisherman's village.

Residents of this neighborhood enjoy a wide variety of accommodations to choose from.

The area south of the beach is known as Bophut Hills and many expats living on this part of the island enjoy breathtaking sea views over a valley of coconut trees.

This is a convenient neighborhood to live in as residents are near the airport without being in the flight path, close to the piers to catch ferries, and sandwiched between two popular beach communities. Top that off with easy shopping and a golf course, and it's easy to see why Bophut is popular with expats, especially retirees.

Koh Samui has all the stuff to do you'd expect a world class holiday destination to have including golf, mini-golf, shooting range, archery range, cooking schools, water park, frisbee golf, soccer golf, Muay Thai kickboxing gyms, tennis, running clubs, cycling clubs, bungy jumping, laser tag, zip lines, and on and on.

Samui is also home to a lot of sailboat enthusiasts. Catamarans are the most popular type. Stroll down the beach near Big Buddha, and you'll see at least a dozen or so bobbing in the peaceful bay. Late in the spring is the Samui Regatta, which attracts competitive sailors from all over the world.

For golfers, the luxurious Santiburi Samui Country Club nestled high in the hills and coconut groves, 180 meters above sea level, between Maenam and Ban Tai is a must visit. Indigenous landscapes, waterfalls, and just a bit of rough are all part of a rare and unique course. On a clear day, you get a panoramic view stretching all the way from Bang Por in the northwest to Choeng Mon at the most northeastern point of the island.

The five-star, 18-hole international standard championship golf course (par 72 and 6,930 yards) is known as one of the most beautiful courses in Asia and ranks as one of the top five courses in Thailand, so it's well worth a visit whether you play golf or not. A leisurely lunch at the clubhouse while enjoying the 270-degree view from the open-air restaurant is sure to be the highlight of any day.

Samui is also home to a golf academy as well as the challenging course at The Royal Samui Golf & Country Club, Ratchaprapha Golf and Country Club, and the more forgiving course at Bophut Hills Country Club.

Hua Hin

For many, Hua Hin fits the bill of the ideal retirement haven. This charming seaside town is nestled along the Gulf of Thailand, offering miles of soft, sandy beaches.

It enjoys warm, sunny weather year-round, which means residents can take full advantage of the excellent recreation opportunities available. Hiking, taking strolls on the beach, water sports, and playing rounds at world-class golf courses are just a few of the highlights of Hua Hin's active lifestyle.

Hua Hin stands out for its elegant, relaxed atmosphere. It's been the preferred retreat for the Thai royal family since the 1920s, and this heritage adds a layer of charm to the city. It also means that Hua Hin is calmer, cleaner, and safer than other places in Thailand, like Pattaya and Phuket, which have reputations as party destinations.

Today's Hua Hin blends traditional Thai charm with modern convenience. The town is steeped in history and culture, which is reflected in the unique architecture, parks, and festivals.

It's well-appointed with solid infrastructure and all kinds of urban amenities—restaurants, shopping centers, internationally accredited medical care, and more. For everything that you can't find in Hua Hin, Bangkok, Thailand's bustling capital city, is only a three-hour drive away.

This combination, as well as the natural backdrop of peaceful beaches and lush green hills, has attracted people from all over the world. Of Hua Hin's 85,000 people, roughly 20% are expats.

The community is vibrant and active, organizing clubs and events—from book clubs to wine tastings to golf groups—so that, on any given day, there's something to do in Hua Hin.

There's an abundance of restaurants here, from seafood spots along the waterfront to steakhouses to Indian restaurants to traditional Thai eateries.

Hua Hin hosts an annual jazz festival on the beach, attracting musicians from around the world. There's also an artist village that features galleries, antiques, artist studios, rare collections, and more.

The main beach is a three-mile (five-kilometer) stretch of soft, clean sand punctuated by rocky outcrops. The waves are calm and the waters are shallow, making them safe for swimming.

Water sports (especially kiteboarding) are popular here. You can swim, take kite or sailboarding lessons, jet ski, sail, windsurf, parasail, kayak, snorkel, and scuba dive. Game fishing and boat trips are also available.

Hua Hin is a golfer's paradise with the Royal Hua Hin 18-hole course just five minutes from the town center.

In the city's radius, you find a further 14 courses, all top of the line, with high-end amenities and beautiful views.

Residency In Thailand

Thailand's visa laws have changed over recent years. It used to be possible to stay indefinitely in the country with a tourist visa, making visa runs to a neighboring country every month or so. However, the government felt that too many people were abusing the system, and changed the laws. Now, foreigners who want to live long-term in the country are only permitted to do so with the proper visa. Fortunately, the requirements for Thai residency are relatively attainable.

Most foreigners can have visa-free entry into Thailand for a period of 30 days. Getting a pre-arranged tourist visa allows for a stay of 60 days. Extensions are possible, however foreigners with single-entry tourist visas will not be able to stay for more than 90 days in any six-month period, and those with 60-day multiple entry visas are only allowed one extension, allowing for a total stay of 120 days.

All foreign-citizen travelers to Thailand, regardless of visa status or stay duration, must obtain a Thailand Digital Arrival Card (TDAC Thailand) before they can legally enter Thailand.

The TDAC was implemented in 2025 in a bid to bolster security for visitors and citizens alike. It also includes a health declaration to help prevent the spread of communicable diseases from outside of the country.

All non-Thai citizens must register for the TDAC before they enter the country. This applies to holders of all kinds of Thai visas including tourist, long-stay, and investment options. Every member of a family traveling together must complete a TDAC. The online system allows for joint applications.

Although the TDAC is essential in order to enter Thailand it is important to note it is not a visa or a travel document of any kind. To enter Thailand, you will still need a visa.

The Non-Immigrant “O-A” Visa

Thailand offers several paths to residency, although for retirees, the most straightforward is the Non-Immigrant O-A Visa. The basic requirement is that you are at least 50 years old and meet one of the following requirements:

- Make a security deposit of 800,000 baht (about $24k) into a Thai bank two months before applying;
- Show monthly income of 65,000 baht (about $2k);
- A combination of the security deposit and annual income that equals 800,000 baht.

This visa is valid for one year at a time, and it can be renewed indefinitely. The application process is relatively straightforward.

The qualifications for the Non-Immigrant Visa "O-A" are as follows:

- You must be age 50 or older at the time of application.
- You must have completed a satisfactory police records check.
- You must have obtained a medical examination and be able to present a certificate of health.
- You must have 800,000 baht (about $25k) deposited in a Thai bank for at least two months prior to applying for the "O-A" visa, or be able to prove that you receive a pension of at least 65,000 baht (about $2k) per month, or a deposit account plus a monthly income totaling not less than 800,000 baht.

When it is time to extend your visa, you will need to show your last three month's bank statements or pay stubs to the Immigration Department, proving that you still meet the same financial requirements. If you are submitting bank statements, you must show an original letter of guarantee from the bank.

If your spouse is applying, they will also need to meet the financial requirements. However, if your spouse is under the age of 50, they will be considered a dependent and will not qualify for the Non-Immigrant Type "O-A" visa. In this case, you will need to provide a marriage certificate that has been notarized by your embassy so that your spouse can apply for a Type "O" multiple entry visa.

Your children may also apply for a Type "O" visa if they will be accompanying you.

The application for the Non-Immigrant Visa "O-A" visa may be submitted to the Thai Consulate or Thai Embassy in your home country or directly to the Immigration Bureau in Thailand.

There is a requirement that the Non-Immigrant "O A" visa-holder check in with Thai Immigration every 90 days to report their location. If there is no Thai Immigration office where you live, you can report to the police department. At the end of the first year, you can apply for a one-year extension. The one-year Non Immigrant Visa "O-A" costs 5,000 baht ($155).

Once you have this visa, you are permitted to leave and re-enter the country, although you'll need to apply at the Immigration office for a re-entry permit before your departure. Without first obtaining this permit, your Non Immigrant "O-A" visa will be void upon departure.

As long as you continue to meet the requirements, your retirement visa can be extended indefinitely. Having any sort of employment is strictly prohibited.

Additional Thailand Visa Options

You can get a Multiple Entry Type "O" Visa, regardless of your age. This visa is valid for 12 months, and requires that the holder exit and enter Thailand at least every 90 days in order to get a new entry stamp. The stamp allows you to stay for another 90 days. If you exit Thailand right before your 12-month visa expires, you will be granted an additional 90 days. In effect, this gives you a total of nearly 15 months in Thailand.

The Multiple Entry Type "O" Visa cannot be issued from within Thailand. It is best to apply through the Thai Embassy or consulate in your home country or your country of residence.

The Type "O" visa is the one that is most commonly used when a spouse is not yet 50 years old and does not qualify for a retirement visa.

There are other ways to legally live long-term in Thailand. Employment visas, student visas, and investor visas are available to applicants who meet the necessary requirements.

Used household belongings can be imported duty-free as long as you have a visa that is valid for one year and they arrive in Thailand within six months of your initial entry. Otherwise, a 20% duty and 7% VAT will be assessed.

Thailand's Digital Nomad Visa

Launched in 2024, Thailand's digital nomad visa is called the Destination Thailand Visa (DTV).

To qualify, you will need to prove you work remotely for a company located outside of Thailand or are self-employed and receive income from non-Thai sources.

You will also need to show sufficient financial assets of at least 500,000 THB ($15,000). This requirement can vary depending on the embassy through which you apply as can the method of proof—some will require a fixed deposit certificate, bank statements, evidence of regular income, tax filings, contracts, and/or recommendation letters.

The DTV is a multiple-entry visa allowing for stays of up to 180 days at a time and is valid for five years.

After 180 days, you can apply for an extension and stay in Thailand for up to 360 consecutive days. For the extension, there is a fee—1,900 THB ($60)—and you will need to provide updated proof of your financial stability, show health insurance, and complete a form.

After a 360-day stay in Thailand you will need to leave and re-enter to reset your stay period.

Under the terms of the DTV, the primary holder can bring dependents to Thailand providing they are your legal spouse or dependent children younger than 20 years old and unmarried. Each dependent must apply separately and pay an additional visa fee.

Applications can be made at the Royal Thai Embassy or through the Thai e-Visa website. The application fee is around $400.

Thailand Investment Visa

You can get a Thai long-term investment visa regardless of your age or income. The minimum investment amount is 10 million Thai baht (about $310,000). Investment visas are valid for one year and can be extended.

The requirements for a one-year investment visa are as follows:

- Invest 10 million baht into a Term Savings account with an approved government bank;

Or,

- Invest 10 million baht into government bonds;

Or,

- Invest 10 million baht into the purchase or lease of a condominium for not less than three years;

Or,

- Invest 10 million baht into a combination of a savings, bonds, or property.

The investment must be for a period of not less than three years.

The money must have originated from overseas.

If you want to purchase a condo for the purpose of securing an investment visa, you will need to provide the title deed of the property, the sales contract, the tax receipt, and your passport.

The easiest way to get an investment visa is to first enter Thailand with a single entry tourist visa. Then, open a bank account at a government bank (either Krung Thai or Government Savings Bank).

Next, transfer 10 million baht into the account from overseas. Be sure to get an official letter from the bank that confirms your account balance and verifies that the money originated from overseas.

Next, go to immigration and apply for a change of visa status based upon your proposed investment. You will be issued a 90-day, non-immigrant "O" visa that can be extended to one year after you have been in the country for 60 days.

At this point, you can shop for a condo. If the total lease or purchase price is less than 10 million baht, you can put the remainder into a fixed term account or government bonds.

After one year, when it is time for your visa to be extended, you'll have no difficulties once evidence of your investment is supplied.

Permanent Residency In Thailand

The Non-Immigrant Visa "O-A" does not give permanent residency. Only 100 people each year of each nationality are granted permanent residency, and having held a valid work permit for three years prior to the application is one of the requirements.

If you have lived in Thailand with a non-immigrant "O-A" retirement visa, you are not eligible to apply for permanent residency. Additionally, you are required to have had three consecutive one-year visa extensions, earn 30,000 baht (about $930) per month if you have been married to a Thai national for five years, or 80,000 baht (about $2,500) per month if you are single. You must provide three years of income tax statements when you submit your application.

The fee for the permanent residency visa is 7,600 baht ($235).

If you want to become a Thai citizen, you'll first need to be a permanent resident. Citizenship is possible after you have been a permanent resident for 10 consecutive years.

Second Citizenship In Thailand

Thai Citizenship through naturalization is a complex process that involves much bureaucracy as well as a language requirement however it comes with many benefits including the right to buy and own property in your name and hold more than 49% of shares in a Thai company.

To be eligible for Thai Citizenship by naturalization you must meet the following requirements:

- Be of legal age (20 years old) both in Thailand and your home country.

- Have lived in Thailand as a Permanent Resident for at least five years. This may be waived in certain circumstances such as if you are the spouse or child of a person who has received Thai Citizenship through naturalization; are the husband of a Thai wife; if you previously held Thai Citizenship; if you have acted in some way that is of benefit to Thailand.

- You can understand, speak, and be able to write the Thai language. This requirement may also be waived if you meet the other requirements set out above.

- You can sing the Thai National Anthem *Sanserm Phra Baramee.*

- You hold a clean criminal record.

- You are employed in Thailand.

- You acquire at least 50 points (out of 100) on the Points Based System of obtaining Thai Citizenship. This test applies to those applying based on having a Thai wife and those who have held permanent residency for a five-year period. This score is determined during a preliminary test and interview. Points are awarded for factors such as age, education, Thai language skills, knowledge of Thailand, employment, personality, appearance, and the duration of your civil registration.

Making An Application For Thai Citizenship

Applications for citizenship can be made at the Department of Provincial Administration (in Bangkok) or your local provincial public administration office. They will provide you with a list of the documents required to make your application.

Once you have submitted the required documentation, your application will be lodged. You will need to pay a processing fee and give your fingerprints.

You will then have to visit the Ministry of Interior for an interview in Thai and to sing the Thai National Anthem.

As part of the application process Thai immigration officers will come to your home to ascertain that the details you provided are correct.

When your application is approved you will be required to take the Citizenship Oath at the Police Headquarters.

Thailand allows for dual citizenship. The processing time for Thai Citizenship applications is between six and 12 months.

Banking In Thailand

For the most part, banking in Thailand (especially online banking) is friendly and hassle-free.

The type of bank account you will be able to open will depend on the visa you're holding (if indeed you have one). As a tourist, you will only be able to open a savings account, whereas if you are a holder of a Thai non-immigrant visa, you will have more options.

Bank accounts can be opened in a day. A variety of accounts are available including ATM cards, credit cards, time deposits, and even car loans.

All major credit cards are accepted here, but you may find that American Express is not accepted as commonly as in the States. Wise and Payoneer are international currency transfer services available here, but PayPal has recently gone through some changes that prohibit foreigners from using it in Thailand.

Several major Thai banks are set up to receive U.S. Social Security payments as direct deposits.

Here are three of the most popular banks used by expats in Thailand.

Bangkok Bank

Founded in 1944, Bangkok Bank is one of Thailand's largest and most established banks. There are some 1,200 branches across the country. In Bangkok and popular expat areas you will find English-speaking staff. They also have documentation in English for many services as well as English language options for their internet banking and mobile banking services.

They offer savings, fixed deposit, current, and foreign currency deposit accounts as well as specialized deposit services.

Requirements for foreigners seeking to open accounts in recent years have tightened so you may need to show a long term visa, proof of property ownership, or marriage to a local.

Kasikorn Bank (KBank)

With a strong focus on digital services, a large ATM network, and over 800 branches, Kasikorn Bank is another popular choice among expats.

Their mobile banking app (K PLUS) offers an English language option and many branches have English speaking staff.

KBank offers savings, fixed deposits, foreign currency deposit accounts, current accounts, and special savings/fixed deposit variants. Requirements for opening an account vary from branch to branch. You will likely need your passport, visa, and work permit. Non-immigrant visas may be sufficient if you can provide other supporting documentation such as proof of address.

Siam Commercial Bank (SCB)

Long-established Siam Commercial Bank offers savings, current, and fixed deposit accounts, credit cards, international transfers, currency exchange, insurance products, and investment and wealth management services.

They have around 600 branches across Thailand, a large ATM network, and solid digital banking services. Online saving accounts can be opened via the app with identity verification. The app has an English language option and branches in larger cities will have English-speaking staff.

Taxes In Thailand

Paying taxes is required for anyone earning income in Thailand. The tax year runs from Jan. 1 to Dec. 31, and returns must be filed and paid by March 31 (or April 8 if filing online) for the previous year.

Your tax rate depends on how much you earn. The first 150,000 baht (around $5k) of annual income is tax-exempt. From 150,001 to 300,000 baht (around $5k to $10k), you're taxed at 5%. Between 300,001 and 500,000 baht ($10k to $15k), it's 10%. From 500,001 to 750,000 baht ($15k to $23k), the rate is 15%. Between

750,001 and 1 million baht ($23k to $30k), it's 20%. From 1 to 2 million baht ($30k to $61k), it's 25%, then 30% up to 5 million baht ($155k). Anything over 5 million baht ($155k) is taxed at 35%.

If you're a tax resident (you stay in Thailand 180 days or more in a year), foreign income is also taxable if it is brought into Thailand in the same year it was earned.

Thailand's income tax rates range from 5% to 35%. Capital gains are generally taxed as income (except in a handful of specific cases). Inheritance and estate taxes run from 5% to 10%. Property tax runs from 0.4% to 1.2%. Thailand has a Tax Treaty with both the U.S. and Canada.

Thailand does not impose a wealth tax, but it imposes an inheritance tax of 10% on legacies valued at over 100 million baht (about $3 million). In the case of heirs, the rate is 5%.

Both the U.S. and Canada have tax treaties with Thailand.

Real Estate In Thailand

Like many Southeast Asian countries, Thailand has some restrictions for foreigners when it comes to buying property.

Foreigners can own property in their name in Thailand. Condominium buildings can have up to 49% of their total deeded space owned by foreign individuals. Foreigners can also own buildings. Land, however, cannot be titled to a foreigner.

Foreigners can secure leases on land and buildings for a maximum of 30 years with two extensions. Foreigners can control Thai companies that own land and buildings. Through all of these mechanisms, foreigners can own a wide array of properties for pleasure or profit.

There is a cottage industry that has been thriving for decades that helps you set up a Thai company to own any property as an asset. Depending on how much capitalization your company needs to own the property you want to buy, the cost to set up a company is between $1,500 and $2,000. It costs about $300 per year to keep up the proper paperwork.

Like most legal processes in Thailand, there's an easy way and a hard way when it comes to buying property. It's not recommended to orchestrate a property transaction in Thailand without the help of local experts.

Enter the property agent.

A property agent who is worth his 5% commission (paid by the seller) will wear several hats and become your "fixer." While the real estate brokerage business in Thailand isn't as rigidly regulated or policed as it is in the United States, there are many reliable firms that have been in business here for decades.

The Thai Property Buying Process

1. Once you find a property, make an offer, and a transaction is agreed upon in principle, a reservation fee is paid by the buyer to secure the property.

   Usually, 100,000 Thai baht will do the trick. This fee is held by the agent. At that point, the seller takes the property off the market and releases relevant ownership documents to the agent to perform due diligence and prepare the sales agreement.

2. The Sales Agreement will determine the price, the terms, and the timing of the transaction. Once the Sales Agreement is prepared, reviewed, and signed by both parties, the buyer will deposit funds which, along with the reservation fee, add up to 10% of the purchase price. (The agent holds all deposits as there are no escrow services available.)

3. Usually within two to four weeks, everybody goes to the Land Office to complete the purchase. Most agents have personnel on staff that are experts at expediting the process and they will walk you through it.

The buyer will present to the seller payment of the balance in the form of a cashier's check in the presence of a Land Office official. The Land Office will then register the property to the buyer and the original title deed will be updated accordingly and presented to the buyer.

4. At the same time as the final exchange of funds and property, any transfer fees and taxes are paid to the Land Office. Which party pays these fees is something that is negotiated and spelled out in the Sales Agreement. Most of the time, parties agree to split the fees 50/50.

   It should be noted that buyers and sellers often give power of attorney to representatives of the agent to complete the transaction in their absence. You could buy or sell a property without even being in Thailand if you have your paperwork together.

What Your Property Agent Does

- Ensures the buyer's funds are transferred into the country accompanied by the appropriate Foreign Exchange Documents from the bank (TT3 documents). This documentation is vital to make sure you can get your money out of the country if and when you sell the property.

- Orders and collects a "free of debt" letter from juristic offices governing condos and homeownership committees.

- Organizes the formation and documentation of a Thai company if necessary for purchase of the property.

- Due diligence on the title and property taxes if any.

- Prepare transfer fees and power of attorney documents if

the purchase is made by an absentee buyer or seller.

- Prepares final balance and cashier's check.

- Final inspection of property, meter readings, and inventory of furniture and appliances.

Some Other Things To Consider...

There is no MLS or Zillow in Thailand. Finding available properties and properly vetting them will require the help of someone with expertise in the local market.

A building inspection is not routine as it is in the United States. New units come with a warranty. Previously owned units may not. An inspection of key appliances like AC units, hot water heaters, etc., is advisable.

For condos, it is prudent to ask for a copy of minutes from the last meeting of the condo association to detect any ongoing disputes or problems and to determine the financial health of the building.

Doing Business In Thailand

Setting up or doing business in Thailand as an expat can be highly rewarding, thanks to the country's growing economy, strategic ASEAN location, and strong government support for foreign investment in targeted sectors.

The tourism, manufacturing, tech, and renewable energy sectors are particularly open to foreign involvement. However, there are restrictions in place under the Foreign Business Act, which limits foreign ownership in certain industries unless specific exemptions or licenses are obtained.

Most expats set up a Thai Limited Company, which typically

requires at least three shareholders and a majority Thai ownership, though workarounds like Board of Investment (BOI) promotion can offer full foreign ownership in approved sectors.

Registering a company in Thailand involves several steps, including reserving a company name, preparing statutory documents, and registering with the Ministry of Commerce.

Expats will also need to secure a work permit and the appropriate visa—typically a Non-Immigrant Business Visa—which requires sponsorship from a Thai-registered company.

Thai Board of Investment (BOI) promoted companies enjoy significant advantages, such as tax incentives, land ownership rights, and simplified visa and work permit processes.

It's advisable to work with local legal and accounting firms to navigate Thailand's regulatory environment smoothly and stay compliant with labor, tax, and corporate laws.

Once the business is up and running, Thailand offers a supportive environment with modern infrastructure, a growing digital economy, and a large pool of skilled, affordable labor.

Bangkok serves as the business hub with world-class office space, luxury accommodations, and easy access to international travel.

Business networking is strong through various chambers of commerce and expat business groups, and digital nomad-friendly hubs like Chiang Mai and Phuket provide additional options for entrepreneurs in lifestyle-focused industries.

With the right legal guidance and sector strategy, Thailand can be a highly attractive base for expat business ventures.

THAILAND

For The Jet-Set Millionaire

Thailand is a premier destination for the jet-set millionaire lifestyle offering a blend of tropical beauty and upscale indulgence.

You can make your home in secluded mountain villages, bustling beach towns, or booming cities. In popular spots like Bangkok, Chiang Mai, Koh Samui, Koh Phangan, and Phuket, you'll find well-connected communities of remote workers as well as co-working spaces with solid Wi-Fi.

Thanks to the large expat communities and thriving tourism trade you won't have issues getting by in English in the aforementioned locales.

From the buzzing rooftop bars of Bangkok to the pristine beaches of Koh Samui, the country caters to luxury seekers with world-class resorts, private villas, and five-star service.

High-end shopping malls showcase global designer brands, while gourmet dining experiences range from Michelin-starred Thai cuisine to exclusive chef's table gatherings. Private yacht charters, helicopter tours, and bespoke spa retreats add to the allure of living lavishly in the Land of Smiles.

You'll never be bored here. The entertainment options are vibrant, diverse, and tailor-made for those with refined tastes and a thirst for adventure. You can spend your days on championship golf courses, island-hopping, or relaxing at wellness escapes in serene mountain resorts.

Whatever your speed and need you'll find it catered to here from private art gallery tours to high-end Muay Thai events. When night falls you can opt for VIP access to upscale nightclubs, live music lounges, and hidden speakeasies... or kick back at the beach with sundowners and new friends.

CHAPTER XIII

MONTENEGRO

Europe's Hidden Gem

Montenegro, a tiny Balkan country of about 5,300 square miles, lies in Eastern Europe, sandwiched between Serbia, Bosnia and Herzegovina, Kosovo, Albania, and Croatia.

In the southwest of the country, overlooking the same stretch of water as Southeastern Italy, is where you'll find the jet-set playground of Kotor Bay.

Its 57 miles of sparkling coastline features towering mountains and stunning fjords. Northern California is the only other landscape that compares...

The Bay is dotted by a charming mix of medieval towns and luxe modern developments, complete with super-yacht marinas. The ultra-wealthy treat this yachting paradise like their own private riviera.

We identify Kotor Bay as the area with the best investment potential in Montenegro right now...

But with its affordable cost of living, gorgeous scenery, easy residency policies, budding expat community, and endless recreation opportunities, it also has major lifestyle appeal.

Montenegro is home to about 620,000 people, and it only officially became a country in 2006 when it got its independence from Serbia.

But big things are on Montenegro's horizon...

It's widely expected to join the European Union in the next few years. (Some say it will happen before 2030.)

If you establish residency or citizenship before then, Montenegro could become the fastest backdoor to an EU passport.

What else makes Montenegro so special?

Jaw-dropping vistas are available from almost every vantage point because of the mountainous geography, and access to the sea is abundant.

The Adriatic is the same body of water that laps the shores of southeastern Italy. It's part of the Mediterranean.

The waters are clear and warm, perfect for swimming, boating, any water-based recreation... or just providing a beautiful backdrop for daily life.

The boating lifestyle is a major draw, with luxury marinas disbursed about the Bay. Even the Saudi royal family relocated its golden fleet of mega-yachts from Monaco here.

The Bay also offers diverse lifestyle opportunities.

One option is the Old World historical appeal found in Kotor Old Town. This UNESCO World Heritage Site is widely regarded as the best-preserved medieval town in the Mediterranean.

It's a compact, triangular area that you access via three gateways through thick stone walls. It's dense with ancient architecture, plazas, and churches. Behind it, crumbling city walls zigzag up the steep mountain, and in front of it is the sea.

Another option is the all-new, high-end, flashy private developments that are dotted around the Bay.

One of the best known is Porto Montenegro, developed by Canadian gold billionaire Peter Munk into the largest marina in Southern Europe.

Luxury penthouses now sell for millions of dollars... the shopping mall features high-end brands such as Dior, Rolex, Burberry, and Balenciaga... A-listers flock here to dock their super yachts.

Between Kotor Old Town's historical charm and projects like Porto Montenegro that target the 1%, there are half-measures, of course, like the normal towns of Tivat, Kotor, and the areas surrounding them.

Inland from Kotor Bay, Montenegro houses even more surprises. Only a few hours' drive away, there are two ski resorts. This is a place where you can ski in the morning and then swim in the Mediterranean in the afternoon.

Montenegro has a burgeoning reputation as an extreme sports destination.

One look at the topography and you'll understand why... Sharp peaks create opportunities to practice wind sports, while national parks, like the UNESCO-recognized Durmitor National Park, provide hiking, abseiling, rock climbing, and whitewater rafting opportunities.

On top of all of this, the cost of living in Kotor Bay is low. Compared to places in Croatia and Italy, where what's on offer is roughly the same, prices here are a downright bargain, especially when it comes to real estate prices.

If you announce to friends and family, "I'm moving to Kotor Bay, Montenegro," you'll probably get some funny looks... Not many people have heard of Montenegro; to move here, you've got to be a little adventurous...

But you'll be rewarded for your boldness.

You'll be among the first to arrive in a place that we predict is going to explode in popularity over the coming years.

You'll enjoy stunning sea and mountain vistas every day... You'll lower your current cost of living... You'll enjoy mild temperatures year-round as well as access to untouched nature...

You'll be able to choose the lifestyle that suits you best among a diverse array of opportunities... you'll have a friendly expat community to lean on... and you'll be making a smart move, as property is still affordable, and it gets you residency and potentially a backdoor to the EU.

Montenegro is largely undiscovered by mainstream tourism. Those who find their way here enjoy the benefits of an undeveloped tourism market (and the resulting non-tourist prices).

Americans are just finding out about it, while British visitors have only recently caught on...

You might think this relative isolation would add up to a low level of English... but the locals are surprisingly fluent.

You'll have no trouble speaking to waiters, real estate agents, taxi drivers, shop attendants, and so on.

Some of the expats have picked up a conversational level of Montenegrin—not an easy language to grasp but seemingly possible. It's similar to Croatian and Serbian and uses the Latin alphabet (in addition to the Cyrillic).

Tivat Airport is the local airport in Kotor Bay. It's tiny and fluctuates hugely in the number of destinations it serves throughout the year.

There are no direct flights to the States or Canada, so making a connection in Europe along the way is a must. That said, it's not the only international airport in the region...

Podgorica Airport in the capital offers flights to more cities (Barcelona, Berlin, London, Istanbul, etc.) and maintains more routes throughout the year.

Dubrovnik Airport, across the border in neighboring Croatia, is about 40 miles (70 kms) from Kotor Bay.

You can also arrive here by boat, whether it's your own boat, the ferry from Bari, Italy, or a cruise ship.

Residency And Citizenship

Montenegro long stood out to real estate investors for its attractive residency option whereby foreigners could qualify with a property purchase of any value. The system operated much like a golden visa program, except for the fact that no minimum purchase threshold was set.

However, that changed in early 2026.

As per new rules brought in by the country's parliament, third-country nationals seeking residency based on real estate ownership must now show that their property has a taxable value of at least €150,000 as determined by the Tax Authority's transfer tax assessment.

Applicants will need to prove ownership and use of the property and all related tax obligations must be settled. Residence granted under this real estate investment category is valid for one year and is renewable.

These are the basic requirements:

- A clean criminal record.
- Receive an income of about €10 per day (or you can deposit €3,650 in a Montenegrin bank).
- A birth and marriage certificate (if you're applying with your partner).
- Proof of accommodation.
- Proof of health insurance.

This will get you a temporary residence permit that's valid for one year and can be renewed.

You can leave the country for more than a month in a year, but you have to let your local immigration inspector know.

After five years as a temporary resident, you can apply for permanent residency, valid for five years and extendable. This gives you the same rights as a Montenegrin, except for the right to vote.

After 10 years of lawful, continuous residence in Montenegro you can apply for citizenship. This is shortened to five years if you are married to a Montenegrin and have at least three years of marriage and residence.

Montenegro also allows for citizenship by descent if you can prove direct Montenegrin ancestry—for example, a parent or grandparent. In this case, Montenegro may allow you to hold dual citizenship but otherwise it's not permitted.

A Montenegrin passport is valuable in its own right, but there's potential for it to become even more valuable in a few years' time when Montenegro joins the EU. It could enhance your access to the 27 member states.

Montenegro's invest-for-residency option is one of the few remaining in Europe.

Taxes In Montenegro

You become a tax resident if you spend 183 days in a tax year in Montenegro, have a domicile there, or use the country as a center of personal or economic activities.

Income is taxed at progressive rates:

- €0 to €700: 0%
- €701 to €1,000: 9%
- €1,001 and up: 15%

A local surtax is due to your municipality in Montenegro, which is 13% unless you base yourself in Podgorica or Cetinje, in which case it's 15%.

Capital gains tax applies to real estate sales and sales of shares in a legal entity and securities. You can avoid paying capital gains tax on real estate sales if the home is your primary residence or you are transferring title to your spouse or children.

For investment income, the same personal income tax rates outlined above apply. For property income, the tax rate is also 15%.

Montenegro does not impose a net wealth or worth tax. It imposes an inheritance tax of 3% on real estate, but if the property is a gift or inheritance to a spouse, children, or parents, it's exempt.

If you're an entrepreneur looking to set up a business in a non-developed region of the country, you can enjoy a tax break of €200,000 for an eight-year period.

Your business can't be related to agriculture, transport, shipbuilding, fishery, or steel production.

Banking In Montenegro

Montenegro's banking system is small but stable. There are 11 commercial banks operating in Montenegro, all headquartered in the capital, Podgorica. The Central Bank of Montenegro (CBCG) acts as the country's central bank regulator.

The majority of the banks are local but there are international banks in the market here too including Austrian-owned Addiko Bank, Turkish-owned ZIRAAT Bank, and Crnogorska Komercijalna Banka, owned by Hungary's OTP Group.

Locally, NLB Banka is highly regarded among expats for its reliable mobile banking, low maintenance fees, and straightforward onboarding process. Hipotekarna Banka is also well rated for its mobile banking app, clear English-language support, and low fees. Lovćen Banka stands out for offering flexible mortgage rates to non-residents.

Montenegro's banking sector is fully euroized—the country uses the euro as its de facto currency despite not being in the Eurozone.

While financial services are modernizing, lending is still relatively conservative, and regulatory oversight is aligned with EU standards. For U.S. investors, the market offers straightforward account setup, but there are due diligence requirements.

Expat residents in Montenegro can set up an appointment at their local branch to open an account. Standard documentary requirements include ID and proof of address and employment.

Non-residents are required to complete an additional form for submission to the Central Montenegrin Bank, along with passport details and contact information.

Most banks require a temporary or permanent Montenegrin residence permit to open an account. Exceptions may be made but will likely come with higher fees and stricter requirements.

Investing In Montenegro

Montenegro offers moderate investment potential mostly due to its small size and regulatory challenges.

That said, this little country is very much open to foreign investment with no restrictions on foreign ownership in most sectors, including real estate, tourism, and banking. Coastal developments and infrastructure tied to tourism particularly in hotspots like Porto Montenegro and Lustica Bay, attract a steady stream of foreign capital.

With EU ascension firmly in its sights, Montenegro's future looks promising.

Real estate is the strongest investment play here. Joining the EU holds the potential to boost property values way beyond their current levels.

That's what happened in Dubrovnik, Croatia, which is right next door. Property values skyrocketed when Croatia joined the EU in 2013.

Today, Dubrovnik's property prices are extortionate, at $4,440 per square meter ($412 per square foot)—about 27% more than Kotor Bay's current prices.

Dubrovnik is only 45 miles (72 kms) from Kotor Bay, and it offers much of the same appeal... although its scenery is less spectacular.

Kotor Bay's property prices should rise to at least match Dubrovnik's when it joins the EU... maybe they'll even go beyond Dubrovnik's prices.

Property owners might only have to wait a few years for a big boost in value...

In 2023, Montenegro elected a young, ambitious new prime minister—Milojko Spajic, who's only 37 years old.

He launched the "28 by 2028" campaign and is taking measures to make Montenegro the 28th member of the EU by 2028.

Anyone can buy real estate in Montenegro and enjoy almost all the same rights as a Montenegrin citizen.

There are some restrictions placed on foreigners: they can't buy certain types of land, like agricultural land, land in national parks, historical monuments, and so on.

You can get around said restrictions (legally) and buy land by forming a Montenegro-based company, purchasing the property through that company, and transferring it to their name after the purchase.

Be aware that forming, registering, and maintaining a company incurs some fees.

MONTENEGRO

For The Jet-Set Millionaire

Montenegro's strategic location in Europe, low cost of living, and favorable tax policies make it an attractive prospect for North Americans looking to diversify overseas.

With approval for EU membership likely in the next couple of years, Montenegro provides early access to a growing market while maintaining visa-free travel to the Schengen Zone.

It offers a business-friendly environment, with no restrictions on foreign property ownership, and a stable currency giving it broad appeal to American and Canadian investors seeking lifestyle and asset diversification outside home borders.

Plus, it has major lifestyle appeal and a range of options from Kotor Old Town's historical charm and projects like Porto Montenegro that target the 1% to charming towns like Tivat and Kotor.

The boating lifestyle is a major draw here with marinas available in Kotor, (Marina Prcanj and Marina Kotor), Tivat (Porto Montenegro and Marina Bonici), Hercig Novi (Portonovi Marina), and just outside Kotor is Lustica Bay.

Within a couple hours' drive of Kotor Bay, there are several national parks. There are also two main ski resorts: Ski Resort Kolasin 1450 and Ski Resort Savin Kuk, with smaller ski centers nearby. Facilities like equipment rentals, ski-lifts, ski schools, and more are all set up here. Montenegro has big potential as Europe's next ski destination.

CHAPTER XIV

★ ★ ★

MALAYSIA

Exotic Charm And Rich Opportunity

Malaysia is a friendly, welcoming country and in no way is this more apparent than in their immigration laws. Foreigners from Europe, North America, Australia, and New Zealand can enter Malaysia through any immigration checkpoint and receive a 90-day Social Visit Stamp. Making visa runs every three months can extend your stay indefinitely.

Malaysia is one of the few countries in Southeast Asia that allows foreigners to live in the country for an extended period of time without requiring that they attain residency status.

Malaysia has a very reasonable cost of living. Most things cost between half to one-third of what they would cost in the west. Utilities, food, entertainment, and health care are all inexpensive, and you can live very well on a low to moderate budget. Malaysia is also the only country in Southeast Asia that allows foreigners to own full titles to landed property.

Here are some of your best options for expat living in Malaysia...

Kuala Lumpur

Kuala Lumpur, located in the heart of the Malaysian peninsula, is a city of contrasts. The shining stainless steel Petronas Towers, two of the tallest skyscrapers in the world, anchor a startlingly beautiful skyline that is truly unique to this city.

Modern, air-conditioned malls flourish, selling everything from beautifully handcrafted batik clothing to Tiffany jewelry. In the shadows of these ultramodern buildings, the ancient Malay village of Kampung Baru still thrives, with free-roaming roosters and a slow pace of life that's usually only to be found in the most rural of villages.

In less than a 20-minute walk from the city center, you can be conversing with monkeys in the city jungle surrounding one of the highest telecommunications towers in the world. A walk of less than 30 minutes will lead you to Chinatown and Little India, where merchants offer their wares, foods, and culture in happy neighborhoods that showcase the amazing diversity of the city.

It may be a big city, if when you go to your neighborhood shop you take your time and talk with the owner, by the second or third time you visit, you're recognized and waved to when you walk down the street. You may be invited to dinner, or at least to share a cup of delicious *kopi* (coffee) or *teh tarik* (a hot milk tea beverage).

Foreigners are genuinely welcomed in Kuala Lumpur, and Malaysia having been a British colony, people here are used to newcomers. The British left an indelible mark on Malaysian culture. Many fine buildings still stand strong, the British-built railway system has been expanded and is still very much in use, driving is on the left side, and English is still the language of commerce, required learning for all Malaysian children, and is the primary spoken language for many Malaysians.

Health care is first-rate, public transportation is modern and efficient, and the tap water is safe to drink.

Beautiful beaches are just a short drive or flight away, and cool mountain retreats can be reached in less than an hour.

The political, commercial, and cultural capital of Malaysia, the vibrant city of Kuala Lumpur, has thrived in recent years and today is most prosperous city in the country. Located at the confluence of the Klang and Gombak Rivers, Kuala Lumpur means "muddy city" or "muddy confluence." Popularly called "KL," and its residents "KLites," the population of the city is just over 2 million, with 9 million in the greater metropolitan area.

Home to the Petronas Towers and a monorail that runs from one end of the city to the other, KL is ultra-modern in some ways, yet still manages to hold onto vestiges of its British colonial heritage and traditional village life.

With so much to do in the city, and its convenience as a transportation hub to almost every place in Asia, expats here find life easy. Welcoming immigration policies makes living here long-term relatively hassle-free. Plus, exceptional health care, the widespread use of English, and advanced infrastructure makes day-to-day life a pleasure.

From mountains to beaches, busy malls to tranquil parks, fine imported foods to tasty street cooking, it's easy to see why so many people find that KL has it all.

Kota Kinabalu

For many, the Island of Borneo conjures up images of an untamed frontier—undeveloped, savage, and wild. This couldn't be further from the reality... Kota Kinabalu is one of the most livable beach cities in the world—civilized, safe, clean, peaceful, and organized.

Kota Kinabalu city itself is home to about 800,000 inhabitants, including the adjacent suburbs, the industrial and commercial hub of Sabah. KK, as it's known, is a lively, vibrant, modern city with every amenity, brand name, food variety, and entertainment option you could want. You won't find orangutans swinging from trees... no Wild Man of Borneo... nobody with bones protruding from pierced nostrils.

KK is Pleasantville or Mayberry brought to life... people stop you on the street just to say hello, perhaps to ask you where you're going and if you need help or directions. Nobody here is in a hurry, it's like a small town frozen back in 1950s America—the land that time forgot. People here are warm and sociable to each other and even more so to the Westerner.

Home to a large number of immigrants from both the Philippines and Indonesia, Malaysian Borneo is a cultural mosaic unparalleled in Asia, with foreign cultures, languages, lifestyles, customs, and foods imported from all over the region and the world. Plus, you'll meet a number of highly educated locals who studied abroad or pursued careers overseas before resettling in KK to enjoy a slower pace of life.

The genuinely warm welcome you'll get from the locals is partly thanks to the positive colonial experience Borneo had as a British colony. North Borneo was a British protectorate from the late 1800s and a British colony from the end of WWII to 1963 when it joined the new Malaysian Federation.

The result of colonization was a strong British influence in city planning and infrastructure. The rainwater goes down the drains, electricity and internet are good, road traffic flows smoothly most of the time, sidewalks are level and wide, and safe pedestrian crossings are prevalent.

Overall, a sense of management and structure is felt throughout the city, imparting a comfortable feeling to the visitor and resident without a sense of overdoing it. The result is a splendid balance between order, safety, and colorful, original local culture.

At the same time, the city retains its traditional look and feel, with markets and independent shops spread throughout, including the old colonial center featuring Gaya Street, the Sunday Market, and all its shopping and dining offerings. The waterfront area offers upscale restaurants, bars and clubs, a row of informal local restaurants, and two new malls. The backdrop for all this is a cluster of five islands just minutes away by boat.

The white-sand beach at Tanjung Aru lies a few minutes south of the city center, while three miles north, a waterfront park offers picnic areas, a seaside walking promenade, restaurants, and bike path with exercise areas flanked by condo developments and shopping.

The cuisine here is simply out of this world. Traditional Malay dishes, Chinese, Indian, Filipino, Indonesian, plus indigenous dishes from the numerous tribes can be found anywhere.

KK is foreigner-ready. Every amenity, accommodation type, attraction, and leisure option is already at hand and implemented; the infrastructure is complete and operational.

It's easy to live a similar lifestyle as in North America here. Pleasant suburbs are home to many installed and happy expats, and you've got easy access to integrated international shopping, restaurants, and condo developments.

George Town, Penang

The island of Penang offers retirees and expats one of the best overseas living opportunities in the world.

You can while away the hours wandering around George Town, Penang's colorful and lively historic state capital. Kick back on the beach, explore stunning mountains and waterfalls, shop till you drop, or partake in some of the finest and most affordable cuisine to be found anywhere in the world. Best of all, you can indulge in the many pleasures of Penang on a budget that is comfortable even with a modest retirement income.

George Town's population is just 800,000—small enough that it's easy to make friends and meet your neighbors, yet large enough to have health care that meets international standards. Year-round sunny, warm weather, First World infrastructure, easy permanent residency, and English-speaking locals make the living here easy.

Penang's various nicknames—The Pearl of the Orient, Garden of the East, and Penang, Island of Pearls—all describe an exceptional location. It's an island of beauty and abundant natural resources, friendly and welcoming people, and a place rich with tradition and opportunity. Of all the places to live in Malaysia, Penang stands out as our top pick if you are a retiree or an expat seeking the good life.

The center of historic George Town is a maze of streets reminiscent of the 19th and early 20th century. Even beyond the city's designated UNESCO Core Area, a cornucopia of Chinese shop-houses, pagodas, temples, clan-houses, churches, mosques, British colonial buildings, and landscaped parks supply a never-ending source of visual treats.

The first documented European discovery of the island was made by Portuguese traders in the early 16th century. They were exploring the Far East in search of spices and found a small, uninhabited island which they named Pulo Pinaom.

The island, located at the strategically important northern entry to the Straits of Malacca, was a safe place to linger during the monsoon months and for traders to replenish their fresh water supplies. Arabian, Chinese, Indian, and European ships all took advantage of the natural harbor, and the population of Penang Island slowly grew. By the 18th century, Penang had become quite prosperous due to the spice and opium trade.

One of the many charms of George Town is that being here really does feel like stepping back in time... The historic old town is filled with buildings dating to the 19th century and remains the center of commerce.

As you wander around the city, it's easy to imagine yourself living in another era and another place. Here, you're in old China and around the corner, you could be in India. Another neighborhood is reminiscent of an old Malay *kampong* (village), and everywhere there is architecture and infrastructure that harkens back to England's colonial heyday.

It's also a fascinating combination of cultures. Shops selling Chinese herbs and traditional medicine, importers and exporters, musical instrument stores, restaurants, and hawker centers specializing in authentic regional Chinese cuisine are scattered throughout George Town.

The early Indian traders have left their legacy as well, with a vibrant Little India that consists of several Hindu and Sikh temples and a commercial district selling material and clothing, incense, fruits, spices, herbal teas, and remedies.

Other parts of the city reflect the Malay culture, with mosques and a wide assortment of clothing, consumables, and retail goods.

The many mansions, banks, churches, and parks have left the British legacy alive in the city, as well.

George Town was officially recognized as a global historical treasure in 2008, when UNESCO declared the old city a World Heritage Site. Today, there is a designated core area that is bordered by a buffer zone, all of which has a protected status due to its historical significance. Even outside of these areas, modern skyscrapers cast shadows on old shophouses and mansions.

You'll never run out of things to do here. Whether you're in the mood for outdoor fun, historical exploration, adventures in eating, taking in the nightlife, or spending an evening at the symphony, there is always something happening here.

Expats will find a lot to like about living here. Whether you're into hiking in the hills, relaxing on the greens, or savoring symphonies or street-food, there is no need to travel elsewhere. English-speaking locals, exceptionally fine food, internationally accredited medical care, and a low cost of living makes this area an appealing choice for almost anyone.

Residency In Malaysia

U.S. and Canadian travelers can come to Malaysia visa-free as tourists and stay for 90 days. To stay longer, you'll need a residency visa.

There are good reasons to obtain permanent residency in Malaysia. You'll need it to open a checking or savings account or obtain a driver's license and insurance, among other things.

Malaysia invites foreigners to apply for permanent residency through their Malaysia My Second Home Programme, or as it is popularly known, the MM2H. If you want to purchase any real estate in Malaysia, the MM2H comes with significant incentives.

You only need to be 35 years old and meet the mandated requirements to obtain permanent residency in Malaysia. Successful applicants will receive a residency pass that is valid for up to 10 years which covers the immigration of spouses, children, parents, and even a housekeeper under the same visa.

Here's an overview of the MM2H's four main categories:

- **Silver** – This is valid for five years and has the lowest requirements and fewest allowances. You need to make a fixed deposit of $150,000 (in a Malaysian financial institution), pay a "participating fee" of $225, and buy a home worth at least $135,000.

- **Gold** – This is valid for 15 years and has moderate requirements and allowances. You need to make a fixed deposit of $500,000, pay a participating fee of $675, and buy a home worth at least $225,000.

- **Platinum** – This is valid for 20 years and has high requirements but generous allowances. You need to make a fixed deposit of $1,000,000, pay a participating fee of $45,000, and buy a home worth at least $450,000.

- **Special Economic Zone** – This is valid for 10 years. You need to make a fixed deposit of $32,000 (for those 50 and above), pay a participating fee of $225, and buy a home sold by developers (not real estate agents or existing owners), meeting the minimum price according to your state.

Note that investment amounts are originally quoted in Malaysian ringgit, so exact amounts are subject to currency fluctuations.

In all cases, you're required to stay in Malaysia for 90 days per year to maintain your residency status. The MM2H has been changed many times across the years, and it has very specific rules. Make sure to read the fine print of any tier you select.

MM2H Benefits

Here are the primary incentives the Malaysian government offers prospective MM2H participants:

Foreigners, regardless of whether they are permanent residents or not, can purchase up to two properties in Malaysia. This includes condominiums, houses, or land. The minimum purchase price for a non-resident foreigner to buy property is 1 million Malaysian ringgit (RM), and may be more depending on where the property is located. That's about $300,000. If you have a MM2H visa, though, you can purchase property valued at much less than this.

As an example, if you have a MM2H visa, you could buy a home in the state of Sarawak for RM300,000 ($65,000) or in the state of Perak for RM350,000 ($76,000).

The minimum purchase price varies from state to state.

If you sell real estate, you are responsible for paying Real Property Gains Taxes (RPGT). The amount varies according to the length of time that you have owned the property. MM2H holders qualify for a reduced rate, and are exempt from paying the RPGT at all if their property has been held for at least five years.

You can apply for a home loan through a Malaysian bank for up to 80% of the value of a qualifying residential property.

You can import your household and personal belongings duty-free.

You can import one automobile duty-free, or buy a locally assembled automobile free of import duty, excise duty, or sales tax.

You may obtain a Malaysian driver's license and bank account.

You can bring one maid into Malaysia, as long as that person meets the basic immigration requirements. You may bring your family with you. That includes your spouse, any unmarried children under the age of 21, and your parents. Only the applicant needs to meet the financial eligibility requirements.

Your unmarried children may attend private schools.

All income from foreign sources such as pensions, interest

and dividend income, and foreign earned income is exempt from Malaysian taxes. However, income received from employment or business within Malaysia is taxable.

You may start a public or private business in Malaysia. The minimum investment capital is RM250,000 ($55,000).

If you are over the age of 50, you may work up to 20 hours per week in a position that the government deems is filling a critical sector—one that would be difficult or impossible to fill by a Malaysian.

You are issued a Malaysian ID card, so you no longer need to carry a passport.

You and your family can reside in Malaysia for up to 10 years with the option of indefinite visa renewals.

You can enter and leave the country as often as you wish. The length of the visa is determined according to the validity of the passport—it will not extend beyond the passport's expiration date.

MM2H Requirements

Applicants must meet certain requirements when immigrating to any foreign country. Malaysia's MM2H Program requirements are as follows:

If you are at least 35 years old, but under the age of 50, you must be able to show that you have liquid assets of at least RM500,000 ($108,170) and an offshore (non-Malaysian) income of at least RM10,000 ($2,164) per month.

Additionally, you will need to open a fixed deposit account of at least RM300,000 ($65,000) at a Malaysian bank. This deposit will earn interest, which is exempt from Malaysian taxes.

After living in Malaysia for one year, you can withdraw half of your deposit and use it for a home purchase, your children's education expenses, or for medical expenses. The remainder of the fixed deposit must remain in a Malaysian bank for the duration of your participation in the MM2H program.

If you are over the age of 50, you must show financial proof of at least RM350,000 ($76,000) in assets and an offshore income of at least RM10,000 ($2,164) a month.

If you are retired, you must show proof of receiving a monthly pension. You have your choice of opening either a fixed deposit account of at least RM150,000 ($32,500) or providing proof of a monthly government pension of RM10,000 ($2,164).

If you have made a fixed deposit, RM50,000 ($11,000) may be withdrawn for approved expenses after one year (as above). The remainder—at least RM100,000 ($22,000)—must be maintained in your fixed deposit account for the duration of your participation in the program.

Regardless of age, you'll need to submit a medical report, which can be obtained from any Malaysian hospital or registered clinic. Additionally, you must have health insurance. This requirement can be waived if you are unable to get insured due to your age or a pre-existing condition.

You must be bonded, which will cost anywhere from RM200 to RM2,000, depending on your nationality.

You'll need to submit certified copies of your passport and marriage license (if immigrating with your spouse).

You'll need to submit copies of your last three month's bank statements, payslips, and pension or income statements.

Finally, you will need to purchase an MM2H Social Visit Stamp, which costs RM90 annually.

Malaysia's Digital Nomad Visa

Malaysia's digital nomad visa launched in 2022. Known as the DE Rantau Nomad Pass or the Professional Visit Pass, the visa allows location-independent workers in the digital sphere to stay in Malaysia for up to 12 months, with the possibility of renewing for a further year.

Under the terms of the visa, you can work as an employee, business owner, or freelancer for companies or clients outside of Malaysia. Tech Professionals (software developers, UX/UI designers, data scientists, digital marketers, etc.), can qualify with an annual income of at least $24,000. For non-tech professionals that figure rises to $60,000.

You will also need a clean criminal record and a valid passport with a minimum of 14 months remaining validity and six blank pages.

Under the terms of the visa, a dependent spouse or children can accompany you. A further requirement is health or travel insurance, which covers you and any dependents for the duration of your stay.

The visa application can be completed online and costs around $220 for the main applicant. The fee for each dependent is around $110.

Permanent Residency For Investors

High-net-worth individuals are also invited to apply for permanent residency. You must be willing to invest at least $2 million in a fixed deposit account at any Malaysian bank and keep it there for at least five years. At the end of that time, you, your spouse, and your unmarried children under the age of 18 will be eligible to receive permanent residency status.

Citizenship

It is possible to obtain Malaysian Citizenship once you have been a permanent resident for at least 12 years (at least 10 of which you spent in-country), however Malaysia does not allow for dual citizenship. In addition to having to renounce your own citizenship (not a decision to be taken lightly) you would also need to be proficient in Bahasa Malaysia.

Taxes In Malaysia

Malaysia can be tax-friendly for retirees who apply for the MM2H program... The MM2H makes you eligible for tax exemptions on most forms of overseas income (investment-related income, retirement income, periodic payments, property and intellectual property income, and other gains and profits).

The cash that you import to meet the MM2H fixed deposit requirement is also tax-exempt.

Income generated from employment (including overseas income) is subject to taxation in Malaysia if you're considered a tax resident—in other words, if you spend 182 days or more in the country. Employment income tax rates range from 1% to 30%.

Malaysia does not levy net wealth or worth taxes, nor does it levy inheritance, estate, or gift taxes. It has a tax treaty in place with Canada but not the U.S.

Banking In Malaysia

To open a bank account, you'll need a passport, national identity card, a sales agreement for your property investment, and your approval letter for the MM2H program. Some banks may require a reference letter from your bank in your home country.

The most popular banks for expats in Malaysia include Maybank, CIMB, and HSBC. All are recognized for their wide branch networks, English-language services, and user-friendly online banking.

Local banks Maybank and CIMB offer expat-friendly accounts and easy international transfers. HSBC may appeal more to those seeking global banking services and premium expat packages.

These banks typically provide multi-currency accounts, investment options, and support for setting up everything from savings to credit cards, making day-to-day financial management smooth for expats in Malaysia.

Doing Business In Malaysia

Setting up a business in Malaysia as an expat is a relatively straightforward endeavor thanks to the country's pro-business policies, strategic location, and well-developed infrastructure.

The Malaysian government actively encourages foreign investment through various incentives, particularly in sectors like manufacturing, technology, tourism, and green energy.

Registering a business is typically done through the Companies Commission of Malaysia (SSM), and foreigners can fully own a company in most industries, although some sectors may require a local partner or special licensing.

Expats can choose from several types of business structures. The most common is a Private Limited Company (Sdn Bhd), which requires a minimum of one director who must be a resident in Malaysia. Many expats apply for a work permit or employ a nominee director until they meet the residency requirement themselves.

Once operational, businesses in Malaysia benefit from a strong banking system, relatively low corporate tax rates, and a multilingual workforce fluent in English, Malay, and often Chinese.

Major urban centers like Kuala Lumpur, Penang, and Johor Bahru offer modern office spaces, business services, and access to regional markets.

Networking opportunities are abundant, with active chambers of commerce and business associations supporting expat entrepreneurs. While navigating local bureaucracy and regulations may require local expertise, most expats find Malaysia a welcoming and cost-effective place to launch or expand a business.

MALAYSIA

For The Jet-Set Millionaire

Malaysia offers a compelling mix of exotic charm and modern luxury, making it an ideal destination for those seeking a jet-set millionaire lifestyle.

Kuala Lumpur, the cosmopolitan capital, is where to go for high-end shopping malls, exclusive rooftop bars, and luxury residences in prestigious districts.

Lavish resorts on the islands of Langkawi and Penang offer private villas, spa sanctuaries, and fine dining by the sea, while the Cameron Highlands is the ideal cool-weather escape with elegant colonial-style retreats and upscale tea plantation tours.

Entertainment in Malaysia runs the gamut from refined relaxation to high-octane thrills. You can tee off at award-winning golf courses, charter private yachts around tropical islands, or indulge in wellness experiences at five-star spas and health retreats.

The nightlife scene in KL includes VIP club lounges, private karaoke suites, and speakeasy cocktail bars. Cultural experiences are equally luxe, with private batik workshops, curated art gallery tours, and chef-led culinary adventures showcasing Malaysia's rich heritage with a sophisticated twist.

CHAPTER XV

★ ★ ★

ITALY

The Home Of La Dolce Vita

Italy is no secret to those of us who love culture, great food and wine, and the beauty of the Old World.

This popular European destination is a haven for expats searching for a dreamy, culture-rich, sunshine-filled retirement.

The country juts out into the Mediterranean Sea, giving it 7,600 kilometers of dazzling coastline. Along with this generous stretch of coastline, Italy offers one of the most varied landscapes on Earth, including scenic mountain ranges like the Alps and the Apennines, and stunning lakes such as Lake Garda and Lake Como.

Home of the Roman Empire, Italy maintains a solid connection to its past, with hundreds of ruins still visible in many cities and towns.

The Renaissance can also be felt in modern-day Italy. Cities like Florence preserve the beautiful Renaissance architecture in buildings such as the Duomo Cathedral.

Italy's historical and cultural side offers hours of discovery and enjoyment through art galleries, museums, and city tours.

Here are our top picks for enjoying *la dolce vita*...

Pisa

A vibrant city nestled in the heart of Tuscany that offers history and culture combined with the conveniences of modern living. If you're considering a move to Italy, you should put the highly livable, underrated city of Pisa on your radar.

Rich in historical and architectural heritage, Pisa is a delight for leisurely strolls with landmarks around every corner. It is of course most famous for its Leaning Tower, but the Piazza dei Miracoli, the UNESCO World Heritage Site where the tower is located, is also home to other iconic buildings like the Pisa Cathedral and Baptistery.

There's a timelessness to Pisa... Narrow medieval streets spill out onto vibrant piazzas where people gather to socialize, enjoy meals, or chat over coffee.

Pisa also has a youthful buzz thanks to the high proportion of students that come here to study. Education is deeply ingrained in Pisa's identity. The University of Pisa is one of Italy's most prestigious schools. Scholars from around the world make their way here and broaden the range of cultural offerings, from live music to art exhibitions to theater performances.

A small city of about 90,000 people, Pisa strikes the ideal balance between a village atmosphere and an urban one. The pace of life is slow, and there's a community feel, yet there are also excellent medical facilities, diverse shopping options, and a well-connected public transportation network.

This includes an international airport that makes trips around Europe easy and a train system that can connect you to Florence, Rome, and beyond in hours. Pisa provides a connection to nature. The Arno River wends gracefully through town, providing scenic walking and cycling paths. It's surrounded by the best of Tuscany—soft hills and valleys covered by rows of grapevines, olive groves, and centuries-old cypress trees. And when you need a dose of sunshine, Mediterranean beaches are only a 20-minute drive away.

With its cultural richness, historical charm, and modern amenities, Pisa is far more than just a place to visit—it's a great place to put down roots and enjoy a well-rounded lifestyle.

Bologna

Bologna is situated in northern Italy, capital of the Emilia-Romagna region. It's one of Italy's wealthiest cities, with a fast-growing economy based on agriculture, finance, and transport. This affluence is reflected in the quality of its public services, namely health care, which is of a very high standard.

Italy is world-famous for its food... and Bologna is its culinary capital. From homemade pasta and delicately folded tortellini to fresh cheese, organic produce, and excellent local wine, the food and drink are reasons enough to come to this city.

Bologna rivals Europe's top gastronomic capitals, like San Sebastian and Copenhagen, for its cuisine.

Eating is a long, drawn-out, almost revered practice here. And indulging in the food and the simple but masterfully prepared dishes is one of the best things about living here...

But this city also offers much more.

Its claim to fame is its historic center—one of the biggest in Europe at 142 hectares. It's also one of the best preserved and was one of the few remaining walled cities in Europe until the 19th century. Viewed from above, the skyline is the color of burnt orange, apricot, and terracotta. The color of the buildings has garnered Bologna the nickname: "La Rossa" or the red.

The historic center is full of incredible architecture, including monuments of the medieval, renaissance, and baroque movements. Your life would be immersed in history just by living among these historically significant buildings and going about day-to-day life.

The area dates back to the 7th and 6th centuries B.C., when Bologna was an Etruscan civilization. It became a Roman colony in 196 B.C., evident in the grid-pattern of its inner streets that are typical of a Roman settlement. Some 180 defensive towers were built in the medieval period; 15 still stand today, including the Due Torri, or two towers—landmarks of the city.

Bologna is famous for its porticos, which are covered walkways—elegantly designed with patterned elements. The historic center has 24 miles of porticos, meaning you can walk the length of them without ever feeling a drop of rain.

Palazzos and piazza, basilicas, churches, towers, theatres, and more... Bologna is an architecturally stunning and historically important place. It's even home to the oldest university in the western world (some say the world), the University of Bologna, open since 1088. This has made Bologna a student town for nearly 1,000 years...

On top of its incredible history, Bologna is a cultural hub. It was the European capital of culture in 2000 and has been a UNESCO City of Music since 2006. Its music scene is thumping, hosting performances from a wide variety of genres: jazz, opera, orchestra, electronic, folk, world music... You can catch shows throughout the year or at annual festivals.

Bologna hosts a number of cultural events throughout the year... celebrating everything from food to film, chocolate, dance, and more.

Bologna's events calendar is packed... It's the type of place where, whatever your interests are, you'll find something that suits them. Or you'll pick up a whole new set of hobbies and interests just by stepping outside your front door and seeing what's on in the streets.

Bologna is a transport hub, sitting at the nexus of major arteries of Italy's highway and railway systems.

This allows for easy access of the boot, getting you to places like Rome or Venice in about two hours. You can fly to Paris from Bologna in under two hours, to London in just over two hours, or to Munich in 70 minutes.

All of this combines to create an above-average quality of life for people who live in Bologna, both local and expat. If you've dreamt of living in Italy (and let's face it, who hasn't at some point?) and want to be surrounded by history, charming architecture, vibrant culture, great people, and great amenities, Bologna deserves your attention.

Città Sant'Angelo

Perched on a gently sloping hilltop, with sweeping views from the Gran Sasso Mountain to the Adriatic, and rolling hills of vineyards and olive groves in between, walking the stone streets of Città Sant'Angelo truly feels like being in a world removed from time.

Quaint storefronts are home to butchers, bakers, pasta makers, and pharmacists, locals popping in from one to the next to get their daily shopping done.

This 9th century medieval town, situated between two rivers, is home to magnificent palazzi, piazzas, churches, and monasteries... but also, more importantly, a way of life that hearkens back hundreds of years... nothing here has changed much in that time, and that's the way folks like it.

Nestled within the verdant hills of Abruzzo, this little hamlet of about 15,000 is one of the culturally richest towns the region has to offer. Abruzzo itself is one of the greenest regions in all of Europe, offering mountains (with over a dozen ski resorts) and 80 miles of coastline (with seven beach resorts—more than any other single European region), and Sant'Angelo is perhaps as ideally located in the region as it could be.

Centrally positioned just 20 minutes from the coast and an hour to the nearest slope—making this town equally ideal for both the rugged outdoorsman as well as the culture vulture.

Thanks to its architecture, Città Sant'Angelo earned the title "*Borgo*" joining the ranks of "*I Borghi più belli d'Italia*," Italy's association of towns of historical interest.

The town that existed on the site of Sant'Angelo was mentioned by Pliny the Elder as one of four Vestini cities, and was known from the 12th century as Castrum Sancti Angeli, "Castle of the Holy Angel." A Guelph city, it was destroyed in 1239 for its loyalty to the Roman Catholic Church.

Reconstruction began in 1240, and the city center became fortified. With the advent and gaining popularity of monastic orders in the first half of the 14th century, local interest became so great as to justify a monastery being established.

By 1528, the town was known as Città Sant'Angelo, and an agrarian bourgeoisie established itself through to the 17th century, the ancestors of whom still occupy the town today.

Sant'Angelo is a designated "Città Slow," referring to its commitment to try to stick to tradition and resist modernization in all ways. The mayor is serious about keeping development at bay, preserving the town's authenticity.

It's also known as a Città del Vino and Città dell'Olio; City of Wine and City of Oil. Surrounded by flourishing crops, the city produces so much excellent wine and oil it's now renowned for them. It's also a serious art town, having hosted works from the Venice and Istanbul Biennales and the Godart project.

The city has several sister cities or official friendship recognitions. It's sister cities with Nicolosi, Sicily, and an officially recognized "friend of the United States."

While small, Città Sant'Angelo is a gem that packs a punch. It's active, with jazz concerts, theater, and an old church that draws worshippers from around the region. There is an outlet shopping center nearby (the biggest in the region that offers free shipping) that also draws visitors who stay in Sant'Angelo.

Thanks to the *autostrade* (highway) passing right by the city, access is easy without spoiling the atmosphere.

While the claim to fame here is the ancient, the modern is just as well represented. The Città Sant'Angelo Village outlet mall, the first of its kind in the region, provides a wealth of shopping opportunities and draws shoppers from miles around. Shop the 100+ stores for anything from home goods to clothes at up to 70% off the retail price—and, remember, the brands are local... all fine Italian craftsmanship direct from the source!

Nearby you'll also find a shopping center with cinema, furniture store, and more.

Offering small-town living, tranquility, a closeknit community, but continued access to modern conveniences, Città Sant'Angelo is the best of all worlds.

Residency In Italy

As a U.S. or Canadian citizen, you're entitled to stay in Italy (or any other Schengen country) for 90 days on your tourist visa, and you may be asked to show proof of return or onward travel before you depart.

If you come to Italy planning to stay beyond 90 days, you need to apply to do so before setting out.

Apply for a residence visa (*visto per ragioni di dimora*) at an Italian consulate before leaving home. This acts as your temporary residency once you arrive, which is renewable for up to five years, after which time you can seek permanent residency.

If you don't apply before coming, you'll have to obtain a permit of stay (*permesso di soggiorno*) within eight days of arriving in Italy—this is the only document that legalizes your stay in Italy beyond your tourist visa.

The Elective Residence Visa

While Italy doesn't have a specific retirement visa it does offer an independent means visa known as the Elective Residency Visa that many retirees use to live in the country long-term.

The basic requirement to qualify is proof of passive income (pensions, dividends, royalties, rents, etc.) of around €32,000 per year (about $33,765 annually or $2,815 monthly). This grants you a one-year residence permit that is renewable.

Under this visa, you aren't allowed to be employed in Italy, though you can continue any remote work or be self-employed—you just have to support yourself without taking anything from the Italian economy.

You must apply in person at your nearest consulate and submit:

- Completed National (Italian) Visa Application Form, signed in the presence of a Consular Officer.

- Passport/travel document valid for at least three months beyond visa expiration date.
- Two recent passport-sized photos.
- Documented and detailed guarantee of substantial and steady private income (pensions or annuities) from property, stable economic and commercial activities, or from other sources.
- Proof of dwelling: a signed rental agreement or proof of ownership of a home.
- A letter specifying the reason for your stay in Italy, length of stay, place of residence, and the names of anyone accompanying your application (spouse and children). The signature on the letter must be notarized.
- Proof of private health insurance to cover you for your stay.
- Certified copy of marriage certificate and birth certificate(s) of children, if applicable.
- Visa-handling fee (ranging from €37.30 to €123.50) to be paid in cash, money order, or cashier's check made out to the Consulate General of Italy.
- A self-addressed (from and to yourself) pre-paid envelope (FedEx or Express Mail) along with this authorization form to have your passport mailed back to you.

All documents must first be translated by a certified translator. The visa costs €75 and is generally granted to anyone applying.

Permanent residency can be requested after living in Italy for five years on *permesso de soggiorno* and is then valid for an indefinite period of time.

You must go to the local town hall and submit your stay permit, original birth certificate (must first be translated and authenticated in your home country), a copy of your passport, and a copy of a deed showing adequate housing in Italy.

Citizenship In Italy

Italian citizenship can be obtained by non-EU citizens after living permanently in Italy for 10 years; EU citizens can apply after four years.

Italy doesn't have a direct citizenship by investment program, but its elective residency visa offers a pathway for individuals with substantial financial means.

Process Overview:

1. **Obtain Residency:** Show proof of sufficient income (€100,000 per year or more) and secure an elective residency visa.
2. **Residency Duration:** Reside in Italy for 10 years to qualify for citizenship.
3. **Integration Requirements:** Pass a basic Italian language test and demonstrate cultural integration.

Italy's lifestyle and cultural appeal make it a top choice for those willing to wait for citizenship.

One of the key advantages of Italy's golden visa program is its potential pathway to Italian citizenship. After residing in Italy for ten years, you may be eligible to apply for citizenship. This period can be shortened in specific scenarios, such as marriage to an Italian citizen or having Italian ancestry.

To qualify for citizenship, applicants must demonstrate integration into Italian society, which generally includes:

- Basic knowledge of the Italian language (B1 level).
- Proof of stable income.

Italian Citizenship By Descent

Your other option in Italy is obtaining citizenship through ancestry. Under recent rule changes citizenship by descent in Italy is now restricted to just two generations. In addition, applicants to maintain an effective bond (*vincolo effettivo*) with Italy which could include residence or direct family ties.

Plus, dual nationals risk losing their Italian citizenship if they don't engage with Italy by means such as paying taxes or voting.

Taxes In Italy

Tax residents of Italy are subject to income tax on their worldwide income.

Qualifiers For Tax Residency In Italy (Any Qualify You)

1. Physically present on Italian territory 183+ days in tax year.
2. Have a residence in Italy (habitual abode).

Or,

3. Have a domicile in Italy (principal center of social interests, e.g. the family).

There are three types of income tax in Italy: national income tax, regional income tax, and municipal income tax.

Regional income tax ranges from 1.23% to 3.33% depending on which region you live in. Municipal income ranges from 0% to 0.9% (according to municipality).

Italy made changes to its property tax laws with the Italian Budget Law 2020. Now, the basic rate for a principal residence is 0.5%, but the municipality may increase or decrease this.

Capital gains taxes vary depending on the type of gain. For the sale of real estate, the gain is taxed at progressive rates or at a flat tax of 26%. If the home is a principal residence or was owned for more than five years, its sale is exempt from capital gains tax.

Inheritance tax rates vary depending on the relationship between the donor and beneficiary. For spouses or relatives in a direct line, it's 4% on the value of assets exceeding €1 million ($1,055,190); for siblings, it's 6% on the value of assets exceeding €100,000 ($105,500).

Italy imposes a wealth tax of 1.06% on real estate owned outside of Italy. Different rules about the tax base apply, so this is something to discuss with a real estate tax specialist.

Italy also imposes a wealth tax of 0.2% to 0.4% on financial investments owned outside of Italy.

Italy has a tax treaty with both the U.S. and Canada.

Income Tax rates run from 23% to 43%. Inheritance and Estate Taxes are variable.

Property Tax is 0.5% of the city valuation on your primary residence, rising to 0.86% for other properties. The city valuation is usually lower than the actual valuation.

Capital Gains is 26% for most investments including Crypto but there are exemptions.

VAT is 22% with essential goods at 4%.

Social Security—about 10% of wages up to a maximum of €120,607. Self Employed people pay up to 25% of their wage in contributions.

Rental Income Tax is complicated but a simpler cedolare secca flat tax is 21% or 10% in certain circumstances.

Wealth on foreign property is 1.06% of purchase price and 0.2% on foreign financial investments.

Corporate tax is 24% and dividends 24%.

Transfer Tax is 2% to 9% depending on the value and your relationship to the assignee.

Inheritance for a spouse or children is taxed at 4% after the first €1 million (per heir). It's 6% for siblings after the first €100,000.

Tax On Interest is 26% and Royalties 24%.

Digital Nomads must earn €30,000 per year and pay social security and a reduced rate local income taxes of either:

a. *Regime Forfettario*—a 5% tax for the first five years on a portion (usually 78%) of gross billings, for the self-employed earning (gross) up to €85,000 per year;

b. *Impatriates Regime*—a 50%/60% exemption in calculating taxable income. For both the employed and the self-employed. For the self-employed the salary/profit reduction also applies for purposes of social security payment calculations.

Loopholes And Deductions

- **Elective Flat Tax Rate:** High-net-worth individuals may elect to pay a flat €200,000 tax per year. However, if you're not rich there are other options for expats.

- **7% Flat Tax for Foreign Retirees:** Foreign retirees who have recently arrived to central and southern Italy may elect to pay only 7% for 10 years on non-Italian sourced income, so long as they move to a town with less than 20,000 inhabitants in one of these 11 regions: Sicily, Calabria, Sardinia, Campania, Basilicata, Abruzzo, Molise and Puglia.

While the income taxes are high in Italy, the 7% retiree flat tax is appealing. With Italy's double taxation agreement, flat tax for wealthy foreigners, low cost of living, and digital nomad tax breaks, it is fairly easy to avoid becoming tax resident if you choose to (if you get good tax advice beforehand).

Buying Real Estate In Italy

There are no restrictions imposed on foreigners when it comes to buying property in Italy. In fact, there are even special programs with low-cost properties that are designed to attract and incentivize foreign buyers.

Here's a quick guide to the property purchasing process:

Enlist The Help Of A Real Estate Agent (And Translator, If Required)

Find a licensed real estate agent (agente immobiliare) familiar with the local market and ideally experienced with expat buyers. While English-speaking agents are available in popular expat areas, having a translator or bilingual lawyer can be helpful when dealing with contracts or negotiations in Italian.

A good agent can help you shortlist properties, schedule viewings, and navigate regional quirks and nuances.

Get A *Codice Fiscale*

Before making any formal property transactions in Italy, you'll need a *codice fiscale* —a tax identification number issued by the Italian Revenue Agency (*Agenzia delle Entrate*).

You will need a *codice fiscale* for pretty much all legal and financial processes in Italy, including opening a bank account and signing contracts. You can apply for one at any local tax office or through the Italian consulate.

Make A Formal Offer (*Proposta d'Acquisto*)

Once you've found your dream home, your agent will help draft a *proposta d'acquisto*—a formal written offer. This usually includes a small deposit (typically around 1% to 5% of the purchase price) to show your commitment. If the seller accepts, the deal progresses; if not, the deposit is usually refunded unless stated otherwise.

Sign the Preliminary Agreement (*Compromesso*)

The *compromesso* is a legally binding contract signed by both parties that outlines the agreed property price, conditions of sale, and a target date for completion.

At this point, a more substantial deposit is paid—typically 10% to 30% of the purchase price. In the event that the buyer pulls out, they forfeit the deposit; if the seller backs out, they must pay double the amount back to the buyer.

Legal Checks And Due Diligence

Hire a notary (*notaio*). They play a crucial role in verifying that the property has a clean title, no outstanding debts, and all the required permits and paperwork.

While the notary is technically neutral, hiring your own offers an extra layer of protection. This is also the time to finalize financing if you're taking out an Italian mortgage.

Both EU and non-EU citizens are eligible to apply for a mortgage in Italy but banks will usually apply stricter criteria for non-EU applicants. You don't need to be a resident, but non-residents typically face more restrictions (e.g. lower Loan-To-Value ratios). Generally speaking, residents can borrow 70%–80% of the property's value, for non-residents it's usually 50%–60% LTV.

Finalize The Sale (*Rogito Notarile*)

The final deed of sale (*rogito*) is signed in the presence of the notary. At this point, the remaining balance is paid, and the keys are handed over.

The notary registers the sale with the land registry, making you the official owner.

For non-EU buyers some additional paperwork or restrictions may apply depending on their nationality.

Register Ownership And Pay Taxes

After completion, the notary will ensure the property is registered in your name.

Buyers are responsible for paying stamp duty, land registry tax, and notary fees —these typically range from 7% to 10% of the purchase price, depending on whether it's going to be your primary residence or second home.

Ongoing costs include IMU (property tax), utilities, and condo fees (*spese condominiali*) where applicable.

Banking In Italy

Banking in Italy as an expat is generally a straightforward process, with a wide range of national and international banks offering services tailored to foreigners.

Major banks such as UniCredit, Intesa Sanpaolo, and international branches like HSBC or BNP Paribas often have English-speaking staff, particularly in larger cities and areas popular with expats. Many banks also provide online and mobile banking platforms in English.

To open a bank account in Italy, expats generally need a valid passport, Italian tax code (*codice fiscale*), and proof of address. Some banks may also request a residence permit or proof of employment, depending on the type of account and your nationality.

While being a resident makes the process easier, certain banks do offer non-resident accounts, though these usually come with more limited features and higher fees.

Minimum deposit requirements vary depending on the bank and account type, but basic current accounts often have low or no minimums, while premium accounts may require larger deposits or regular income.

Some banks charge modest monthly maintenance fees, while others waive them if you maintain a minimum balance.

Private banking and wealth management services are also widely available for high-net-worth individuals, offering personalized investment advice, tax planning, and international banking options.

Doing Business In Italy

Italy welcomes foreign entrepreneurs, but the process of starting a business can—like so many processes in Italy—be bureaucracy-heavy and time-consuming.

Expats typically choose between setting up as a sole trader (partita IVA), forming a limited liability company (SRL), or establishing a branch of a foreign company.

Key requirements include obtaining a tax identification number (*codice fiscale*), registering with the Chamber of Commerce, opening a business bank account, and securing any necessary licenses depending on the industry.

Italy offers some incentives for foreign investors and business owners, particularly in underdeveloped regions in the south. These include tax credits, EU-funded grants, and support for startups, especially those involved in innovation, sustainability, or digitalization.

In recent years, the Italian government has also introduced visa options like the "Investor Visa" and "Startup Visa," designed to attract foreign capital and talent. Navigating the local legal and tax system is best done with the help of local consultants and accountants familiar with the Italian business environment.

Taxation in Italy can be tricky, with corporate tax rates around 24%, plus a regional production tax (IRAP) of roughly 3.9%. Self-employed individuals and small businesses must also comply with VAT, social security contributions, and strict invoicing regulations.

ITALY
For The Jet-Set Millionaire

Italy is a dream destination for the jet-set millionaire, offering a seamless blend of old-world elegance and modern luxury. From the fashion capital of Milan to the historic grandeur of Rome and the coastal splendor of the Amalfi Coast, Italy is filled with exclusive experiences...

Opulent villas, five-star resorts, and private estates in Tuscany or Lake Como offer the ultimate in comfort and privacy, while luxury shopping in Via Monte Napoleone or designer ateliers in Florence caters to the most sophisticated tastes.

Entertainment in Italy caters to everyone from culture vultures to hedonists...

Choose to attend private opera nights, exclusive art exhibitions, or VIP events at the Venice Film Festival...

Sip a chilled Negroni on a candle-lit rooftop lounge in Rome or sink your toes in the sand at a glamorous beach club in Sicily...

For something slower-paced, private vineyard tours and truffle hunting experiences add a touch of rustic luxury.

Adventure and indulgence go hand in hand in Italy. You can hit the slopes in the Dolomites with luxury chalet access, cruise the Mediterranean aboard a superyacht, or explore the countryside by Ferrari or vintage Alfa Romeo.

High-end wellness retreats in regions like Umbria and South Tyrol offer world-class spa treatments and holistic programs.

Whether it's fine dining at Michelin-starred restaurants, bespoke culinary tours, or sailing sun-kissed islands, Italy delivers an iconic and indulgent lifestyle.

PART IV

THE CRYPTO MILLIONAIRE

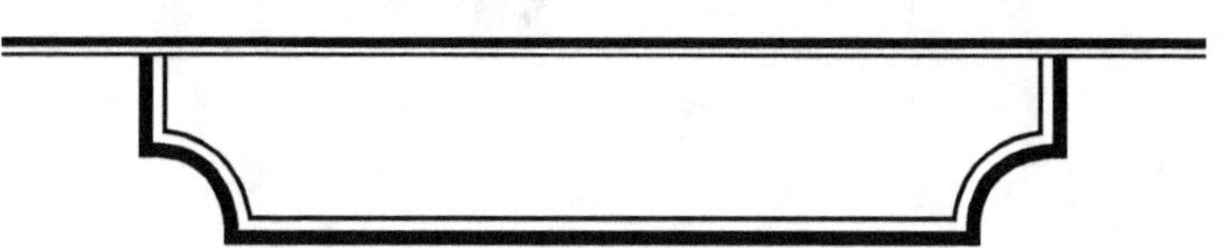

CHAPTER XVI

★ ★ ★

EL SALVADOR

The Bitcoin Vanguard

About the same size as New Jersey and wedged between Guatemala and Honduras, lies the smallest country in Central America: El Salvador.

Here, majestic panoramas of emerald cane fields stretch for miles, often with the perfectly-shaped gray cinder cone of a volcano off in the distance. The country's Pacific coast is lined with black-sand beaches, dotted with regal palm trees, leafy banana trees, and riotous colors of bougainvillea.

Most mornings, the country's magnificent volcanoes are kissed by clouds that gently blow away like some kind of ethereal cotton candy. There's more than 20 volcanoes here, though only three are considered active.

Once famed for civil war, gang violence, and being the murder capital of the world, this little country's fortunes have changed dramatically in recent years most notably since 2019 when businessman and one-time mayor of the country's capital, San Salvador, Nayib Bukele, swept to power as president with 53% of the vote.

Bukele's policy of *mano dura*—iron fist—drove an aggressive zero-tolerance policy on gang activity. Tens of thousands were jailed and today El Salvador is one of the safest countries in Latin America. The country's homicide rate is 1.9 homicides per 100,000 people which is about on par with Canada. For the U.S., it's 4.7 homicides per 100,000 people.

While his regime hasn't been without controversy—something Bukele embraces, calling himself "the world's coolest dictator"—he's not going anywhere anytime soon. Still in his early 40s, he was re-elected in 2024 with more than 84% of the vote.

In 2021, two years into Bukele's first term, El Salvador became the first country in the world to adopt Bitcoin as legal tender but the country was already on the map of crypto enthusiasts thanks to a pioneering initiative in the beach town of El Zonte which had begun back in 2019.

It was there that, thanks to anonymous donation of Bitcoin to a local charity led by U.S. expat Michael Peterson, this unassuming beach town became a real-world testbed for cryptocurrency adoption.

The donor stipulated that the Bitcoin he was handing over was not to be cashed in for U.S. dollars but rather used to support the community in its digital form and thus Bitcoin beach was born.

It started small. Local kids were given Bitcoin stipends for chores like beach clean ups and for getting good grades in school and in turn local businesses began accepting it as payment.

Then, the pandemic hit and to ensure nobody would go hungry or lack necessities, each local family was given some Bitcoin as a sort of universal basic income and more local stores began accepting it.

In time, word spread across the wider crypto community and Bitcoin payments platform Strike launched in the country. Ultimately, the project came to the attention of Bukele who cited it as his inspiration for making Bitcoin legal tender in 2021.

For all these strides forward in Bitcoin adoption, in recent years there has been a dial back of the country's crypto ambitions. In order to secure a $1.4 billion loan from the IMF, El Salvador dropped Bitcoin as legal tender in 2025, reverting it to an optional payment method for the private sector and amending legislation so that taxes could once again only be paid in U.S. dollars.

That said, El Salvador continues to stack Bitcoin and holds

more than $600 million worth... depending on the day.

So, while it may not be the high-profile, government-driven Bitcoin hub it once was, it still offers plenty of attractions for crypto holders and adventurous expats...

El Salvador Residency And Citizenship

El Salvador offers a number of residency options including a retirement visa, an independent means visa, a digital nomad visa, and a citizenship by investment program.

Rentista Visa

El Salvador's *Rentista* Visa is designed for individuals with a reliable passive income.

To qualify, you must demonstrate a stable monthly income of around $1,600 from pensions, passive investments, or annuities. The official figure is set at four times the minimum wage in the country's commerce and services sectors.

Applicants must provide proof of income, a valid passport, clean criminal records from both El Salvador and their home country, and health insurance coverage.

To maintain and renew the *Rentista* Visa, holders are required to spend at least 90 days per year in the country. These days may be accumulated over multiple visits or completed in a single stay and are necessary to maintain legal residency status.

The visa is typically valid for two years and can be renewed, provided the income threshold is met and residency requirements are maintained.

A financially dependent spouse, financially dependent children under 25, and financially dependent parents over 65 can accompany a *Rentista* Visa holder.

Pensionado Visa

For retirees, the *Pensionado* Visa is the obvious choice. To qualify, applicants need to show a monthly pension of at least $1,100, though higher incomes are generally preferred.

To maintain the visa, holders are generally required to spend at least 90 days per year in El Salvador, either consecutively or cumulatively. In order for the pensionado visa to remain eligible for renewal, applicants must meet the annual physical presence requirement.

Applicants must also provide proof of health insurance valid in El Salvador, clean criminal records from both El Salvador and their home country, and a local address for registration purposes.

While the *Pensionado* Visa is intended for retirees, holders are legally allowed to work or start a business if they wish, although additional registration or licensing may be required depending on the type of work or business.

The *Pensionado* Visa is granted for one year initially and, on renewal, for two years providing your residency obligations are maintained.

This visa allows retirees to live legally in El Salvador, own property, access local banking, and provides a pathway to permanent residency and eventual citizenship after meeting the country's residency requirements.

A financially dependent spouse, financially dependent children under 25, and financially dependent parents over 65 can accompany a *Pensionado* Visa holder.

Digital Nomad Visa

To qualify for El Salvador's Digital Nomad Visa you will need to show a minimum monthly income of approximately $1,500 from international clients or employers.

This visa allows holders to live and work remotely in El Salvador. It typically requires evidence of ongoing contracts, bank statements, or proof of business ownership. Health insurance and a clean criminal record are also mandatory.

This visa usually grants an initial residency of one year, renewable annually, for a maximum of four years.

El Salvador does not tax foreign-earned income.

General Requirements For All El Salvador Residency Visas

- Valid passport and visa application.
- Proof of income, investment, or pension (depending on visa type).
- Clean criminal records from El Salvador and your home country.
- Health insurance coverage recognized in El Salvador.
- Some programs may require proof of local address or a registered business.

El Salvador Citizenship

El Salvador permits dual and multiple citizenship without restrictions.

The country offers several pathways to citizenship, including naturalization, marriage, descent, and special programs for significant economic or cultural contributions and investment.

Citizenship provides full access to Salvadoran civil rights, property ownership, and business opportunities.

Citizenship By Naturalization

The most common route for foreigners is naturalization. To apply, you generally need to have legally resided in El Salvador for at least five years.

Applicants must demonstrate good moral character, have a clean criminal record, and show integration into Salvadoran society, including a basic knowledge of the Spanish language, culture, and civic responsibilities.

Naturalization involves submitting required documentation such as proof of residence, identity, financial stability, and police clearance certificates, followed by a review process that can take several months to a year.

Citizenship By Marriage

Foreigners married to a Salvadoran citizen can apply for citizenship after three years of marriage. Residency in El Salvador is generally required only during the application process but proof of a stable and genuine marital relationship is a non-negotiable.

Applicants must provide a marriage certificate, evidence of cohabitation or joint financial activity, and good character references.

Citizenship By Descent

If your parents or grandparents are citizens of El Salvador you may be eligible for citizenship by descent.

Children born abroad to Salvadoran parents can usually claim citizenship at birth, while grandchildren may need to register their claim through a consulate. Adoption under Salvadoran law can also create eligibility for citizenship for minors.

Citizenship by descent often allows for a faster process than naturalization with proof of lineage being the primary requirement.

Citizenship By Merit

El Salvador has recently introduced programs aimed at individuals who make significant economic, cultural, or social contributions to the country. This includes entrepreneurs, investors, philanthropists, and professionals with exceptional skills in areas such as science, technology, arts, or sports.

Applicants typically need to demonstrate a measurable impact on the national interest, such as creating jobs, investing in strategic sectors, or supporting cultural and social initiatives. Approval is discretionary and involves evaluation by the Ministry of Foreign Affairs and other relevant government bodies.

El Salvador Freedom Visa Program

El Salvador's Freedom Visa Program is a premium fast-track citizenship route aimed at high net worth individuals, particularly within the crypto space.

Applicants apply through an authorized agent, undergo due diligence and security checks, and if approved, make the required $1,000,000 contribution in Bitcoin (BTC) or Tether (USDT).

There is no language test, interview, or residency requirement before or after approval and a spouse and dependent children under 18 can be included for a fee of around $1,000 per person.

The program is limited to 1,000 applicants per year.

Taxes In El Salvador

El Salvador operates a residence-based tax system: residents are generally taxed on their worldwide income, while non-residents are taxed only on Salvadoran-source income.

For crypto holders, recent legislation and guidance treat Bitcoin and other digital currencies in ways that can affect both income and capital gains taxation.

Tax Residency

In El Salvador, you are considered a tax resident if you spend more than 183 days in the country during a calendar year.

Residency can also be established through permanent ties, such as owning a home, maintaining a local business, or having family in the country.

Tax residents are liable for tax on all income, whether earned locally or abroad, while non-residents are only taxed on income sourced within El Salvador.

El Salvador Tax Rates

- **Income Tax:** Progressive, 10% to 30% for individuals on local income. Foreign-earned income is generally exempt for tax residents unless it is remitted to El Salvador.
- **Value Added Tax (VAT):** Standard rate is 13% and applied to most goods and services.
- **Social Security Contributions:** 7.5% employee contribution and 7.5% employer contribution for most workers. Self-employed individuals pay 15% of declared income.
- **Capital Gains Tax:** Generally, 10% for local securities; exemptions may apply for certain asset sales.
- **Property Tax:** 0.25%–0.5% of registered property value annually.
- **Rental Income:** Taxed as part of personal income at standard rates (10% to 30%).
- **Dividends:** 10% withholding tax for non-residents; tax residents include dividends in taxable income.
- **Inheritance and Gift Tax:** Currently 0% for close family members; others may be taxed at 10%.
- **Cryptocurrency:** Capital gains on crypto transactions are not subject to capital gains tax but businesses and individuals using crypto for commercial purposes must account for VAT and income tax on profits.

Tax Treaties

El Salvador has limited double taxation agreements, including one with the U.S., which means you won't be taxed twice on the same income.

Canadians may need to rely on foreign tax credits when filing both Salvadoran and Canadian returns.

El Salvador's tax system can be particularly favorable for foreign retirees and digital nomads. Income earned abroad by residents and not remitted locally is often exempt from local tax.

Crypto-savvy expats can also benefit, as digital currency gains from private transactions are largely untaxed, though businesses transacting in crypto must, of course, comply with reporting requirements.

Expats can generally deduct business expenses, social security contributions, mortgage interest on Salvadoran properties, and charitable donations. Using foreign income exemptions and legal corporate structures can help to reduce overall effective taxation.

Banking In El Salvador

Banking in El Salvador has been evolving rapidly in recent years, particularly since 2021 when the country adopted Bitcoin as legal tender alongside the U.S. dollar (though this status has since been rescinded).

Still, traditional banking in El Salvador continues to coexist with digital currencies, offering flexibility in how you manage and move your money.

While the U.S. dollar simplifies everyday transactions, many Salvadoran banks are increasingly offering services that cater to both crypto enthusiasts and conventional banking clients.

Traditional banking in El Salvador is generally reliable, with several institutions offering English-language services, online banking, and international wire transfers.

Popular choices among expats include Banco Agrícola, one of the country's largest banks, which provides a wide range of accounts, debit and credit cards, and mortgage services.

Another option is Davivienda, which has embraced modern banking tools and mobile apps, making it easier to manage accounts remotely.

Both banks allow you to open accounts as a non-resident, although documentation such as a passport, proof of address, and a local reference or income statement is typically required.

Some private financial institutions offer crypto-friendly accounts and ATMs, attractive to expats who want to leverage Bitcoin for savings, remittances, or investment purposes.

El Salvador Real Estate

Property prices in El Salvador have risen steadily in recent years, driven by increased demand, a growing expat presence, and limited real estate supply in the most desirable areas.

In the capital, San Salvador, a modest apartment or small home in a well-connected neighborhood now typically costs between $150,000 and $250,000, while larger houses in secure, upscale suburbs can reach $300,000 to $450,000, depending on size and condition.

Coastal properties command higher prices still due to their scarcity and lifestyle appeal. Ocean-view lots and completed homes in these areas can range from $200,000 to over $600,000, with luxury developments approaching the upper end of that scale.

There are few restrictions on foreign real estate investors here. Ownership rights are fully recognized and most residential and commercial properties are sold freehold. Exceptions exist primarily for very large agricultural plots or land within public coastal zones, which require special government approval.

Buyers must obtain a local tax identification number and finalize the purchase through a notary, who prepares the deed and registers it in the national property registry.

Real estate transaction costs are reasonable. Buyers pay a one-time transfer fee based on the property value, plus notary and registration charges. Agent fees are typically negotiated and often paid by the seller. Total closing costs generally range between 5% and 8% of the property price.

Ongoing costs are low and there is no nationwide property tax but rental income and short-term tourist accommodations are subject to local taxes.

Real estate agents in El Salvador are widely used but not centrally licensed, so standards vary wildly. Experienced local agents can provide valuable market insight and access but it's always a smart move to retain independent legal support when it comes to contracts and title verification.

Construction quality in El Salvador runs the gamut, too. New developments in the capital and along the coast tend to be to a good standard while older homes and rural builds generally require upgrades or more extensive maintenance.

Construction costs for new homes are generally lower than in North America, though imported materials and high-end finishes naturally increase costs.

Expats tend to concentrate in certain neighborhoods and regions. In San Salvador, secure suburbs with reliable infrastructure, shopping, and services are preferred. Coastal towns with surfing, beaches, and tourism-oriented amenities have attracted both lifestyle buyers and investors seeking rental income. Outside these hotspots, supply is more limited, properties are smaller, and the market is less liquid.

In the country's most desirable areas, prices are at levels generally comparable with the U.S. and Canada.

Doing Business In El Salvador

Running a business in El Salvador as an expat generally involves fewer layers of administration than in many developed economies though the system relies heavily on formal compliance and local intermediaries.

While company incorporation and tax registration are clearly defined in law, most foreign owners depend on local lawyers and accountants to navigate filings, labor registrations, and ongoing reporting obligations. Digital platforms have improved access to government services but many procedures still require in-person validation and sequential approvals.

El Salvador's use of the U.S. dollar eliminates currency conversion risk and simplifies cross-border accounting for U.S. and Canadian entrepreneurs.

Corporate profits are taxed at a standard national rate, with smaller companies qualifying for a reduced rate. A value-added tax applies to most commercial transactions and must be reported and paid monthly.

Businesses are also subject to advance income tax payments based on gross revenue, which are reconciled against annual tax returns. Although electronic filing is the norm, tax compliance is closely monitored and penalties for errors or delays are enforced.

Labor regulations are formal and protective. Statutory minimum wages vary by industry and are set at levels well below North American standards. The legal work-week is capped at 44 hours, and employees are entitled to paid leave, public holidays, and severance in cases of termination without cause.

Employers must register workers with the national social security and pension systems and remit monthly contributions, with the employer portion exceeding that of the employee.

Foreign participation in the workforce is restricted. Salvadoran law requires that the majority of employees be local nationals, with exceptions typically granted for executive, technical, or highly specialized roles.

Certain economic activities and professions require licenses or government recognition, particularly in regulated sectors.

Self-employed individuals are responsible for their own tax and social security obligations.

EL SALVADOR

For The Crypto Millionaire

El Salvador combines lush landscapes, colonial charm, and modern urban centers and offers accessibility, forward-thinking innovation, and a range of lifestyle options.

The climate is tropical, with warm temperatures year-round. English is widely spoken in business circles and expat neighborhoods, and the country's legal system is increasingly accommodating to overseas investors.

The cost of living is lower than in most of North American, health care is accessible and improving, and international schooling options are available.

Internet speeds are strong in urban areas, mobile networks are reliable, and travel connections throughout Central America are expanding. Here, you're just a short flight from Mexico City, Miami, Bogotá, and beyond.

While not tax-free, the country offers favorable conditions for certain digital asset activities. There is no capital gains tax on Bitcoin and crypto transactions are increasingly integrated into the financial system.

Residency options are flexible and if you've got the $1 million budget for the freedom visa you can get citizenship within a matter of months.

For investors and remote professionals looking for a bold, dynamic base in Central America, El Salvador is a compelling choice.

CHAPTER XVII

★ ★ ★

THE CAYMAN ISLANDS

A Classic Tax Haven

Legend has it that in February 1794, 10 merchant ships sailing from Jamaica to England struck the reef off Grand Cayman. The Caymanians saw the ships sink and, without hesitation, headed into the sea and bravely rescued those on board, saving almost all their lives.

This moment in history has been named "The Wreck of the Ten Sail".

As the story goes, one of the passengers rescued was a royal prince. To reward their courage and express his gratitude, King George III declared the people of Cayman should forever be free of taxes and the draft.

Caymanians explain their valor and compassion as "Caymankind." A reflection of their goodwill toward all people. And global investors are happy to use the friendly Caymans as a tax haven. They've found a home on these islands for centuries.

A philosophy of kindness and financial freedom are both solid reasons to consider the Cayman Islands, but there's something for everyone here... quiet, secluded beaches with achingly blue, pristine waters and world-class scuba diving, rollicking nightlife, rich history and culture, active retirement communities, excellent schools, and such family-oriented activities as kite festivals and snorkeling with stingrays.

With year-round sunshine, a safe and clean environment, lively community spirit, and a stable government, how could one not love these islands?

It was Christopher Columbus who put the Cayman Islands on the map, recording the Sister Islands on May 10, 1503, when his ship was blown off course during a trip between Hispaniola and Panama. The turtles crawling the islands prompted him to name them "Las Tortugas." Sir Francis Drake, who spotted them 80 years later, called them "Caymanas", the Carib name for crocodiles. That name stuck—even though most believe it was rock iguanas he saw, not crocodiles. Plenty of iguanas still roam the islands today—especially on Little Cayman, where the speed limit is 25 mph to assure their safety.

Pirates promptly scared off early settlers, who arrived from Jamaica in late 1660, and the islands weren't permanently inhabited until the 1730s. The Cayman Islands were officially a dependency of Jamaica until that island's independence from England in 1962, after which the Caymans voted to become a self-governing Crown colony of the United Kingdom.

Today, each of the three Cayman Islands has its own personality. There's Grand Cayman, the largest and most boisterous of the group with a bustling capital of George Town and world-renowned Seven Mile Beach. And then there are the Sister Islands Cayman Brac and Little Cayman, with populations of around 2000 and 160, respectively, which are notably toned down a notch.

Grand Cayman is an easy place to get to, and its Owen Roberts International Airport has direct flights everywhere from London and Toronto to Los Angeles and Atlanta, as well as several one-hour flights daily to Miami.

Cayman Brac's Charles Kirkconnell International Airport offers direct flights to Miami as well. Cayman Airways connects Grand Cayman to Cayman Brac and Little Cayman.

Public transportation on Grand Cayman and Cayman Brac consists mostly of a public mini-bus transport system. It's pretty relaxed: You can flag down a bus and let the driver know when you'd like to get off. Fares are CI$2 to CI$2.50 (around $2.40 to $3) for short trips and up to CI$8 (around $10) for longer ones on Grand Cayman, and CI$3 (around $3.60) on Cayman Brac. If you ask your driver for any sort of detour (which is totally OK to do), it'll cost you CI$1 to CI$3 (around $1.20 to $4). Additionally, the Purple Ribbon Bus Service is free on New Year's Eve.

Public transportation is more limited on Little Cayman, but it's not difficult to arrange travel in such a small community. Its cheerful 11-seater mini bus taxi service provides pickups and drop-offs to beaches, bars, restaurants, and the airport, as well as land tours and food delivery.

A car is nice to have on all three of the islands, but gas is expensive at CI$5.99 (around $7.19) per Imperial gallon, locals have a reputation for bad driving, and Grand Cayman's traffic can be heavy during peak hours.

Bikes, scooters, and mopeds can also be rented easily, and electric scooters are available on Grand Cayman. The cost for renting a scooter is CI$1 (around $1.20) to start and then CI$0.15 (around $0.18) per minute.

Digital nomads will have no problems with internet service. There are plenty of options here, and reliable internet is one of the many reasons for this. Still, some residents in the more remote areas of the Sister Islands play it safe and keep their landlines.

Banking In The Cayman Islands

The Cayman Islands is one of the world's largest and most respected financial centers boasting a wide variety of offshore bank accounts and wealth management options.

The proverbial offshore bank account in Cayman Islands was made famous (or infamous) by too many books and movies to count and has become synonymous with tax cheats and money launders. Adding insult to injury, Obama pandered to this pop culture image when he attacked Mitt Romney in 2012 for his use of the island as a home for his money.

The truth about the offshore bank account in the Caymans is far removed from these fairy tales sold to the uninitiated.

The Islands are one of the most transparent and professional of the tax neutral jurisdictions, allowing large corporations and sophisticated investors to maximize the international tax benefits available to them from their home country (i.e. loopholes in the U.S. tax code for Americans). If you are thinking about incorporating a business or investing abroad, you might open an offshore bank account in the Cayman Islands as a place to park retained earnings or as a base of operations for your global tax plan.

Offshore companies and offshore bank accounts in Cayman remain a major part of the island's economy. With around 100,000 registered corporations and a population of about 87,866, there are more companies than residents.

International financial services contribute approximately 40% of the island's GDP, are responsible for a significant portion of the 50%–60% share from finance and tourism combined, and generate nearly 50% of government revenue. The sector also supports a large share of local employment, with subsectors like insurance alone accounting for 256 direct jobs and contributing 5% of GDP.

The Cayman Islands is one of the world's leading offshore financial centers, with around 79 licensed international banks and over 40 of the world's top 50 banks holding licenses locally.

Of these banks, the vast majority are what we call offshore banks (only allowed to do business with people and companies outside of Cayman), with institutions representing jurisdictions across Europe, North America, and South America.

Then there are the hedge funds and captive insurance companies, which are also significant contributors to Cayman's diversified financial services industry. There are over 30,000 regulated investment funds with more than $8.2 trillion in assets, which represents strong growth in recent years. Rounding out the industry, there are 697 international insurance entities with $153 billion in assets, of which the majority are from North America.

Of these, a large portion insure medical malpractice and workers compensation accounts.

This emphasis on high-end financial management services has paid off. With an average income of around $58,800, Caymanians have the highest standard of living in the Caribbean. In fact, the Cayman Islands' GDP per capita ranks among the highest in the world.

Opening A Bank Account

A good rule is to never open an offshore bank account at an institution with a branch in the United States. Holding funds at any offshore bank with a U.S. branch exposes you to IRS levy and civil creditor judgments. If you're going offshore, then go offshore.

For this reason, and because of their diverse investment options and excellent customer service, Cayman National Bank (CNB) is a solid option for those who want an offshore bank account in the Cayman Islands.

Founded in 1974, CNB has assets exceeding $2 billion, with shareholders' equity of $261 million. Total deposits stand at $1.7 billion. The Cayman Islands dollar remains pegged to the U.S. dollar at CI$1.25 to US$1.

CNB offers wealth management and business banking services to U.S. persons who are operating through tax compliant structures. The use of a U.S. tax expert or a U.S.-based lawyer to form your company and open an offshore bank account in the Cayman Islands with CNB is required. Using an online incorporator who is not approved by the bank will cause significant delays and additional reporting requirements.

CNB will open an account after receiving the required documents by courier, so a personal interview is generally not necessary. Documents must be notarized, but an apostil is not required. CNB does not charge to open an account. Minimum opening deposits with CNB are $1,000 for non-residents and CDs usually start at $5,000.

You may hold funds in Cayman dollars, U.S. dollars, Canadian dollars, sterling, and other major currencies. Some currencies may require higher minimum account balances.

Cayman National considers more than $250,000 a premium account. Benefits include dedicated relationship managers, preferential rates on loans and overdrafts, priority processing on applications, and access to exclusive Visa Infinite credit and debit cards.

Here is a list of the documents required from each signatory to open an offshore bank account in the Cayman Islands:

- Completed application.
- U.S. tax compliance referral and IRS Form W8-BEN if applicable.
- Notarized copy of your passport.
- Notarized copy of a utility bill reflecting your name and home address (no P.O. Boxes and not older than two months).
- Notarized copy of your bank statement.
- Bank reference letter.
- Personal or business reference letter, and
- A notarized copy of your offshore trust or corporation or Certificate of good standing will be required if your structure is older than one year.

Taxes In The Cayman Islands

The Cayman Islands have a long history of tax freedom and neutrality. For this reason, Americans may be able to maximize the offshore loopholes in the U.S. tax code by opening an offshore bank account in the Cayman Islands.

This demand for tax and personal freedoms has been a part of Cayman life for centuries. For example, local lore claims that King George III rewarded the island with a promise to never introduce taxes as a reward for saving his son Prince William when his ship wrecked upon a reef in February 1794.

Whether this story is true is up for debate, but the "Wreck of the Ten Sail" is deeply engrained in Cayman culture and tells you a lot about the local mindset.

Whatever the history, the government of the Cayman Islands has always relied on indirect taxes, never passing an income tax, capital gains tax, or wealth tax.

It's a thriving offshore financial center as well. Multinational companies do not pay corporate, income, payroll, or withholding taxes. Thousands have found it the perfect place to avoid taxation and establish an offshore subsidiary. Especially popular among hedge fund managers, there's no taxation on interest or dividends earned on investments either.

Offshore corporations are subject to an annual licensing fee, paid to the government, and, of course, doublecheck your home country's tax laws. (U.S. citizens can sometimes exempt a portion of their foreign income from their U.S. obligations, for example.) Lucky for investors, like all tax havens, privacy laws are taken very seriously.

If you decide to open an offshore bank account in the Cayman Islands, never use the phrase "tax haven" in polite conversation. Ask a Cayman banker about his country being a tax haven and you'll likely get an angry diatribe about how pop culture has vilified Cayman. Locals call it the Grisham effect... ever since his book "The Firm" in 1991, Americans have believed Cayman is a pirate's paradise.

That divisive term, which implies a country with laws blocking the sharing of information and a lack of honesty or compliance, is far from the truth and a sign of ignorance. In fact, Cayman is on the OECD "white list" of countries, along with the U.K. and the U.S., for their acceptance of internationally recognized tax standards in their laws.

Cayman has been cooperating with the OECD since 2000, signed tax exchange agreements with the United States covering all civil and criminal cases in 2001, and is party to a number of other treaties in the years since.

As to FATCA, the Caymans elected the U.S. Treasury's Model I

Intergovernmental Agreement back in 2013.

The proper term for the efficiencies offered by Cayman is "tax neutrality." Cayman will not tax you or your business and your offshore bank account in Cayman will integrate with the laws of your home country, allowing you to minimize taxes when available. If you are an American living and working abroad, an offshore corporation in Cayman may afford you significant tax benefits.

These tax savings, and the advanced financial services industry described above, are not founded on secrecy. They require political and economic stability, tax efficiency, a responsive legal system, a stable banking environment, a sound regulatory regime, and sophisticated service providers.

They are based on an integrated approach where tax neutrality, combined with the tax code of your home country, results in tax efficiencies. This is what Cayman offers the investor, not backroom deals or hidden assets.

And this is why the Islands take such offense when they are attacked for being a tax haven. The Caymans is simply a tax neutral country that doesn't bury its citizenry in taxes. For Americans, it is the U.S. tax code that allows companies to hold billions offshore and incentivizes high-net-worth individuals to minimize taxes and protect their assets abroad.

Many global wealth management firms have offices in Cayman, including Butterfield Bank, Royal Bank of Canada, Scotiabank, and the asset management arm of Cayman National Bank, the only bank headquartered in Cayman, Cayman National Securities. These institutions can provide access to a wide array of investment choices and will be familiar with the tax and regulatory issues of your home country.

For example, if you want to take your IRA offshore, you might follow the lead of Mr. Romney and use a Cayman Islands structure. Note that you don't need to be a millionaire, the size of your IRA doesn't matter, and anyone can take advantage of these benefits.

If you are a sophisticated investor, Cayman's advanced wealth management and captive insurance industries may allow you to access major tax incentives embedded in the U.S. tax code.

Many of these opportunities, such as captive insurance, require an investment of $1 million and Cayman has the best in the field to assist you.

In recent years, this same philosophy of tax neutrality and regulatory pragmatism has extended into digital assets and cryptocurrency.

The Caymans have quietly become one of the world's most important jurisdictions for crypto funds, blockchain startups, and digital asset investment vehicles. Rather than banning or loosely ignoring crypto, the Caymans chose a third path: clear rules without punitive taxation.

The Cayman Islands does not impose capital gains tax, income tax, or withholding tax on cryptocurrency transactions conducted through properly structured entities. For investors and fund managers, this means gains realized from trading or holding digital assets are not taxed locally, allowing Cayman structures to integrate efficiently with your home-country tax obligations—much like traditional hedge funds and private equity vehicles have done for decades.

In 2020, the Cayman Islands introduced the Virtual Asset (Service Providers) Act (VASP), which established a regulatory framework for businesses involved in crypto exchanges, custody, issuance, and related services. This law brought digital assets under the supervision of the Cayman Islands Monetary Authority (CIMA), signaling to global investors that Cayman intended to be credible, compliant, and institution-friendly, not a regulatory free-for-all.

As a result, many of the world's largest crypto hedge funds, Web3 venture funds, DAOs, and token-issuing entities are legally domiciled in Cayman. The familiar Cayman exempted company and foundation company structures are now commonly used for:

- Crypto investment funds.
- Token issuances and DAO governance.
- Digital asset holding companies.
- Blockchain infrastructure projects.

For U.S. investors in particular, Cayman's approach mirrors what made it dominant in traditional finance: tax neutrality combined with legal clarity.

The Caymans don't help you evade taxes, obviously, but nor does living here add an extra layer of taxation on top of your U.S. obligation. Rather, the system allows investors to take advantage of efficiencies already embedded in U.S. tax law.

Importantly, Cayman's crypto ecosystem is not built on secrecy. KYC, AML, and compliance requirements apply to virtual asset service providers, and information exchange agreements remain firmly in place.

What Cayman offers is predictability—a stable legal system based on English common law, sophisticated service providers, and regulators who understand modern financial products.

Many of the same global law firms, banks, administrators, and auditors that service traditional hedge funds now support crypto and blockchain structures in Cayman. This continuity has made the Islands especially attractive to institutional investors who want exposure to digital assets without regulatory uncertainty.

In short, Cayman has become for crypto what it has long been for hedge funds: a neutral, respected jurisdiction where innovation can occur within a clear legal framework. Just as with traditional finance, the advantages come not from secrecy, but from stability, compliance, and tax neutrality—principles that have defined the Cayman Islands for generations.

Residency And Citizenship In The Cayman Islands

Although most visitors do not require a visa, check before you go. Citizens of the United States, Costa Rica, and Panama won't need one, for example, but those from China, India, and Jamaica do.

Technically visitors can legally stay for six months, after which they can apply for an extension. However, most visitors are in fact only given permission to stay 30 days when they arrive, unless they own property on the islands and can prove they can take care of themselves financially.

If you'd like to settle in for a while, your best bet is to arrive with a letter demonstrating financial security, health insurance, and your island address. Frequent visitors (looking at you, snowbirds) are often granted six months, but will have to show a return ticket. If you aren't approved for more than 30 days upon arrival, you can fill out an extension form at the Customs and Border Control office on Grand Cayman; the cost is CI$50 for the first extension, CI$100 for each additional application.

You can apply for Permanent Residency with the right to work after eight years of living here, or immediately if you are the spouse or child of a permanent resident or Caymanian. This is granted through a fairly complicated point system based on exigencies like age, community involvement, and education, as well as financial stability. There's even a history and culture test.

If you are willing to invest significantly in a business or property, however, you can apply straightaway to the Director of Workforce Opportunities and Residency (WORC) for permanent residency with or without the right to work in four different ways.

Following is a brief description of each...

The first three are specifically declared for "persons of independent means" and the last for "persons of independent means with substantial business presence." You'll need deep pockets for all four, but the first requires the deepest. Be sure to doublecheck details and requirements before moving forward.

First, the Certificate of Permanent Residency is the easiest way to acquire permanent residency and the right to work. This option has no expiration date, but it's expensive: You are required to invest at least CI$2,000,000 in developed real estate and prove you can support you and yours financially. You'll also need to confirm your good health and good character. Only 250 of these certificates are granted annually; application fee is CI$500 with CI$100,000 due at close and an additional CI$1,000 for each dependent, payable annually.

Second, if you want to live here and not work, you can apply for a Residency Certificate, renewable and valid for 25 years; the initial application fee is CI$500. You're required to show proof of an annual income of at least CI$120,000 (or deposit at least CI$400,000 in a local bank) and invest at least CI$1,000,000, half of which must be in developed real estate. (Applicants typically buy a property that meets that entire requirement.)

It's a little less expensive to live on Little Cayman or Cayman Brac, where you'll need proof of an annual income of CI$75,000, as well as to invest CI$500,000, half in developed real estate.

Wherever you live, expect a one-time fee of CI$20,000 and an additional CI$1,000 for each dependent.

Your third option is to obtain the Certificate of Direct Investment, valid for 25 years and renewable and intended for investors interested in investing in employment that specifically generates business in the Cayman Islands. You're required to demonstrate an existing or planned investment of CI$1,000,000 in such employment.

Before you apply for a full certificate, you are permitted to obtain an Approval in-Principle Certificate, valid for six months, which allows you to reside in the Cayman Islands and work in the business in which you've invested. The application fee is CI$1,000, with an additional CI$20,000 due upon receipt of the certificate, plus CI$1,000 per dependent.

Finally, the Residency Certificate (Substantial Business Presence), valid for 25 years, is designed to be more amenable than the Certificate of Direct Investment, and allows residency to anyone who owns at least a 10% share in an approved category of business in Cayman (these are listed online) or will be employed at such a business. You must prove you and your spouse have no criminal record and are in good health. The fee is CI$5,000, with an additional CI$1,000 per dependent.

After you've been a permanent resident 12 months and have lived in Cayman for at least five years, you can apply for naturalization as a British Overseas Territories Citizen (BOTC). Once naturalized, you'll receive a BOTC passport and can register for

British citizenship.

Note: Living "off island" for more than 90 days in a year, or 540 days over five years, could affect your application.

After five years as a BOTC (or you've been 15 years in Cayman—whichever comes first), you can apply for the Right to be Caymanian. This is decidedly not the same as being naturalized. The Right to be Caymanian officially grants you the right to reside and work in the Cayman Islands, while naturalization simply declares you a BOTC and allows a Caymanian passport, which only functions as a travel document.

Real Estate In The Cayman Islands

The Caymans make it easy to buy property. There are no restrictions on foreign ownership, and anyone can and even is encouraged to buy property here. You do not have to live here to do it. It's no surprise that many expats already have. It's safe, clean, and beautiful, and, of course, owners do not pay property, income, or capital gains tax.

Really the only fee you'll encounter is a one-time stamp duty fee, currently 7.5% of the purchase price or the market value of the property, whichever is higher. (Market value is determined by a Valuation Office and is open to review.) If you require financing, be aware that although banks in the Cayman Islands do offer mortgages to foreign buyers, they often have strict regulations concerning deposits and income verification. Secured mortgages are subject to a one-time stamp duty at 1% or 1.5%, depending on the amount of the loan.

You can purchase a property yourself or through a company or trust. You'll register any foreign company (incorporated outside of the Cayman Islands) as a foreign entity here before beginning the process. Title to property can be arranged one of two ways: Freehold is the conventional arrangement, where the owner owns the land and any buildings on it forever. Leasehold means the owner will lease it to you for a fixed period, offering, in some cases, periodic options to extend. You might find some properties along Seven Mile Beach leasehold.

The Cayman Islands Land Registry holds all land ownership information, guarantees the legitimacy of property titles, and protects every buyer's purchase. The Registry is public and easily available, and an on-hand registry map lists the details of each parcel of land. Still, it's always safest to work with a local real estate agent and attorney. CIREBA (Cayman Islands Real Estate Brokers Association) manages the Multiple Listing Service (MLS) where most properties are listed. Have your lawyer doublecheck any restrictions that could potentially affect the property and possible licensing requirements for, say, non-residential or rental properties.

Obviously, location matters. You'll see insane prices in well-known areas like Seven Mile Beach—as astronomical as $50 million—where neighbors include the Ritz and the Kimpton Seafire. The newest five-star residences at the Grand Hyatt here are priced on average at $1,450 per square foot.

If you are considering renting your new investment, the Cayman Islands never seem to go out of style but don't forget to review local regulations regarding short-term rentals and potential rental income.

Note: If you are considering an apartment or condominium, you'll likely be required to follow a registered strata plan and bylaws. The strata corporation manages the building insurance, as well as the maintenance of the common areas. Eyes wide open and read the fine print.

Overseas Business Incorporation In The Cayman Islands

Setting up a company in the Cayman Islands offers many advantages, including tax neutrality, a welcoming business environment, and political stability. The company formation process is pretty straightforward but it's important to carefully follow the jurisdiction's legal and regulatory requirements.

Here's a quick guide to registering a company in the Cayman Islands...

Step 1: Choose Your Company Type. Select the most appropriate offshore company structure for your needs, such as an Exempted Company, Limited Liability Company (LLC), or a Special Economic Zone Company.

Step 2: Pick A Company Name. Verify that your desired company name is available and complies with Cayman Islands naming rules. The name should be unique and must include a suffix that indicates limited liability.

Step 3: Appoint A Registered Agent. You will need to hire a licensed registered agent located in the Cayman Islands. This agent manages legal correspondence and serves as a link between your company and the government.

Step 4: Prepare And Submit Incorporation Documents. File the required documents with the Cayman Islands Registrar of Companies. These typically include the Memorandum and Articles of Association, information about directors and shareholders, and the registered office address.

Step 5: Pay Government Fees. Initial registration and ongoing annual fees must be paid to keep the company compliant and in good standing.

Step 6: Meet Regulatory Obligations. Depending on your business activities, you may need to obtain licenses or permits. Compliance with regulations such as anti-money laundering (AML) and know your customer (KYC) is also necessary.

Step 7: Understand Financial Responsibilities. Be aware of taxation rules, fees, licensing requirements, and banking options relevant to your company.

Step 8: Open A Bank Account. Although not mandatory for incorporation, opening a bank account is typically necessary for business operations. This can be done locally or in another jurisdiction, depending on your needs.

Step 9: Maintain Proper Records. Keep thorough company records and fulfil any reporting obligations, including filing annual returns or financial statements as required.

Step 10: Seek Professional Guidance. Due to the complexities involved in international business and Cayman Islands regulations, consulting with legal and financial professionals experienced in offshore company formation is highly recommended.

THE CAYMAN ISLANDS

For The Crypto Millionaire

For a true jet-set lifestyle, the Cayman Islands are hard to beat. Grand Cayman is arguably one of the most active entertainment capitals in the Caribbean today. In addition, it offers excellent schools, world-class doctors, fantastic restaurants, developed infrastructure, and everything you could possibly need for a comfortable life.

For crypto investors and founders, that last point matters more than you might realize. Cayman is not a remote island in any meaningful sense. Internet connectivity is fast and reliable, power outages are rare, and professional services—from legal and accounting to fund administration—are accustomed to working with global, time-sensitive financial operations, including crypto funds and blockchain companies.

Of course, you'll pay for your beautiful views and tax-free status. As on most islands where everything has to be imported, prices are high. Import duties (the government's primary source of revenue) are about 22%, and while some items are exempt, others are taxed at a higher rate based on their value. Duty tax on an expensive car, for example, may be as high as 42%.

For high-earning investors—including those whose wealth is largely digital—this trade-off is often acceptable. There is no local income tax, no capital gains tax, and no tax on crypto trading or long-term holdings at the Cayman level. For many crypto investors, that means daily life may be expensive, but the jurisdiction itself does not erode portfolio gains.

The jet-set lifestyle on offer here is standout and the residency requirements ensure you can afford it. That said, the locals themselves are not a wealthy group. The minimum wage is CI$6 (around $7) an hour, and a drive across Grand Cayman exposes the socio-economic disparity.

There are really two faces to Grand Cayman. Its western side is home to touristy Seven Mile Beach, with active nightlife and world-class dining, as well as the busy port of George Town—also the heart of the financial services industry. This proximity is appealing for crypto investors who want to live close to banks, law firms, and regulators that understand complex investment structures.

The cliffs and marshland on the island's East End and North Side are quieter, offering privacy and space for those who prefer a lower-profile lifestyle.

No wonder it appeals to so many vacationers—you can holiday at the luxurious Ritz-Carlton or stay in a low-key West Bay Airbnb. And it's safe, friendly, and family-oriented—there is no gambling here or casinos. For crypto investors used to volatility in markets, the predictability and calm of daily life in Cayman is often an underrated benefit.

Grand Cayman is breathtakingly beautiful, and even though it's the most developed of the three islands (with a population of roughly 67,000), naturalists will be happy here as well. Like its Sister Islands, Grand Cayman offers excellent diving and snorkeling sites, as well as some of the largest untouched mangrove glades in the Caribbean. It's not unusual to take a morning call with Asia or the U.S., then spend the afternoon underwater.

For crypto investors, Cayman's time zone is another low-key advantage. Operating on Eastern Time makes it easy to stay aligned with U.S. markets, regulators, and counterparties, while still being globally accessible. Flights to major financial hubs are frequent and direct, which matters when your assets—and opportunities—are international.

In short, it's beautiful, tax-free, and friendly... plus it's an easy place to live and get around. Things work. People care. There's a small-town feel with a strong sense of community, and it's super safe. Cayman proudly boasts one of the lowest crime rates in the Caribbean.

CHAPTER XVIII

★★★

MALTA

Blockchain Island

Malta has always intrigued me...

Thanks to its central location in the Mediterranean, this little island nation has a complicated history. Over the centuries, every regional power has wanted to control the islands of Malta...from the Phoenicians in the seventh century B.C. to Carthage, Rome, the Vandals, the Byzantines, the Ottoman, and, most recently, the Germans and the Italians in World War II.

Malta remains a sought-after destination, though no longer among those who would try to rule it. Today Malta, part of the European Union, is an offshore haven, an interesting choice for someone looking to establish residency, set up a corporation, open a bank account, and pay no or little local tax, all in a country where English is one of the official languages.

The Maltese archipelago (made up of three main islands) is one of Europe's smallest countries but it has a lot to offer. Its rugged coastline boasts dramatic cliffs and tiny coves dotted with ancient forts and quaint fishing harbors. Inland, walls of coffee froth dry stone separate fields cut into strips of olives, wheat, and potatoes. Wine production is also popular and vines hang heavy with grapes all over the island.

Malta's Mediterranean location means its scenery changes dramatically over the course of the year. The islands enjoy a daily average of around 12 hours of sunshine in summer going down to five to six hours in midwinter. It makes for a landscape that switches from green and verdant to dry and parched in the height of the summer.

The Maltese language, Malti, is thought to derive from the language of the ancient Phoenicians who arrived in Malta in 750 B.C. Peppered with many foreign words, particularly English, Italian, and Arabic, it has been a source of fascination for linguists and historians for many years in that it is the only Semitic language written in Latin characters.

English, however, is also an official language and is widely and fluently spoken. The level of English fluency among the population is remarkable—literally everyone is fluent. And it's not just used in casual conversation—business, banking, and legal affairs are all conducted in English.

Malta is a member of the European Union and the currency used is the euro. While Ireland lays claim to being the only English-speaking country in the Eurozone, the fact that Malta has English as a second official language means it too has a good case to make. That positions Ireland and Malta as the gateway countries for major companies—particularly from the United States—looking to access the Eurozone market via an English-speaking base. For such a tiny nation, that's a major attribute to have in its favor.

The Maltese Islands have always been outward-looking. They went through a golden era during the Neolithic period some 7,000 years ago. The remains of this civilization, which predates the Egyptians and the people who built Stonehenge by several thousand years, are a number of mysterious temples dedicated to the goddess of fertility. Later, the island would fall to the Phoenicians, the Carthaginians, the Romans, and the Byzantines, all of whom left their mark on the islands.

The Maltese people are overwhelmingly Roman Catholic and the religion's presence on the islands dates back to 60 A.D. when St. Paul is said to have been shipwrecked there while on his way to Rome.

The Maltese Islands found themselves marooned in the middle of the empire carved out by the Arabs in the ninth century and after repeated raids and failed attacks. Malta finally fell to Muslim invaders in 870 A.D.

After subsequent periods under the Normans and the Aragonese, the islands were gifted to a band of knights called the Sovereign Military Order of St. John of Jerusalem by Charles V in 1530.

The group, which had been established to provide protection and health care to religious pilgrims arriving in Jerusalem from the Christian regions of Europe before being banished by the Arabs, took the island into a new golden age and much of its most prized historical buildings date from the period.

The islands took their place as a hub of Mediterranean artistic and architectural excellence and artists such as Caravaggio, Mattia Preti, and Favray were commissioned by the knights to embellish churches, palaces, and auberges.

The era of the knights came to an end in 1798 when Napoleon Bonaparte swept into Malta en route to Egypt. The French didn't stay long—they were ousted by the English after the Maltese requested their help. The English would remain in control of the islands right up until 1964 when Malta secured its independence.

Although steeped in history, Malta is very much a modern European nation. The standard of education in Malta is high and its people are industrious and outward looking.

Another big positive for anyone planning on spending time here is that Malta has a fantastic standard of medical care. The knights who ruled the country for 300 years were first established to provide care to the often ragged pilgrims turning up in Jerusalem. During World War I, the island acted as a hospital providing high level care to injured and sick soldiers.

Today, it is home to a number of state-of-the-art public and private facilities with highly-trained staff who are all fluent in English. While health care coverage normally comes as a residency requirement for foreigners, you can expect to pay considerably less than you would in the United States.

Malta Residency

U.S. and Canadian citizens are automatically granted a 90-day tourist visa when entering the country. This is a short-stay Schengen visa, allowing you 90 days within the Schengen Zone at large, not just Malta.

For longer stays, Malta offers a number of Residency and Citizenship options.

Global Residence Program (GRP)

Launched in 2013, the Malta Global Residence Program allows non-EU/EEA/Swiss nationals and their dependents to settle in Malta.

The program offers the applicant a flat rate tax of 15% on income remitted to Malta with a minimum tax liability of €15,000 per year. This amount also covers all dependents.

Qualifying dependents may include the spouse or partner of the main applicant, dependent children under the age of 25, and dependent brothers, sisters, and direct relatives (provided that the Director of Inland Revenue is satisfied that these are genuine dependents of the beneficiary of the program). The scheme even allows for employees (anything from a caretaker to a butler) as long as you have been employing them for the preceding two years.

As well as giving you the right to reside in Malta for as long as you like, the Global Residence Program has the key advantage of offering those who secure it the ability to move freely throughout all the other Schengen countries in the EU. In effect, it's a gateway program that gives you the keys to the entire continent.

Qualifying Requirements

- You must be a third-country national (non-EU/EEA/Swiss).

- You may not already benefit from or be enrolled in any other Maltese special tax/residence schemes.
- You must have sufficient, stable, and regular financial resources for you and your dependents.
- You must hold adequate health insurance covering all risks across the EU for you and your dependents.
- You must undergo due diligence and background checks.
- You must be able to communicate in English or Maltese.

You will also need to hold a qualifying property in Malta or Gozo as your principal residence. This property cannot be sublet.

For real estate purchases, the minimum purchase price is €220,000 in Gozo/South Malta and €275,000 for the rest of Malta.

For rental properties, the minimum annual rental is €8,750 in Gozo/South Malta and €9,600 in the rest of Malta.

You will need to pay a one-off administrative fee of €6,000 though this is reduced to €5,500 if your qualifying property is in Gozo/South Malta.

The Minimum annual tax of €15,000 is payable on foreign income remitted to Malta.

Applicants must not reside in any other jurisdiction for more than 183 days in a calendar year.

Applicants must continue to hold their qualifying property and health insurance, and meet their reporting/tax obligations annually.

Malta Permanent Residence Programme (MPRP)

The Malta Permanent Residence Programme—a residency by investment program for non-EU/EEA/Swiss nationals—was launched in 2021.

To qualify, applicants must show proof of assets of at least €500,000—a minimum of €150,000 of which are in the form of financial assets. Alternatively, the applicant may show capital of

€650,000 of which at least €75,000 is held in financial assets.

Under the MPRP there is no minimum physical stay requirement in Malta but qualifying real estate must be held for five years.

MPRP applicants are also required to:

- Undergo due diligence and background checks.
- Hold adequate health insurance.
- Pay a one-time government administrative fee of €60,000 with an additional €7,500 payable for each adult dependent. Qualifying dependents include the main applicant's spouse or partner, dependent children up to the age of 28, and dependent parents and grandparents.
- Pay a government contribution of €37,000 within eight months of Approval in Principle.
- Rent a property in Malta for a minimum of €14,000 per year or purchase real estate valued at a minimum of €375,000. Beneficiaries who purchase property under the MPRP are free to rent out their qualifying property in line with Residency Malta Agency guidelines.
- Donate €2,000 to a local registered philanthropic, cultural, sport, scientific, animal welfare, or artistic NGO.

In order to apply, applicants must appoint a Licensed Agent and the process typically takes around six months.

Malta Retirement Programme (MRP)

The Malta Retirement Programme (MRP) allows retirees to live in Malta and enjoy certain tax benefits. To qualify, applicants must rent or buy property of a set minimum value, hold adequate health insurance covering Malta and the EU, and show proof of financial stability. Those in the program pay a 15% tax on foreign pension income sent to Malta with a minimum yearly tax of €7,500 (plus €500 per dependent).

The real estate requirements are purchasing a home worth at least €275,000 in Malta or €220,000 in Gozo/South Malta or renting a property for at least €9,600 per year or €8,750 in Gozo/South Malta.

Holders must reside in Malta for at least 90 days per year (averaged over five years) and not spend more than 183 days a year in any other country. For the most part employment is not permitted with the exception of some certain directorship roles.

MRP Eligibility Requirements:

- Applicants must be in receipt of a pension making up 75% of their taxable income.
- Applicants must make Malta their primary residence.
- Hold comprehensive health insurance for Malta and the EU.
- Hold a clean criminal record with no prior visa denials from countries with a visa waiver agreement with Malta.
- Must not be profiting from another Malta residence program.
- Must own or rent qualifying property as a primary residence.
- Must have sufficient financial resources to support themselves.
- Must speak English or Maltese.
- Must pay minimum tax per year, including for dependents.

Key Benefits Of The MRP:

- Flat 15% tax rate on foreign income remitted to Malta.
- No tax on foreign income brought into Malta.
- No inheritance, wealth, or estate tax.

Malta Nomad Residence Permit (MNRP)

Malta also offers a digital nomad visa—the Nomad Residence

Permit—to those who can prove a minimum gross annual income of €42,000 from a source outside of Malta.

The permit is issued for one year and can be renewed providing the applicant continues to meet the qualifying criteria and can show that they resided in Malta for a minimum period of five months over a 12-month period.

The permit may be renewed a maximum of three times allowing for a total stay of four years.

Family members of Malta Nomad Residence Permit applicants or holders may also apply for a residence permit. Qualifying are the applicant's spouse, minor children, and dependent adult children, however gaining residency in this way does not grant dependents the right to work in Malta. Additionally, parents of the main applicant and/or spouse are not eligible to be included in the application as dependent family members.

The fee for the MNRP is €300 for the main applicant and an additional €300 for each family member.

Malta's Nomad Residence Permit allows you 12 months of income-tax-free living in Malta and a low 10% flat rate thereafter.

Malta Startup Residence Programme (MSRP)

Malta also offers a Malta Startup Residence Programme (MSRP) for non-EU startup founders and employees.

To qualify for this three-year visa (renewable for a further five years), business activities must be in one of the followings sectors:

- Manufacturing.
- Software development.
- Industrial services analogous to manufacturing.
- Health, biotechnology, pharmaceuticals, and life sciences.
- Eco startups involved in the blue, green and sustainable industries.
- Other innovative economic activities which are enabled

through knowledge and technology providing services or products which are currently not readily available in the relevant market or which shall be provided through a process which is novel.

The startup incorporated in Malta is required to have a tangible investment or paid-up share capital of at least €25,000. If more than four co-founders apply for the MSRP, an additional €10,000 must be invested for each additional co-founder.

Beneficiaries of the MSRP must live and pay taxes in Malta, and are subject to statutory Maltese tax rules.

Malta Citizenship

Maltese citizenship can be obtained through naturalization, marriage, descent, or through the country's citizenship-by-merit program. There are no restrictions on dual citizenship in Malta.

You can apply for Maltese citizenship after fulfilling standard residency and integration requirements which are generally several years of legal residence, language ability, and proof of good character.

In Malta, citizenship by marriage happens through a process known as "registration." To qualify, you will need to have been married to a Maltese citizen for at least five years and you will need to also have lived together for five years preceding your application. You do not have to have lived together in Malta to apply.

If you have Maltese ancestry (e.g., a parent or grand-parent born in Malta) or were adopted under Maltese law, you may be eligible for citizenship by descent.

Malta Citizenship-By-Merit Program

In 2025, Malta's golden visa program was terminated and its

citizenship-by-merit program was introduced.

In order to qualify you will need to be able to show "an exceptional contribution to the national interest" of Malta by showing significant services, contributions, or talents in fields such as philanthropy, sport, culture, the arts, science, technology, or entrepreneurship.

Banking In Malta

The Maltese banking system is very safe and Malta has never been forced to seek any bailouts for its financial institutions. In fact, Malta came out of the downturn smelling of roses. In the wake of the banking crisis that hit Europe, the EU put together a series of stringent stress tests to check the viability of financial institutions around the Union. Malta's banks passed the stress tests with flying colors.

Malta's banking sector is well set up to provide services to international clients.

The main banks in Malta today include:

Bank of Valletta (BOV)

BOV is the largest, most established bank in Malta. It offers a full range of retail, business, and wealth services and has an extensive branch and ATM network making it a go to for everyday banking and mortgages.

HSBC Bank Malta

HSBC Malta is the local subsidiary of the global HSBC Group, known for its international banking capabilities, multicurrency accounts, and global connectivity.

APS Bank

APS Bank is a long standing Maltese institution with a strong presence in retail and corporate banking. It's known for good customer service and is generally well-regarded by expats.

BNF Bank

Formerly Banif Bank, BNF Bank offers everyday banking products and mortgage options. Expats appreciate the bank's easy account setup process and responsive customer service.

MeDirect Bank

MeDirect (formerly Mediterranean Bank) focuses on savings, investment, wealth management, and personal accounts. It offers online banking and is considered a good choice for investment oriented clients.

Lombard Bank Malta

Domestic bank Lombard offers a range of retail and business banking services. It's smaller than BOV and HSBC but well-regarded for its flexible business banking solutions and personalized service.

In general, foreigners will normally be required to provide a reference from bankers in their home country in addition to the usual documents when setting up an account in Malta. The account opening process can be slower than in some other EU countries so some expats also use EU online banks such as Revolut or Wise in conjunction to their in-country account.

Banks are normally open until early afternoon from Monday to Friday, and until midday on Saturday. Some banks or branches work longer hours. International bankcards are accepted and foreign currency is easily exchanged. Banks, ATMs, and exchange bureaus can be found all over the islands. The majority of hotels, larger shops, and restaurants also accept payment in the main international currencies.

Taxes In Malta

Taxes in Malta may appear stiff at first glance because of the relatively high marginal tax rate but there are plenty of legal loopholes to get your tax rate down to 15%.

Malta operates a residence-and-domicile-based tax system. Individuals who are resident and domiciled in Malta are taxed on their worldwide income, while residents who are not domiciled in Malta are taxed only on Maltese-source income and on foreign income that is remitted to Malta.

Malta has an extensive double-tax treaty network, including treaties with both the United States and Canada, which helps prevent double taxation.

In addition, Malta offers special residence and retirement programs that can provide flat or reduced tax rates on qualifying income, making the system particularly attractive for retirees and internationally mobile investors.

Are You A Tax Resident?

In Malta, tax residency is determined by a combination of residence and domicile status.

You are generally considered a resident for tax purposes if you live in Malta for six months (183 days) or more during a calendar year. However, even if the physical presence threshold is not met, you may be deemed a tax resident in Malta if you are considered to have a "durable connection" with Malta.

Domicile status can be established by birth, by intent to make

Malta your permanent home, or by long-term presence.

Married individuals where one spouse is both resident and domiciled in Malta may also be subject to taxation on worldwide income, as the couple's combined status affects their overall tax liability.

Tax residents are generally liable for tax on their worldwide income, while non-residents are only taxed on income arising in Malta.

Malta Tax Rates

- **Income Tax:** 0% (income under €12,000) to 35% (income over €60,001).
- **VAT:** 18% (standard) with reduced rates of 5%, 7%, and 12% on some goods and services.
- **Social Security:** 10% up to a max of €55.93 per week, and max €83.89 per week if self-employed.
- **Capital Gains Tax:** Generally taxed as ordinary income, except transfers of Maltese property, which are subject to an 8% tax.
- **Real Estate Tax:** 0%.
- Rental Income Tax: 15% optional flat tax, otherwise taxed at ordinary income rates (0%–35%).
- **Wealth Tax:** 0%.
- **Corporate Tax:** 35% but if you trade locally you can get a rebate of up to 6/7ths of the taxes you pay.
- **Dividends:** Taxed at ordinary rates, with credits for foreign taxes.
- **Transfer Tax:** 8% standard; 5% on primary residence, with the first €86,000 of the value exempt if you are reinvesting in another Maltese property.
- **Inheritance Tax:** 0% on securities; property transfers on death are subject to stamp duty (~5%), with a reduced effective rate (~3.5%) on part of the value for close heirs.
- **Interest:** 0% on bank accounts.

- **Royalties:** 0% for qualifying IP; otherwise taxed at normal rates.
- **Exit Tax:** Anti Tax Avoidance Directive (ATAD) based. Applies to unrealized gains on certain assets if an individual or company moves tax residence out of Malta; not triggered for ordinary bank accounts or fully taxed income.

Malta Loopholes And Deductions

Several of Malta's residency programs offer a 15% flat tax on foreign sourced income remitted to Malta.

Certain persons employed in Malta in the financial services, gaming, aviation, maritime, and offshore oil and gas get a flat 15% rate.

Malta's digital nomad visa allows holders 12 months of income-tax-free living and a low 10% flat rate thereafter.

Artists can claim a flat rate of 7.5% on their first €50,000 in income.

Malta allows specific personal deductions for certain fees (with caps) against taxable income including private school fees, childcare, sports, creative and cultural activities for children, and homes for the elderly, and interest paid on money borrowed for investing. Alimony payments are also tax deductible.

Reat Estate In Malta

Investment in a property (unless you go the route of renting your residence) is, as mentioned, a requirement for those looking to stay in the country long-term under the Permanent Residence Programme, Global Residence Programme, and Retirement Programme.

Malta's real estate market has historically shown strong long-term growth in property values. From 2013 to 2023 values more than doubled. Over the past three years, Malta's Residential Property Price Index (RPPI) has continued to grow year-on-year, with prices up around 5.7% in 2025 versus 2024.

Significant downturns have been rare. During the 2009 global financial crisis property prices dropped around 5%.

Around 75% of Malta's residents own their own homes and about 50% of the remaining population lives in rent-controlled properties.

Malta's limited supply of developable land has kept upward pressure on property prices and there is strong demand from both local buyers and international investors.

Buying property in Malta is generally a pretty straightforward process, but non-EU/EEA citizens (and EU nationals who do not meet the five-year residency criteria) will need to acquire an Acquisition of Immovable Property (AIP) permit when buying a property.

This permit allows you to purchase one property which cannot be rented out.

The minimum purchase value for AIP properties as of 2026 is €174,274 for apartments and maisonettes and €300,619 for other immovable property.

However, if you look within Special Designated Areas (SDAs), you can buy multiple properties and rent them out without needing an AIP permit and without minimum investment thresholds.

In Malta a 5% stamp duty is applied to property purchases. Sales are subject to an 8% capital gains or final withholding tax.

For sellers, properties that have served as their primary residence for at least three years are exempt from the 8% tax, while properties sold after less than three or five years may qualify for a reduced rate of 2% or 5%, respectively.

Taxes on property transactions are calculated on the full sale price.

As of 2026, Malta's residential property market continues to show moderate price growth, with official data indicating annual increases of around 5%–7 %.

The average house price falls roughly between €220,000 and €550,000 depending on the property size and location.

Doing Business In Malta

Starting a business in Malta is relatively straightforward. While the country's legal system is primarily based on civil law, it incorporates significant English legal principles in commercial and corporate matters, which makes it familiar to investors from common-law jurisdictions.

Malta has developed a reputation as a business-friendly environment within the EU, with a strong focus on sectors such as financial services, information technology, online gaming, and knowledge-based industries. Its strategic location, multilingual workforce, and EU membership make it an attractive base for international companies.

The Maltese economy has remained resilient in recent years, maintaining stable growth and low unemployment. Corporate taxation is competitive: the statutory rate is 35%, but Malta's full imputation system and refund mechanisms can reduce the effective tax on distributed profits to as low as around 5% for many companies.

Personal income tax is progressive, reaching up to 35% at higher income levels, while a variety of incentives exist for foreign investors and certain professionals.

Setting up a company in Malta can be completed within a few days once the necessary documentation and compliance checks are in place, and the costs are relatively low compared to many other EU countries. Both local and international service providers offer guidance on company formation, tax planning, and regulatory compliance.

Malta encourages entrepreneurship, but regulated industries—such as financial services, insurance, and certain medical or pharmaceutical professions—require licenses or authorizations. For most commercial activities, no special permits are needed. The most common corporate structure is the private limited company (Ltd), though sole traders and partnerships are also options.

The Companies Act incorporates elements of English company law but has been modernized to meet EU directives and standards. Companies benefit from Malta's full imputation tax system, which eliminates economic double taxation: shareholders can claim a tax credit for the corporate tax already paid, and many are eligible for refunds, enhancing the overall attractiveness of the jurisdiction for both trading and holding entities.

MALTA

For The Crypto Millionaire

For North Americans looking for a European base with global reach, Malta offers a rare combination of lifestyle, legal certainty, and strategic positioning.

Sitting at the crossroads of Europe, North Africa, and the Middle East, Malta feels both distinctly European and refreshingly international. English is an official language, the legal system is based on English common law influences, and daily life is easy to navigate for newcomers.

From a quality-of-life perspective, Malta punches above its weight. Health care is excellent and affordable, private schools are widely available, and the island enjoys more than 300 days of sunshine a year.

The pace of life is slower than in major North American cities, but the infrastructure is modern: reliable Internet, strong mobile coverage, and easy access to the rest of Europe via frequent flights. You can be in London, Zurich, or Paris in a few hours, making Malta an appealing base for globally mobile professionals and investors.

For crypto investors in particular, Malta has spent the last several years positioning itself as a jurisdiction that understands digital assets. Early on, the government chose to regulate blockchain and crypto activity. Today there is a clear legal framework for exchanges, custodians, and other virtual asset service providers, giving investors and founders a level of certainty still lacking in many countries.

While Malta is not tax-free, its tax system can be highly efficient when properly structured. There is no wealth tax, no inheritance tax, and no tax on long-term capital gains in certain circumstances. For North Americans who organize their affairs carefully and take professional advice, Malta can serve as a low-friction European hub rather than a high-tax trap.

Residency options are another draw. Malta offers multiple pathways for non-EU nationals, including programs tied to investment, remote work, or financial self-sufficiency. For crypto investors who do not need local employment and whose income is largely portfolio-based or generated online, this flexibility is especially valuable. You can live legally in Malta without being forced into a traditional employer-employee model.

Lifestyle-wise, Malta has its contrasts. Coastal areas like Sliema and St. Julian's are lively and cosmopolitan, with modern apartments, marinas, and an active dining scene. Other parts of the island remain quiet and traditional, with stone villages, local markets, and a strong sense of history. Whether you prefer a social, urban environment or something more low-key, the island offers options within a short drive.

Safety is another key advantage. Malta has low violent crime rates and a strong sense of community. For investors managing significant digital or financial assets, such stability matters. It's an environment where discretion is the norm and wealth is not generally flaunted.

Ultimately, Malta appeals to those seeking European access without cultural friction, and to crypto investors who prize regulatory clarity, legal predictability, and a comfortable lifestyle.

For investors seeking a credible, livable base within the EU, Malta remains an appealing choice.

CHAPTER XIX

★ ★ ★

PORTUGAL

Europe's Old World Treasure

With its mild, almost Mediterranean climate, over 300 days of sunshine a year, a beautiful coastline with 150 great sandy beaches, status as one of the safest countries in the world, with friendly locals, great cuisine, fine local wines, and a low cost of living with easy residency options, it's easy to understand why Portugal is the number one choice for so many North American expats.

Portugal stands out among expat havens for the following key reasons:

1. The Weather

Portugal's Algarve enjoys one of the most stable climates in the world and 3,300 hours of sunshine per year, meaning more sunny days than almost anywhere else in Europe. As a result, the Algarve has a long-standing reputation as a top summer destination among European sun-seekers and a top winter retreat for those looking to escape Northern Europe's coldest months.

The Algarve has no bad weather months, but it does have a winter. January and February can be cold enough that you'll want a coat. The best months can be September and October, when the summer crowds have gone but the weather and sea temperature are still ideal.

2. Safety

Portugal ranks as the seventh safest country in the world. Violent crime is rare, and petty crime is limited to street crime during the busy tourist season.

3. Solid Infrastructure

Portugal has enjoyed important infrastructure investments in recent years, specifically to do with the country's highway network and airports. As a result, this is an easy region to get around and also a great base for exploring all of Europe and North Africa.

4. Excellent Health Care

Medical tourism is a growing industry in Portugal, in particular for cosmetic, hip replacement, and dental specialties.

5. Golf

Portugal is home to more than 90 golf courses in different regions, many of which were developed by famous architects. The Algarve region boasts 42 courses in less than 100 miles and is recognized as a top golfing destination in continental Europe and the world.

6. Beaches

The Algarve's 100 miles of Atlantic coastline are punctuated by jagged rock formations, lagoons, and extensive sandy beaches, many awarded coveted Blue Flags from the European Blue Flag Association. The water off these shores is azure, and the cliff-top vistas are spectacular. Most beaches have lifeguards during the summer season.

The Alentejo coast, running from the Algarve to the Setúbal region, is a bit less crowded and more rugged than its southern neighbor. It's a place where cliffs meet untamed beaches and the pace of life slows down.

The beaches of northern Portugal may have cooler waters, but they make up for it with unique settings, rich cultural backdrops, and fewer crowds.

Stretching between Lisbon and Porto, the Silver Coast (Costa de Prata in Portuguese) is known for its surf spots, lagoons, and picturesque seaside towns. It sees fewer tourists than the Algarve but offers equally captivating experiences.

Even the area surrounding the capital, Lisbon, offers a surprising number of excellent beaches. Located just north of Cascais, Praia do Guincho is famous for its strong winds and large waves, making it a hotspot for wind and kitesurfers.

7. Healthy Living

The Portuguese are the biggest fish eaters per capita in Europe, and fresh fish of great variety is available in the ever-present daily markets. The abundance of sunshine in this part of the world means an abundance of fresh produce, too, also available in the local markets.

Meantime, pollution rates are low, and streets, towns, and beaches are kept clean and litter-free.

8. Crypto-Friendly

For a long time Portugal was a standout haven where investors could hold crypto free of capital gains taxes. In 2023, that changed with the introduction of a 28% tax on short-term gains. However, long-term holdings (over 365 days) remain tax-free in most cases.

Although crypto activities are increasingly integrated into

the tax code and subject to reporting, Portugal's overall framework—coupled with its strategic location inside the European Union—offers a balance between innovation friendliness and legal certainty casual investors and entrepreneurs in the blockchain space can respect.

Banking In Portugal

Portugal offers a sophisticated banking system that's integrated worldwide and with international markets. The largest bank is state-owned *Caixa Geral de Depósitos*. For regular banking *Banco Comercial Português* (BCP), *Banco Santander Totta*, and *Novo Banco*. Wealth management banks include *Banco BPI* and Bison Bank.

Portugal's ATM network is considered one of the best in the world. Cheques are rarely used in Portugal. Direct debit is usually used for utilities and other recurring bills. Debit and credit cards are widely used.

Guaranteed Funds

The Central Bank guarantees €100,000 per depositor, per account, per institution.

Banks in Portugal adhere to strict Anti-Money Laundering and Counter-Terrorist Financing regulations which involve thorough customer due diligence and reporting of suspicious activities.

SEPA And SWIFT

SEPA is the Single Euro Payments Area. It facilitates electronic payments, like credit transfers and direct debits, by standardizing procedures and requiring International Bank Account Numbers (IBANs) for all bank accounts.

Transfers within the EU will have the same cost (often €0) and transfer speed of domestic transfers. The SEPA system is for euro-denominated transactions only.

SWIFT is the Society for Worldwide Interbank Financial Telecommunications. It is a secure, global messaging network that facilitates international money transfers between banks and financial institutions. The SWIFT network enables secure international money transfers in any currency.

Opening A Bank Account In Portugal

Opening a bank account in Portugal is a fairly straightforward process. You'll need to provide several key documents, including proof of address, a tax identification number (*Número de Identificação Fiscal*, NIF), and valid ID (such as a passport). Proof of employment may also be required where applicable.

For certain banks an FBI report may also be required, particularly in the case of investment banking.

When opening an account for business purposes you will need to provide ID and proof of address for both the Ultimate Beneficial Owner (UBO) and manager. Also required are articles of incorporation, the taxpayer number of the company and director, documents attesting binding powers and resolution, and compliance verification.

Types Of Account

Checking / Current Account (*Conta Corrente*)

- Allows withdrawals and deposits.
- Connected to debit card.
- For everyday transactions such as purchases, bills, and ATM services.

- Most are free but some banks charge fees.
- Low to nil interest rates.

Instant Access Savings Account (*Conta Poupança*)

- Standard rates of interest.
- Easy access of funds.

Time-Deposit Savings Account (*Conta de Depósito a Prazo*)

- Higher rates of interest.
- Minimum deposits and time periods that funds must stay in the account.
- For long-term savings.

International Money Transfers

There are no limits on the amount of money that can be transferred in or out of Portugal and no FX controls.

Transfers between Portuguese banks and banks within EU, the EEA, and Switzerland cost no more than a domestic transfer, providing the money is paid in Euros and is less than €50,000.

Outside the EU/EEA transfers will be subject to fees applied by Portuguese banks, the fee amount will depend on the country.

Residency In Portugal

Portugal is one of the easiest places in Europe to establish residency. You can qualify for residency simply by showing proof that you have reliable ongoing income (whether from financial investments, a pension, or rental income) of at least €1,200 per month. This is known as the D7 Visa, or Passive Income Visa. It's intended for people who wish to live in Portugal, rather than pure investors.

The D7 Visa grants its holders pretty much the same rights as the now-suspended Golden Visa property option once did without making an investment, but it also does not prevent you from doing so. It leaves the choice to you. Once in the country, as a successful D7 Visa holder you can acquire any kind of property at whatever amount you want. However, going that route means you must spend at least 183 days in the country each year, making you a tax resident in the country.

The visa is valid for two years, after which it can be renewed for three years. You can spend six consecutive months or eight non-consecutive months in Portugal to be able to renew your permit. Residency applications must begin in your home country.

In addition to your passport and a visa application, you must do the following:

- Be in Portugal legally (have an address to show).
- Show that you are covered by health insurance.
- Prove that you have a clean criminal record in Portugal and your country of origin.

Before applying for a visa, you must create an online account and pre-register so that you can submit the remaining documents online. The website is VSFGlobal.com.

The Golden Visa

Portugal's Golden Visa program was introduced in 2012 to bolster foreign investment and boost the economy by granting residency to non-EU citizens who made a qualifying investment in Portugal. As of 2023, real estate is no longer eligible, but other investment options remain, such as cultural contributions, scientific research, and certain business or job-creation categories.

For investment in qualifying funds, the minimum amount is €500,000. For scientific research or business investment you will need to commit €500,000. Alternatively, applicants can make a non-refundable contribution of €250,000 to cultural or artistic projects.

Under the program, Golden Visas investors could generally apply for Portuguese citizenship after five years of holding residency however legislation in the works as of mid-2026 looks set to increase this timeline to 10 years.

Citizenship In Portugal

Any person aged 18 or over can apply to be naturalized as a Portuguese citizen after a minimum 10 years of legal residency. That period is reduced to seven years for nationals from the Community of Portuguese Language Countries (CPLP) and three for those who are married or in a common law partnership.

To qualify to become a citizen of Portugal, you'll have to pass a test in Portuguese.

You don't have to be fluent, but you'll need to be able to hold a conversation with the interviewer and take the Portuguese language test to ensure that you have a basic understanding of Portuguese. This is known as the A2 Level *Certificado Inicial de Português Língua Estrangeira* (CIPLE) test.

A history or constitution of the country test is not required.

The whole process of obtaining Portuguese citizenship by naturalization from start to finish takes about a year. The Minister of Justice makes the final decision on the application for citizenship. If the application is approved, they will notify the National Archives of Portugal that your citizenship has been granted.

The applicant is notified via the contact details they provided. The applicant will receive an ID card that includes a fingerprint chip and their personal information such as their social security, health insurance, and tax identification number. After receiving the ID card, you can apply for a passport at the nearest passport authority office with your ID card.

Portugal allows you to hold multiple citizenships, meaning foreigners can obtain Portuguese nationality without having to give up their previous citizenship.

Citizenship By Descent

Portugal recognizes *jus sanguinis* as well as *jus soli* in certain circumstances. Parents must have been legally resident in the country for five years in order to seek citizenship for their children born in the country; children born in Portugal to parents on tourist or short-stay visas are ineligible to seek citizenship.

Children born to Portuguese parents overseas must be registered with the country or declare their desire to obtain citizenship in order to gain it. This step can be skipped if the child has a Portuguese parent and grandparent. Children and grandchildren of Portuguese citizens that have their birth registered with the civil registry and indicate they want to be recognized as citizens are accepted under this liberal arrangement.

Portugal began granting citizenship to foreign-born grandchildren of Portuguese citizens in 2006. Individuals from the former Portuguese colonies of Macau, East Timor, and Estado da India can apply for citizenship, too.

Note that Portuguese citizenship obtained by naturalization cannot be transmitted to descendants already over the age of 18 at the time of their parent's naturalization. Children under the age of 18 can apply upon the naturalization of at least one of the parents.

Portugal also offers a citizenship-through-ancestry option for anyone who can prove a Sephardic Jewish connection in his/her family tree. Portugal (and Spain) expelled their Jewish population more than 500 years ago. In 2015, Portugal enacted a new citizenship regime designed to make amends with its inquisitorial past.

Tracing your Jewish origins back to Portugal is the key requirement for citizenship. Evidence of ancestry may include Sephardic Jewish traditions, family names, family trees, synagogue records, ketubahs, objects, and documents that allow applicants to prove a Portuguese Sephardic ancestral origin.

A Portuguese Jewish community must validate the applicant's Jewish ancestry. The process is then filed with the Central Registry Offices in Lisbon for final approval. Only adults or emancipated persons can apply for citizenship under this special regime. Minors and spouses can later apply for citizenship under the general naturalization rules.

Citizenship By Marriage

A foreign national married to a Portuguese can apply for naturalization after three years of marriage. A foreigner can also apply if they're in a common law partnership if the union is proved in court first. Portugal recognizes same-sex marriages since 2010.

Taxes In Portugal

Portugal has a progressive income tax regime that goes from 13% all the way up to 48%, but on the plus side it's generally even cheaper to live in Portugal than Spain or France.

In Portugal, you are a tax resident if you spend 183 days or more per year in the country, whether you're a legal resident or not.

Qualifiers for Tax Residency in Portugal
(Any of these qualify you)

1. Your Primary Residence is in Portugal
2. You spend 183 days in any 365-day period in Portugal

The United States has a tax treaty with Portugal (as it does with many countries). The treaty with Portugal has the United States taxing the Social Security income of Americans resident in Portugal… and Portugal taxing their pension income.

If your home country has a Double Taxation Agreement (DTA) with Portugal, you won't pay any tax on dividends, interest, royalties, capital gains, rental income from real estate outside Portugal, or income from employment in another country. These are paid in the country where the income is from. For example, if you're working for an American company, you won't be paying income tax in Portugal under the Double Taxation Agreement.

Residents in Portugal pay personal income tax on their earnings. Married couples should submit a joint return. The couple's collective income is divided in two to calculate the tax rate. Income taxes apply to earnings in employment, self-employment, investments, rental income from properties in Portugal, capital gains from selling properties, assets or shares, and pensions in Portugal (including private pension plans).

Income Tax

From €0 to €8,059: 12.5%
From €8,059 to €12,160: 16%
From €12,160 to €17,233: 21.5%
From €17,233 to €22,306: 24.4%
From €22,306 to €28,400: 31.4%
From €28,400 to €41,629: 34.9%
From €41,629 to €44,987: 43.1%
From €44,987 to €83,696: 44.6%
From €83,696 up: 48%

* An extra rate, from 2.5% to 5% applies to income from €80,000 to €250,000. Benefits in kind are taxed as income.

VAT: 23%; reduced rates of 6% and 13%.

Sales Tax (*Imposto Sobre o Valor Acrescentado* or IVA) is charged nationally, based on the type of product or services. IVA rates are high, ranging from some zero-rated services to 6% for basic products, 13% at the intermediate tier, and 23% at the highest tier. IVA is included in all products and services. However, due to the high rates, some service providers don't issue a formal IVA-compliant receipt unless specifically requested to do so.

Social Security: 11% and 21.4% for self-employees.

Capital Gains: 28% for individuals, but this can be 0% if the property is your primary residence for the last 12 months and you reinvest the proceeds into another primary residence in the EU within 36 months. 10% to 30% of gains may be excluded if you held the assets for between two and eight years. Non tax-residents get a 50% deduction on gains on real estate but pay the marginal income tax rate thereafter. You get a 50% tax break on profits from shares in small companies.

Crypto Taxes: Even with increased regulation, Portugal keeps crypto taxes relatively simple. If you hold your crypto for more than a year, any gains you make are generally tax-free. Sell or trade crypto you've held for less than 12 months, and profits are usually taxed at a flat 28% rate.

Income from activities like staking, lending, or frequent trading can also be taxed, especially if it looks more like a business than a hobby.

Rental Income Tax: Rental income is taxed at 28%, but you can deduct all expenses except finance costs, depreciation, furniture, appliances, and decorations. You can even claw back eligible expenses from up to 24 months prior to the rental. As a taxpayer, you can choose to add it to other categories of income and have all taxed at progressive rates. Foreign rental income is exempt if it's already taxed in your home country.

If you own property in Portugal, you must pay the *Imposto Municipal Sobre Imóveis* (IMI). Rates vary according to the municipality and are levied on the tax assessed value of the property. It ranges from 0.3% to 0.45% for urban property; 0.8% for rural property; 7.5% for property owners residing in a "low-tax" jurisdiction or "tax haven."

Property Wealth Tax is known as *Adicional Imposto Municipal Sobre Imóveis* (AIMI). It affects owners with a share in Portuguese property worth over €600,000. If you're a married couple that owns the property, you'd only pay AIMI if the value is over 1.2 million euros. The rates are 0.4% on the total amount for properties held by companies, 0.7% for individuals, and 1% for those owning property valued over 1 million euros.

Transfer Tax: 0% to 7.5% based on value

Inheritance Tax: Portugal eliminated inheritance tax many years ago but a stamp duty known as *Imposto do Selo* may apply at a rate of 10%. This must be done within three months from the date of death. You may have to pay a fine if you don't pay it within three months.

Business Taxes: If you own a business in Portugal, there's a flat rate of 21% of any taxable profits. Local municipality surcharges of up to 1.5% apply. If your company has profits of more than 1.5 million euros, additional charges apply.

A 17% corporate tax rate is applied for small- and medium-sized companies in mainland Portugal, 11.9% in Madeira, and 12.5% in other areas on their first €25,000 of taxable profit.

If your business has less than €200,000 turnover you can elect to only pay 0.15% of sales of products or 0.75% of income arising from business and professional services, and 0.95% for crypto.

Tax credits are available for foreign taxes paid on foreign-source income.

VAT Rebates: You can claim VAT rebates of between 1% and 100% on a myriad of expenses, too long to mention here.

Crypto: No tax on cryptocurrency held for more than 365 days.

Portugal's higher progressive tax rates for residents than non-residents means it may be cheaper to snowbird into Portugal but not become tax resident. The cost of living is very low but even with the taxation agreement with the U.S., the rate of taxes you would pay could be more than in the U.S.

Doing Business In Portugal

Anyone operating a business in Portugal after having run one in the U.S. or the U.K., for example, will find it more difficult. Although new Citizen's Stores (*Loja do Cidadão*) are intended to ease the burden of red tape by allowing one-stop shopping for government services such as company registration and financial filings, the myriad of obligations are complicated and many require validation by a TOC (an 'official' accountant registered with a central professional body).

The government is working on methods of simplifying this and automation has seen a huge improvement in service levels, but the underlying procedures and multi-stage approvals are still cumbersome.

The minimum wage in Portugal is €920 per month. The standard workweek is 40 hours. Typically, work days begin at 9 a.m. and ends at 7 p.m. with a two-hour lunch break in the middle of the day. Regular salaried employees are entitled to 22 days of paid vacation annually along with 12 public holidays.

All workers must pay social security taxes. Employees contracted either full-time or part-time to a multinational company, Portuguese company, or foreign company operating in Portugal will have those contributions deducted automatically from their monthly salary. The employee pays between 11% and 15%; the company matches it with a contribution of about 24%.

Workers in certain trades are required to have professional

certifications recognized by the Portuguese government. This is true of trades (electricians, for example) as well as professions like law that may require passing certain written examinations. Real estate agents are also regulated and licensed.

Self-employed individuals are responsible for paying their own social security contributions, as well as deducting income taxes and value-added taxes. These can be paid at post offices or via ATM *Multibanco* machines. Workers wishing to operate in Portugal as sole traders are strongly advised to get professional advice before doing so.

Buying Real Estate In Portugal

Though prices have gone up in recent years, real estate in Portugal remains among the most affordable in Europe.

Further, Portuguese real estate has one of the most favorable price-to-rent ratios (a measure of the profitability of owning a house) and price-to-income ratios (a measure of affordability) in the region. What that means is that housing is cheaper to buy and investors can make more money from rentals than in many other European countries.

Buying and selling real estate in Portugal is a simple, transparent process, but it takes time. The property market in Portugal is well-established and there are no restrictions on the purchase of real estate, and transaction costs are generally low. Most property is sold freehold. The country's property registry system is centralized and very reliable. The law protects property, property rights, and the right to access and use one's own property.

To start the property purchase process, you'll need a personal fiscal number from the local tax office—if you got a local bank account then you were automatically assigned one.

While many countries overseas do not require credentials for real estate agents, Portugal does. You'll find agents in the city with licenses issued by the government.

Stamp duty is 0.8% of the purchase price. Transfer tax is 0% to 8% and can be avoided through the use of a holding company—but offshore companies have maintenance fees, so make sure you understand the costs of the holding company (and be sure they are lower than the transfer tax cost) before committing to this route. Agent fees are between 3% and 5% (plus tax), legal fees between 1% and 2%. The registration fee will be between 0.2% and 1.2%. In total, the buyer can expect to have to pay between 8% and 10% of the property's total value in fees.

Annually, municipal taxes (called IMI or *imposto municipal sobre imóveis*) are charged on properties using a formula accounting for variables which include the size of the property and how many amenities or entertainment items (such as pools, tennis court, etc.) it contains. Each municipality has the right to charge a slightly different IMI value, which range from 0.3% to 0.5%. Older rustic buildings (whose taxable values are normally very low) pay a value of 0.8%.

The Property Purchase Process

1. Upon finding a property you wish to buy you'll sign a letter of intent in the presence of a local lawyer.

2. Once a price has been agreed to by both parties the lawyer will then write the promissory contract with the seller *contrato de promessa de compra e venda*).

   In order to complete the promissory note you'll need the following:

   - Property Registration Certificate (*Certida o de Teor*).
   - Property Tax document (*Caderneta Perdial*).
   - License of Use (*Licenca de Utilização*).

3. You'll have to put down a deposit, usually 10% to 30% of the

total purchase price (you may need a lawyer to negotiate a deposit in the lower end). The deposit is forfeited if the purchaser does not proceed; if the vendor withdraws from the transaction double the deposit is paid back to the purchaser.

4. The buyer pays the remaining balance of the purchase price, transfer tax (*imposto de sisa*), and any attorney or notary fees.

5. Once everything has been paid (usually within about four weeks of signing the promissory note) you'll be able to complete and sign the deed (*escritura de compra e venda*).

6. Finally, you will have to register the deed at the public land registry and tax office. This should be done as soon as possible after signing the deed.

PORTUGAL

For The Crypto Millionaire

Portugal is a land of superlatives. Consistently ranked among the most peaceful countries in the world, it pairs that calm with some of Europe's best beaches, year-round sunshine, championship golf, and famously welcoming locals.

Long before crypto was mainstream, Portugal was an expat hub offering easy residency options, low costs, and playing host to many English-speakers, making it an easy place to move to.

That lifestyle appeal is one reason Portugal has become especially attractive to crypto investors and digital entrepreneurs. The country offers a relaxed pace of life alongside modern infrastructure, strong private health care, and reliable banking—ideal for those managing global assets or working remotely.

Add Portugal's favorable treatment of long-term crypto holdings and it's easy to see why Lisbon and the Algarve in particular are home to a growing community of crypto investors, founders, and funds.

Portugal's blend of Old World charm and modern luxury has also made it a low-key favorite among high net worth individuals. From Lisbon's cobbled streets to the sun-drenched Algarve, the country is awash with elegant villas, boutique hotels, and Michelin-starred restaurants.

Private wine tastings in the Douro Valley, rooftop cocktails in Lisbon, or a marina berth in Cascais all feel effortlessly accessible—without the flashiness of some wealth hubs.

For those who like their freedom as much as their comfort, Portugal delivers. You can spend mornings on championship golf courses or surfing world-class Atlantic breaks, and evenings in members-only clubs, jazz bars, or intimate *Fado* houses...

Whether arriving by private jet, aboard a superyacht, or simply enjoying the flexibility that comes with decentralized wealth,

Portugal offers a refined, discreet lifestyle that suits modern crypto investors perfectly—historic at heart, but built for a globally connected future.

CHAPTER XX

★ ★ ★

THE UNITED ARAB EMIRATES

A Glittering Oasis Of Options

Home to playboy princes and a favorite of fashionistas, the United Arab Emirates (UAE) is a playground of the uber rich and famous… where you'll find glittering skyscrapers, glitzy malls, sparkling superyachts, and purring supercars. This booming corner of the globe also offers world-class infrastructure, safety, and business opportunities.

Comprised of a federation of seven Emirates—Abu Dhabi, Ajman, Dubai, Fujairah, Ras al-Khaimah, Sharjah, and Umm al Quwain—the UAE is located along the eastern coast of the Arabian Peninsula.

Each Emirate is ruled by a Sheikh who is an absolute monarch. Of these seven Sheikhdoms, the capital, Abu Dhabi, has by far the largest area and oil reserves. Dubai is the most populous (home to around 35% of the total population of the UAE), more liberal, and is the tourism and commercial center of the federation.

In Dubai you can marvel at the Burj Khalifa (the world's tallest building) and the iconic Palm Jumeirah—the world's largest man-made island. Experience the sprawling Dubai Mall, the rush of skiing in the Mall of Emirates' vast indoor ski park, and bask in the opulence and entertainment of Global Village where the traditions of some 90 cultures are celebrated.

You can also enjoy desert safaris in ATVs, dune buggies, or atop a camel... and revel in water sports facilities, including flyboarding, fishing, parasailing, and even a jet car, at Jumeirah Beach. And unlike jet-set destinations like Monaco or Switzerland, it won't cost you millions to secure residency here either.

The UAE is a Sunni Muslim state strategically located between Europe, Africa, and Asia. It's a country of dreams built in the desert floating on an ocean of oil money, and offers lavish entertainment and lifestyle opportunities. It has a robust financial system, and a low VAT and corporate tax regime. There are no personal taxes and foreigners don't pay social security either.

The UAE has rapidly positioned itself as a crypto friendly jurisdiction with a clear regulatory framework designed to encourage innovation while ensuring compliance and investor protection.

Cryptocurrency activities are overseen by multiple authorities including the Virtual Asset Regulatory Authority (VARA) in Dubai, the Securities and Commodities Authority (SCA) at the federal level, and other regulators such as the Central Bank of the UAE (CBUAE).

Licensed exchanges, wallet providers, and other virtual asset service providers (VASPs) must follow robust anti money laundering (AML) and know your customer (KYC) requirements and comply with international standards such as the Financial Action Task Force (FATF) Travel Rule for larger transactions.

UAE Residency And Citizenship

Prior to applying for a Residence Visa, you must first get a UAE Entry Permit. This is issued for multiple entries for a duration of six months. You can apply for this permit online and once you are in the UAE you may apply for the residence permit of your choosing.

The UAE offers long-term residency visas, including a Golden Visa, for investors, entrepreneurs, and highly-skilled professionals.

UAE Golden Residence Visa

The UAE Golden Residence Visa is issued for a five- or 10-year period, depending on the eligibility category of the applicant, and includes multiple pathways for investors, entrepreneurs, and specialized talent.

- The 10-year option is available to individuals who invest at least AED 10 million (around $2.7 million) in approved UAE investments, or to those recognized under the specialized talent category, which includes doctors, scientists, and engineers.

- The five-year option is available for investors in real estate or for entrepreneurs with an existing project that has a minimum capital of AED 500,000 (around $136,000).

Investor Category (10-Year Golden Residence)

For the 10-year Golden Residence investor category, qualifying investments may include:

- A deposit in an accredited UAE investment fund.
- Establishing a new company in the UAE with a minimum capital of AED 10 million.

Or,

- Holding shares in an existing UAE company worth at least AED 10 million.

Key Requirements:

- The investment must be fully owned (cannot be financed through a loan).

- The investment must be maintained for a minimum of three years.
- Visa holders may sponsor their spouse and children.

Five-Year Property Investor And Entrepreneur Category

- For the five-year Golden Residence, applicants must invest in qualifying real estate (minimum value AED 5 million/$1.4 million) or have an existing business project with capital of AED 500,000.
- Investments must not be financed through loans and must be retained for at least three years.
- Visa holders may sponsor their spouse and children.

Self-Sponsorship

Unlike work or student visas, which require an employer or academic sponsor, the Golden Residence Visa is self-sponsored, giving investors full flexibility.

Super Yacht Golden Visa

Abu Dhabi offers a 10-year Golden Visa pathway for high-net-worth individuals connected to the luxury yachting sector. Eligible applicants include owners of private yachts measuring 40 meters (131 feet) or longer, as well as key figures in the maritime and yacht industry, such as CEOs or major shareholders of yacht-building companies, central agents, and maritime insurance specialists.

The visa is valid for 10 years and renewable, and immediate family members may also be included. To apply, candidates must be nominated by Yas Marina and the Abu Dhabi Investment Office (ADIO) through the *Golden Quay* initiative.

UAE Retirement Visa

Foreign retirees aged 55 and older are eligible for a five-year renewable UAE Retirement Visa providing they meet the following criteria:

- An employment history of no less than 15 years inside or outside the UAE

And,

- Own a property/properties to the value of no less than AED 1 million (around $272k)

Or,

- Have savings of no less than AED 1 million

Or,

- Be in receipt of a monthly income of AED 20,000 ($5k) (reduced to AED 15,000 ($4k) a month for Dubai).

UAE Company Formation Visa

The UAE Company Formation Visa allows entrepreneurs and business owners to obtain residence by establishing a company in the UAE. Applicants must register a legally recognized business, meet the minimum capital requirements for their chosen free zone or mainland jurisdiction, and maintain active operations.

The visa typically includes the ability to sponsor family members and is valid for two to three years, renewable providing that the company remains in good standing. It provides a straightforward pathway for foreign investors and business founders to live and work in the UAE while running their enterprise.

UAE Digital Nomad Visa

The UAE Digital Nomad Visa allows remote workers and freelancers to live in the UAE while working for companies abroad.

Applicants must show proof of employment or freelance contracts, meet a minimum income requirement (around $5k), and have valid health insurance.

The visa is typically valid for one year and is renewable, offering the flexibility to live in the UAE without needing a local employer, while enjoying full access to the country's infrastructure and lifestyle.

UAE Citizenship

While the UAE does not offer a direct citizenship by investment program, long-term residency visas allow foreign investors, skilled professionals, and entrepreneurs to live within the region tax-free. After an extended period of residency (typically 30+ years for standard applicants), naturalization may be considered.

Taxes In The UAE

The UAE is one of the most attractive zero income tax destinations in the world. With no personal income tax, no capital gains tax, and no inheritance tax, the UAE has positioned itself as a global hub for business, innovation, and luxury living.

To maintain tax residency, you need to spend at least 90 days per year in the UAE.

Even though you live in a country with no income tax, you may still be liable for foreign tax reporting depending on your citizenship: U.S. Citizens must file IRS tax returns and report offshore accounts under FATCA (Foreign Account Tax Compliance Act) no matter where in the world they live.

EU Nationals are subject to Common Reporting Standard (CRS) regulations, meaning banks will report foreign held assets to their home country.

The UAE is one of the best tax havens for those looking to build wealth while enjoying an ultra-modern lifestyle and a strong business ecosystem.

Crypto Taxes In The UAE

From a tax perspective, the UAE offers a highly attractive environment for both individual crypto investors and businesses. Residents do not pay personal income tax or capital gains tax on cryptocurrency activities, meaning profits from trading, staking, or holding digital assets are typically tax free for individuals.

Most crypto transactions—including buying, selling, and converting virtual assets—are exempt from VAT.

Businesses engaged in crypto activities are subject to the UAE's 9% corporate tax on profits above AED 375,000 (around $102k) though companies in qualifying free zones may benefit from a 0% rate under specific conditions.

Banking In The UAE

The UAE has a sophisticated banking system that is FATCA complaint so you may be able to make assets harder to reach from foreign creditors in the UAE but not from Uncle Sam or the IRS.

Popular banks among expats include Emirates NBD, known for its extensive branch network and online banking and HSBC UAE, which offers international account access and wealth management services. Mashreq, Standard Chartered, and First Abu Dhabi Bank are also excellent options.

Opening an account is straightforward for residents, and many banks provide multi-currency options, contactless payments, and digital banking apps to make managing finances seamless.

To open an account, you'll need your passport, residence visa, Emirates ID, and proof of address and employment.

Real Estate In The UAE

Property is the most expensive consideration when living in the UAE. The median property price is AED 23,600 (around $6k) per square meter for apartments and AED 15,300 (around $4k) per square meter for houses with Dubai being most expensive emirate, followed closely by Abu Dhabi.

Only in designated Freehold Areas can foreigners own title, outside these areas, expats must either hold:

- A long-term lease (up to 99 years);
- Musataha—a 50-year lease;

Or,

- Usufruct—the right to occupy but not alter the property for 99 years.

The areas designated for freehold in Abu Dhabi are Yas Island, Saadiyat, Reem, Mariya, Lulu, Al Raha Beach, Sayh Al Sedairah, Al Reef, and Masdar City.

The designated freehold areas in Dubai include Al Barari, Jumeirah, Palm Jumeirah, Jumeirah Beach Residence (JBR), DAMAC Hills, Dubai Hills Estate, Dubai South, International City, Jumeirah Village Circle (JVC), Dubai Silicon Oasis, and Dubai Sports City.

The UAE, particularly Dubai, has exploded in popularity for real estate investors. The market is known for cutting-edge infrastructure, high rental yields, and investor-friendly regulation.

Highlights include:

- No annual property tax.
- One-time 4% property transfer fee.
- 5% VAT on commercial properties.
- 5.27% gross rental yield (Dubai).

With continued foreign investment inflows, the UAE is a top-tier choice for those seeking long-term exposure in a no property tax locale.

Doing Business In The UAE

The UAE is one of the world's most business-friendly environments for expats. Entrepreneurs can take advantage of free zones, which allow 100% foreign ownership, 0% import or export taxes, and full repatriation of profits.

Investors who establish a company in a free zone can also secure renewable residency, making it easier to live and work while building their business.

There are 21 Free Zones in the UAE, with 20,000 companies operating from them representing industries like automotive, biotechnology, financial, media, logistics, and textiles.

Outside Free Zones businesses considered to be "strategic" must have 51% UAE ownership, though non-strategic and Free Zone businesses are unrestricted.

While the UAE introduced a 9% corporate tax in 2023, most small businesses and free-zone companies remain largely exempt, preserving its reputation as a tax-efficient jurisdiction.

Beyond taxes, the country offers a modern lifestyle, a robust business ecosystem, and a forward-looking economy—with 74% of GDP now coming from non-fossil fuel sources—making it an attractive destination for those seeking wealth creation alongside innovation and growth.

THE UNITED ARAB EMIRATES

For The Crypto Millionaire

The United Arab Emirates has rapidly become one of the most attractive global destinations for crypto investors thanks to its zero personal tax environment.

Unlike many Western countries, the UAE does not impose income tax or capital gains tax on crypto trading, holding, or profit realization, allowing individuals to retain 100% of their crypto earnings.

This tax friendly status, combined with recent exemptions on many crypto transaction taxes, gives investors a significant financial edge compared to jurisdictions with heavy tax burdens.

In terms of a cultural shift, a move to the Middle-East will likely take more adjustment than a move to Latin America or Europe but the lifestyle on offer can offer a serious upgrade and the business opportunities are vast.

With modern infrastructure, world class health care, and one of the lowest crime rates in the Middle East, the UAE offers a secure and comfortable base for international investors and their families.

Its strategic location between Europe, Asia, and Africa makes it a natural hub for global business and travel while major cities like Dubai and Abu Dhabi host welcoming international communities and an array of lifestyle options.

For crypto investors, the regulatory clarity is a big draw. Authorities such as the Virtual Assets Regulatory Authority in Dubai provide structured licensing and compliance rules for exchanges, custodians, and blockchain firms. These clear legal frameworks help mitigate the uncertainty that often surrounds digital asset markets elsewhere, giving investors greater confidence to operate and innovate.

The UAE's broader crypto ecosystem continues to grow with

dedicated hubs and innovation zones such as the DMCC Crypto Centre, ADGM, and DIFC, attracting hundreds of blockchain companies and fintech startups.

Coupled with attractive residency options like the Golden Visa for tech entrepreneurs and investors, the UAE combines financial freedom, regulatory transparency, and quality of life in a way that few other jurisdictions can match.

EPILOGUE

★ ★ ★

Where A Big Idea And A Pioneering Spirit Can Take You

I grew up in a lower-middle-class home, the son of a single mother. There was no trust fund to give me a leg up in life.

I saved long and hard to be able to pay for my first car, and I worked two jobs to cover college tuition... then grad school.

I tell you this to prove the point that you don't need to be born with a silver spoon in your mouth to take advantage of the kind of wealth-building strategies I've followed.

I had a pioneering spirit in me from an early age. I simply had an idea that I wanted more out of life than growing up, going to school, working, and dying in the same place.

I had that idea for the first time when I was in high school.

I could have achieved my objective—of not spending my whole life in one place—by moving to another state. But something in my head told me to push for more.

I wanted options... as many as possible.

Beyond-the-border options.

I heard about a school called, at the time, the American Graduate School of International Management. You might know it as Thunderbird. I decided in high school that that's where I'd go after college.

The school has since merged with Arizona State University, but it still offers one of the best international MBA programs in the world.

That was as far as my thinking went at the time.

After graduating college and getting into Thunderbird, my

plan began to expand; my focus was on job opportunities overseas.

Let someone pay me to see the world, I figured… so I could either find a job in another country or join the Navy, as my best friend had decided to do.

I knew myself well enough to realize that I wouldn't be much good as a link in the chain of anyone's command.

I finished the program at Thunderbird and got what I thought was an ideal offer of employment from an international oil drilling company. Just as I'd hoped, they wanted to pay me to see the world… at least the world where they operated.

The trouble, I found, is that oil seems to be in places where humans probably shouldn't hang out in the long-term.

That drilling outfit sent me to work in Chad, the Tengiz oil fields in Kazakhstan (where it is minus fifty degrees in winter), and northern Argentina in a town so close to Bolivia that that's where we shopped for most things.

The experience was great. Unfortunately, the company wasn't. So, I quit and returned to the United States. But that initial international experience was all I needed to confirm that that was the life for me.

I spent the next four years living in Chicago (another place humans probably shouldn't be in winter… at least not this boy from Arizona) regrouping.

Finally, I felt ready to look overseas again.

I signed up for a tour of Ireland. I had an idea for a property development project… and, from my research, Ireland seemed like a good place for it.

That tour was led by Kathleen Peddicord, who, coincidentally, was also considering a move to the Emerald Isle. We met in June, were married in November, and headed to Ireland together two weeks later.

Whereas the jobs with the drilling company had been short-term gigs, that move to Ireland was indefinite. That meant obtaining legal residency, setting up a bank account, buying a car, getting a local driver's license, and all the other fun things you do when you move to another country.

Ireland became my first real experience at internationalizing my life.

In the nearly three decades since, I've gone offshore completely and thoroughly. At this point, I've done just about everything one could think about doing in another country...

I have obtained residency (in four countries), opened bank accounts (more than 25 accounts in 15 countries), launched and operated businesses (in seven countries), bought real estate (in 24 countries), educated my children (in four countries), and obtained a second citizenship (in Ireland).

I don't tell you all this to brag... but to show you that—unlike other "offshore experts" you may find out there on the Internet—I have real-world, firsthand experience with the offshore world. It's my everyday life.

None of this happened overnight, and here's a secret...

Much of it was not according to any plan.

Kathleen and I have built our offshore life organically, step by step. Each step has opened new doors and led to more options... and we've sifted and filtered and made choices, one after another, that have gotten us from where we were all those years ago to where we are today.

What have I gained?

Well, I've built my fortune overseas—primarily in real estate.

But more than that, I've been able to protect my fortune through the international diversification strategies I've discovered.

A key to making money is making sure you're not losing it. I've worked for decades to increase my understanding of asset protection and identify the best places in the world in which to diversify and grow my wealth.

The result?

Not only has it helped make me money, it ended up saving me a fortune... three fortunes, actually...

This method allowed me to make money during the 2000 dotcom crash, the 2008 financial crisis, and even the global pandemic of 2020...

You know as well as I do that each of those events devastated millions of retirement plans and businesses across the United States. They forced a lot of folks out of retirement... and many more out of their homes.

And, sure as shooting, you can bet another crisis is coming down the road. To eliminate its potential impact on you, find a part of the world where you can have a Plan B in place and you'll sleep well at night knowing you'll be all set for whatever lies ahead...

No matter who's pulling the strings in the White House...

No matter how high taxes rise... Or how far the stock market falls...

No matter when the next recession strikes—or how hard it hits... I am not worried.

And you shouldn't be either.

Pick your place. Make your move. And I look forward to meeting with you somewhere down the road.

Stay diversified,

Lief Simon.

www.ingramcontent.com/pod-product-compliance
Lightning Source LLC
LaVergne TN
LVHW020654110826
845149LV00012B/1987

* 9 7 8 1 9 5 8 5 8 3 1 3 5 *